Heike Hartung (ed.)
Embodied Narration

Aging Studies | Volume 15

The series is edited by Heike Hartung, Ulla Kriebernegg und Roberta Maierhofer.

Heike Hartung (ed.)
Embodied Narration
Illness, Death and Dying in Modern Culture

[transcript]

The printing of this book was supported by the Vice President for Research and Junior Academics at the University of Potsdam, Germany, the Committee on Research and Young Academics (FNK) at the University of Potsdam, Germany, and the University of Graz, Austria.

Karl-Franzens-Universität Graz/University of Graz

Bibliographic information published by the Deutsche Nationalbibliothek
The Deutsche Nationalbibliothek lists this publication in the Deutsche Nationalbibliografie; detailed bibliographic data are available in the Internet at http://dnb.d-nb.de

© 2018 transcript Verlag, Bielefeld

Cover concept: Kordula Röckenhaus, Bielefeld
Typeset by Michael Rauscher, Bielefeld
Printed and bound in Great Britain by Marston Book Services Ltd, Oxfordshire
Print-ISBN 978-3-8376-4306-0
PDF-ISBN 978-3-8394-4306-4

Content

Acknowledgements | 7

Introduction
The Concept of Embodiment in Modern Culture
Heike Hartung | 9

Embodied Narrations of the End of Life
Toward A Thanatological Biopolitics of Modern Culture
Heike Hartung | 21

'About Suffering They Were Never Wrong, The Old Masters'
Human Pain and the Crucible of Representation
Rüdiger Kunow | 51

How We Imagine Living with Dying
Margaret Morganroth Gullette | 67

Disgust in Samuel Beckett's *Molloy*
Sarah J. Ablett | 85

'Blue with Age'
Dis- and Dys-appearance of the Body in Eudora Welty's "A Worn Path"
Ellen Matlok-Ziemann | 103

Growing Bodies
Narrating Death and Sexuality in Contemporary Young Adult Fiction
Mirjam Grewe-Salfeld | 119

When Mother Is Dying
Miljenko Jergović's *Kin*
Dagmar Gramshammer-Hohl | 141

Storytelling in the Age of AIDS
Narrative Possibilities and the Exigencies of Loss in Dale Peck's *Martin and John. A Novel*
Ariane Schröder | 157

Realism and the Soul
The Philosophy of Virginia Woolf's Illness
Vira Sachenko | 177

The Illness Is You
Figurative Language in David Foster Wallace's Short Story "The Planet Trillaphon"
Anita Wohlmann | 203

Reading the Assault on the Lived Body in Hilary Mantel's *Giving up the Ghost*
Monika Class | 227

Contributors | 255

Acknowledgements

The idea for this book has emerged from several postgraduate seminars on the topic of "Embodied Narration" in modern and postmodern fiction and film held at the Department of English and American Studies at the University of Potsdam. Two of the gifted students from these seminars are also represented in the volume. Aspects of my own chapters were presented in several talks at the Center for Inter-American Studies at the University of Graz. The scope of the volume was made possible by the scholarly exchanges facilitated by the development of the European and North American Networks in Aging Studies (ENAS & NANAS).

I want to thank my colleagues at the University of Potsdam and the University of Graz for their feedback and support during the work on this project, most particularly Anke Bartels, Ulla Kriebernegg, Rüdiger Kunow, Roberta Maierhofer, Friederike Offizier, Ariane Schröder, Eva-Maria Trinkaus, Nicole Waller and Dirk Wiemann. Thanks are due also to the numerous age scholars whose work has been a constant inspiration. My deepest gratitude is due to the contributors to this volume on whose collegiality and rigour the book depends.

I acknowledge with gratitude the financial support of the Vice President for Research and Junior Academics at the University of Potsdam, Germany, the Committee on Research and Young Academics (FNK) at the University of Potsdam, Germany, and the University of Graz, Austria.

I dedicate this book to my mother, Hannelore Hartung (1942–2018).

Introduction
The Concept of Embodiment in Modern Culture

Heike Hartung

In response to the perceived neglect of the body as a category of cultural analysis, the concept of embodiment has been theorized in recent years in an attempt to move beyond the Cartesian dualism and to overcome the nature/culture split. Feminist theory and gender studies have been concerned with the cultural implications of embodiment, arguing for a move from viewing the body as a "nongendered, prediscursive phenomenon that plays a central role in perception, cognition, action and nature to a way of living or inhabiting the world through one's acculturated body" (Weiss and Haber xiii–xiv). Since the 1980s, this relationship has been very much at the centre of interest, with a special focus on theorizing the body. Many disciplines have been interested in this theorizing, branching into the history of the body, but also focusing on philosophical, sociological and, above all, gendered and feminist engagement with the cultural implications of "embodiment". The term "embodiment" is not simply a rephrasing of "body", but rather a term that indicates the cultural framework in which the physical is always situated. Thus "embodiment" indicates a movement beyond the nature/culture binary.

Moving away from the Cartesian dualism of body and mind, contemporary psychologists and neuroscientists offer empirical evidence that "the body thinks", arguing that what they refer to as "embodied cognition" may be non-conscious rather than conscious, but can nevertheless influence conscious action as well as initiating thought (Cuddy-Keane 680). The neuroscientific discipline more closely concerned with narrative, the "Philosophy of Mind", has introduced the term "embodied narrative" to refer to another aspect of the connection between body and mind: The narrative self, introduced by David Dennett as an abstraction of the conscious mind, is described by this term, first, as an embodied consciousness, self or agent, whose experiences are available for narration, and, second, as a narrative which plays a role in the agent's psychological life. According to Richard Menary, "this embodied narrative view makes more sense of ourselves as complex biological, historical and social beings whose experiences and actions are ready for narration" (64).

With its focus on a person's being "aged by culture" (Gullette), age studies has extended this view to the embodied experience of ageing, while drawing attention to the ways in which the ageing body in both its materiality *and* plasticity restricts the possibilities of (de-)constructing subjectivity. Therefore, the Foucaultian notion of "biopower", with its treatment of the body as a projection screen for the playing out of power and knowledge structures, has been extended into more flexible conceptions of embodiment focusing on "biosociality" (Rabinow) or "the somatic self" (Rose). As a consequence, the new emphasis on the materiality of both body and mind in contemporary "neurocultures" has to be taken into account critically in relation to shifting notions of biopolitics.

In order to briefly explore the concept of "embodied narration" in this introduction, I will draw on theoretical concepts that can be made useful to age and disability studies. The interdisciplinary construct of embodiment should enable the analysis of literary representations of liminal embodied experiences such als ageing, illness and dying. My starting assumption is that these liminal experiences affect literary representation in significant ways: they problematize and shift the limits of narration itself. Or, in other words: liminal experience challenges narrative form as well as what we perceive as readers as narrative. Implicitly, therefore, this volume wants to open up the question of what can be defined as narrative.

The modern view of life and the body has been defined by Michel Foucault as "biopower". In the essay "Right of Death and Power over Life" (1976), Foucault describes a transformation from the classical juridical form of power—or, in other words: the law of sovereignty, which extends its power over the life and death of its subjects—to a new, modern form of power that is "exercised at the level of life, the species, the race, and the large-scale phenomena of population" (137). This shift leads to the paradox, as he observes, that modern wars, which have become more devastating than ever, are no longer waged in the name of the sovereign. Instead, power is exercised at the level of life: "It is as managers of life and survival, of bodies and the race, that so many regimes have been able to wage so many wars, causing so many men to be killed" (137). In his essay, Foucault points to a transition from a premodern life or embodied existence, which was regulated by the hierarchical forms of sovereign power, but also exposed to arbitrary and haphazard forms of death (through contagion, plague, or the death penalty), to a modern individualized life, which is turning into an ever more controllable form of biological existence. The extension of power, he argues, has shifted from the sovereign's right to take life—the "right of death"—to an extensive (technological, medical) control and power over life. This has affected the meaning of death, which has turned from a public spectacle into a private affair: "One might say that the ancient right to take life or let live was replaced by a power to foster life or disallow it to the point of death. [...] Now it is over life, throughout its unfolding, that power establishes its domination; death is power's limit, the moment that escapes it; death becomes the most secret aspect of existence, the most 'private.'" (138) The shifts in the forms of embodiment hinted at in Foucault's term "biopower", and which he distinguishes as two basic forms that concern the disciplining of the individual human body and the regulation of the "species body" (139), have extensive cultural repercussion that affect the experience of ageing, but also those of illness and dying.

Foucault's brief remarks on biopower have been extended in recent years from various perspectives. Paul Rabinow has incorporated the concept into his anthropological critique of modernity. In his *Studies in the Anthropology of Reason* (1996), Rabinow argues that the category of life itself is subjected to modernization. Therefore, he focused his ethnographic research in the 1990s on the expansion of biotechnology, and more specifically, on examining the sequencing of DNA. He argues that after the Second World War questions concerning life and death, health and illness, the pathological and the normal were turned, in Western societies, into concerns of the nation state, which led to the institutionalization of national welfare. This concern has been reformulated, since the 1990s, into an economic, scientific and political interest in 'life'. The commercial and technological interest in life has, in its turn, changed the relationship between science, economy and the state. Rabinow's studies of DNA sequencing, in which he pursues the question how this global research project has affected our social and ethical practices, describe a shift from an early twentieth-century "sociobiology" to a more recent "biosociality" (99). Sociobiology refers to modernist eugenic projects, which encompassed liberal philanthropic attempts to moralize and discipline the poor and the so-called 'deranged'. But they also led to the institution of racial hygiene, and to the elimination of whole social and ethnic groups in the Holocaust. Rabinow describes these modernist projects as social constructions using biological metaphors, in which the construction of a new society was at issue. The new genetics, he argues, is no longer concerned with biological metaphors of a modern society, but is transforming itself into a network of identity concepts, from which a new form of autoproduction emerges, which Rabinow terms "biosociality":

"In the future, the new genetics will cease to be a biological metaphor for modern society and will become instead a circulation network of identity terms and restriction loci, around which and through which a truly new type of autoproduction will emerge, which I call 'biosociality.' If sociobiology is culture constructed on the basis of a metaphor of nature, then in biosociality, nature will be modeled on culture understood as practice. Nature will be known and remade through technique and will finally become artificial, just as culture becomes natural. Were such a project to be brought to fruition, it would stand as the basis for overcoming the nature/culture split." (99)

The shift from sociobiology to biosociality as a form of embodiment is interesting for cultural analysis because of the notion of the social Rabinow employs. He refers to Raymond Williams's use of the social (and of society) in *Keywords*, as concerning the "whole way of life of a people (hence open to empirical analysis and planned change)" (Rabinow 102). In this broad sense of the social as the common life practices of a people, the relationship of the social to embodiment becomes visible. What is at stake in these and other recent reformulations of Foucault's notion of "biopower" are new concepts of modern subjectivity which affect the relationship between nature and culture, the biological and the social as well as cultural. This is also apparent in Nikolas Rose's concept of the "somatic self", with which he describes how the meaning of human life has changed the notion of humanism emerging in the nineteenth century by changes in biology, biomedicine and biotechnology that have occured since the twentieth century:

"Selfhood has become increasingly somatic—ethical practices increasingly take the body as the key site for work on the self. From official discourses of health promotion through narratives of the experience of disease and suffering in the mass media, to popular discourses on dieting and exercise, we see an increasing stress on personal reconstruction through acting on the body in the name of fitness that is simultaneously corporeal and psychological. [...] I have termed this 'somatic individuality' (Novas and Rose, 2000). The new genomic and molecular vocabularies of ourselves—like earlier biomedical languages of intelligence, or depression, or 'hormones'—are being incorporated within these relations of the somatic self to itself." (18).

Thus the concept of the body is being extended to include both the corporeal and the psychological, but also political, social and cultural dimensions. This inclusive concept of embodiment, on which both Rabinow's term "biosociality" and Rose's term "somatic individuality" draw, has recently been related to "the shifting boundaries between life and death" by Rosi Braidotti ("Dying" 201). She argues that current notions of biopower concern not only "the government of the living" but also "practices of dying" ("Dying" 201). Braidotti's reformulation of the concept of biopower is part of her notion of the posthuman. She incorporates the liminal concept of death into these biopolitical reformulations of subjectivity, for which art becomes a crucial reference point:

"By transposing us beyond the confines of bound identities, art becomes necessarily inhuman in the sense of non-human in that it connects to the animal, the vegetable, earthy and planetary forces that surround us. Art is also, moreover, cosmic in its resonance and hence posthuman by structure, as it carries us to the limits of what our embodied selves can do or endure. In so far as art stretches the boundaries of representation to the utmost, it reaches the limit of life itself and thus confronts the horizon of death. To this effect, art is linked to death as the experience of limits." (*The Posthuman* 93)

These contemporary concepts involve a move towards a more inclusive concept of embodiment which encompasses the physical and the psychological. Foucault's notion of biopower has also traveled further: from a shift between premodern and modern notions of life and death to different approaches to the political, social and cultural repercussions of concepts of human—as well as posthuman—subjectivity. These current debates on embodiment have a strong counterpart in literary representation. Therefore, this volume aims to investigate how liminal embodied experiences such as illness, death and dying affect literary form. Proceeding from the assumption that these experiences problematize and shift the limits of narration itself, contributions explore exemplary works of art from the period of literary modernism onwards to include also contemporary culture. With its focus on experimentalism, the fragmentary and a reduced aesthetics, modern and postmodern literature seems particularly appropriate for studying liminal experience. Furthermore, modernist experimentalism has been seen in a dialogic exchange with similarly experimental tendencies in medical psychology and physiology of the late nineteenth and early twentieth centuries. Together, these approaches have shaped modern concepts of embodiment, thus providing a bridge to our contemporary critical engagement with the acculturated body and embodied mind.

The contributions in this volume look at embodiment from different perspectives, focusing on the interrelations between illness, death and dying. The first chapter, my essay "Embodied Narrations of the End of Life: A Thanatological Biopolitics of Modern Culture" provides a brief overview of approaches to death and dying from the disciplinary perspectives of sociology, cultural studies, history and philosophy in the twentieth and twenty-first centuries. Describing the material turn in the modern attitude towards death, the essay goes on to sketch a preliminary phenomenology of embodied death and dying in a cumulative reading of exemplary texts by Henry James, Samuel Beckett, Christopher Isherwood and Julian Barnes. The essay thus turns from James's ghost stories, in which the ghost materializes as an absent presence and the ghostly presence of the dead determines their remembrance, to Beckett's aesthetic concern with the interrelationship of births and deaths, beginnings and endings, which are prominent as a cultural matrix in his early work. Isherwood focuses on homosexual embodiment turning to embodied consciousness and physical materiality, while Barnes promotes different forms of "death writing" in an ironic inversion of life writing. The second chapter, Rüdiger Kunow's "'About Suffering They Were Never Wrong, The Old Masters': Human Pain and the Crucible of Representation", focuses on suffering as an "emphatic now" in human embodiment. Looking at the body in pain and its representation in art leads him to a consideration of the negotiations of the border that pain expression entails. He traces the artistic representation of pain with an emphasis on how, where, and why the balance of power between the body in pain and the body in representation shifts, and in what direction it does. Focusing on Seth Kaufman's novel *The King of Pain* (2012), he argues that the text illustrates how the human body is "being ruthlessly commodified" and subjected to commercialization. He thus delineates the outlines of an ethics of representation and comes to the conclusion that pain in representation is "both a necessary practice and one that must remain incomplete, unfinished".

In the third chapter, Margaret Morganroth Gullette poses the question of "How We Imagine Living with Dying". In the first part of her essay, Gullette investigates how "living with dying" is represented in British and American nonfictional writing. She points out that there is a new kind of "eagerness to learn the particulars of dying" in the American cultural context that has moved beyond religion. In the second part of the chapter, Gullette turns to Marilynne Robinson's novel *Gilead* (2004) to explore what this text implies about what general readers want to learn about living with dying. In focusing on the protagonist John Ames's enhanced form of living with dying in his gentle life review, the novel provides an example of the good death. Sarah J. Ablett, in the fourth chapter on "Disgust in Samuel Beckett's *Molloy*", argues that Beckett in this novel "navigates in the liminal spaces of body and mind". Her focus is on the tragical rather than the comical aspects of an aesthetics of disgust in *Molloy* (1955). Drawing on Julia Kristeva's notion of the abject, Ablett employs Beckett's novel as an exemplary text to explore the embodiment of the "dualistic struggles of life and death, body and mind, nature and culture, as well as attraction and repulsion". She concludes that the narrative voice in Molloy functions both on a physical and cognitive level to draw the reader's attention to the difficult areas of embodiment, such as ageing, illness and dying.

Chapter five, Ellen Matlok-Ziemann's "'Blue with Age': Dis- and Dys-appearance of the Body in Eudora Welty's 'A Worn Path'", focuses on the specificities of the ageing body and, in particular, on representations of older women in literature. Drawing on Maurice Merleau-Ponty, Simone de Beauvoir and Drew Leder's phenomenological investigations, Matlok-Ziemann reads Eudora Welty's short story as an example for overcoming the binary of decline stories and progress narratives of successful ageing. Rather, Welty's "A Worn Path" is analysed as a text which makes its ageing female protagonist paradoxically visible in her lived embodied experience, in spite of the contradictory tensions in the text which entail her body's disappearance. Mirjam Grewe-Salfeld in chapter six, "Growing

Bodies: Narrating Death and Sexuality in Contemporary Young Adult Fiction", turns to the question of how the representation of death and dying is related to sexuality in the genre of Young Adult novels. With reference to four texts of this genre—Alice Sebold's *The Lovely Bones* (2002), Gayle Forman's *If I Stay* (2009), Jenny Downham's *Before I Die* (2007) and John Green's *The Fault in Our Stars* (2012)—she argues that the embodied experience of dying in these young protagonists becomes a "process and site of growth". As she points out in her conclusion, the aspects of embodied growth in these novels become "enmeshed with mortality and pain" and sexuality in its closeness to death "becomes dually inscribed as dangerous and desired".

Chapter seven, Dagmar Gramshammer-Hohl's "When Mother is Dying: Miljenko Jergovic's *Kin*", argues that in the Bosnian-Croatian writer's novel, which is an autobiographical family saga of a thousand and one pages, the main motif is death. Gramshammer-Hohl shows that this motif brings together the dying of the author's mother with the dying of his family, "the dying of a city (Sarajevo), a country (Yugoslavia), and of what once meant home to the narrator". In an attempt to orientalize his subject, the narrator employs multiple digressions and arabesque interpolated stories to "delay his mother's death as long as possible, as if telling it would make it definite and irrevocable". Furthermore, the essay illustrates in a close reading that the "proliferation" of the narrative mimetically "embodies" what it depicts: the narration, which tries to circumvent the imminence of the mother's and the motherland's death, becomes itself "metastatic", spreading ever further away from its center, the multiple deaths. Ariane Schröder, in chapter eight, begins her essay "Storytelling in the Age of AIDS: Narrative Possibilities and the Exigencies of Loss in Dale Peck's *Martin and John. A Novel*" by pointing out that the representation of AIDS as a literary subject entails encountering specific biomedical, political, ethical and aesthetic discourses. With reference to the specific experimental text she focuses on it is her aim to illustrate how Peck is "able to liberate his narrative [...] from the discursive limits of AIDS" and the stereotypical tropes associated with the disease. She first gives an overview of the development of the genre of AIDS literature, which turned from an early focus on activist texts to more complex renderings in the mid-eighties. As she shows, the focus of the genre is on "'the act of bearing witness' to both individual suffering and the potential demise of a whole [gay] subculture of American life". In her reading of Peck's novel she points out that the author evades the frequent focus in AIDS narratives on "irreversible decline" and destabilizes the "commonly assumed link between homosexuality and death in the age of AIDS". In her conclusion she argues that *Martin and John* is a novel that represents "an elaborate elegy on loss, grief and the potential for self-healing".

In chapter nine, Vira Sachenko's "Realism and the Soul: the Philosophy of Virginia Woolf's Illness", the focus is on Virginia Woolf's approach to her own mental illness and its consequences for her writing. This topic is explored with reference to George Lukács's writing on realism, drawing connections between the materialism of both Lukács and Woolf. In order to illuminate the relationship between Woolf's writing style and her treatment of illness, Sachenko provides readings of Woolf's essays "Modern Fiction" (1921) and "On Being Ill" (1926). She argues that Woolf's concern with materialism, realism and the body was shaped by her reading of Russian literature. Furthermore, she proposes that Woolf draws on the concept of the soul as an unknown quantity to which body and mind are related in illness. She concludes that illness, for Woolf, was "the experience that revealed her embodied difference from all other beings". Anita Wohlmann, in Chapter ten, "The Illness is You: Figurative Language in David Foster Wallace's Short Story 'The Planet Trillaphon'", examines the uses of figurative speech in describing and explaining illness in narrative. In her close reading of Wallace's postmodernist text, which is an imaginative investigation of depression personified as "the Bad Thing", Wohlmann explores the move "from comparison (as in simile and metaphor) to equation or identification (as in synecdoche) by focusing on the relational nature of the two things that are brought together". Rather than regarding metaphor and narrative as two unrelated theoretical endeavours, Wohlmann brings metaphor theory and narrative theory together in her reading in order to explore how narrative criteria can inform metaphor analysis, thus developing a rich critical vocabulary. Drawing on the critique of metaphor in the field of Health Humanities, in which metaphors have enjoyed an ambivalent reputation, she argues that figurative speech can be put to different uses in illness writing—courting both the danger of appropriation and colonization but also opening up the potential of identification. In her conclusion she points out that Wallace's unnervingly open-ended story illustrates the "ambivalences involved when similarity and difference turn into identification and sameness".

In chapter eleven, Monika Class focuses on "Illness and the Assault on the Lived Body in Hilary Mantel's *Giving Up the Ghost* (2003)" in her reading of the British writer's memoir of chronic illness. With reference to phenomenological approaches she defines the concept of embodiment as referring to the "lived body as experienced subjectively" and as connoting "embodied consciousness which is psychological, physiological and social in kind". In her reading of the illness memoir, Class points out how Mantel constructs embodiment as a means of emancipation, while the writer encounters in her depiction of her endometriosis and the difficult way to diagnosis epistemic, testimonial and hermeneutic injustice. In fighting against the self alienation that chronic illness entails, Mantel's language crosses the boundaries of politeness in order to fend off the invasiveness of medical examination. Thus Mantel employs literary narrative to evoke an embodiment that "advocates the epistemic and social recognition of the experience of illness". Taken together, the chapters in this volume delineate a phenomenological inventory of the embodied narration of illness, death and dying in modern culture.

WORKS CITED

Braidotti, Rose. "The Politics of 'Life Itself' and New Ways of Dying." *New Materialisms. Ontology, Agency, and Politics*. Ed. Diane Coole, Samantha Fox. Durham: Duke UP, 2010. 201–218. Print.

Braidotti, Rose. *The Posthuman*. Cambridge: Polity P, 2013. Print.

Cuddy-Keane, Melba. "Narration, Navigation, and Non-Conscious Thought: Neuroscientific and Literary Approaches to the Thinking Body." *University of Toronto Quarterly* 79.2 (2010): 680–701.

Dennett, Daniel C. *Consciousness Explained*. London: Penguin, 1993. Print.

Foucault, Michel. *The History of Sexuality. Vol. 1: An Introduction*. New York: Vintage Books, 1978. Print.

Gullette, Margaret Morganroth. *Aged by Culture*. Chicago: U of Chicago P, 2004. Print.

Menary, Richard. "Embodied Narratives." *Journal of Consciousness Studies* 15.6 (2008): 63–84.

Rabinow, Paul. *Essays on the Anthopology of Reason*. Princeton: Princeton UP, 1996. Print.

Rose, Nikolas. "The Politics of Life Itself." *Theory, Culture & Society* 18.1 (2001): 1–30.
Weiss, Gaill and Honi Fern Haber (eds.). *Perspectives on Embodiment. The Intersections of Nature and Culture*. New York: Routledge, 1999. Print.
Williams, Raymond. *Keywords. A Vocabulary of Culture and Society*. [1976] London: Fourth Estate, 2014. Print.

Embodied Narrations of the End of Life
Toward A Thanatological Biopolitics of Modern Culture

Heike Hartung

The theorizing of the body has differentiated our knowledge of the historically changing human attitudes towards death (Ariès), enabling investigations into the liminal experience of dying in modernity (Elias). Whereas the topic of death has been a continuous aesthetic and existential focus of art, literature and philosophy, the interdisciplinary focus on dying can be dated to the second half of the twentieth century. This is closely related to biopolitical developments: modern technologies lead to an "industrialization" of killing during the First World War (Bourke; Audoin-Rouzeau/ Becker). In a parallel development, the individual life expectancy gradually and steadily increased from the late nineteenth century onwards. Since the mid-twentieth century, the end of life has increasingly been determined by medical and legal discourse which replaced the religious and social meaning of death and dying (Gehring; Lacina; Macho, *Todesmetaphern*). In the twenty-first century, the industrialisation and medicalisation of death leads to a further paradigm shift which raises questions concerning the relational aspects of dying from the different perspectives of a posthuman concept of the species (Braidotti), the postcolonial notion of necropolitics (Mbembe), the deconstructionist view of living and dying (Derrida) and the performative view of dying (J. Butler; Offizier).

The historiography of the body in cultural studies is closely related to a focus on material culture. From this perspective, the body is turned into a "thing among things", as Bill Brown states in his "Thing Theory" with reference to Maurice Merleau-Ponty's phenomenology (4). In more recent theoretical discourse the material quality of the body is once more in the focus of a new discussion of biotechnological and biopolitical developments (Coole/Frost; Bennett; Beistegui/Bianco/Gracieuse). The notion of the body as part of material culture has repercussions for the modernist and postmodernist relationship to death. Theories of death and dying in the twentieth and twenty-first centuries are frequently narratives of disappearance. Examples are the sociological analyses of death and grief in modern society (Elias; Nassehi/Weber). The focus in these studies is on secularism and on loneliness—both in the attitude towards death and the experience of dying. Set against this narrative of disappearance are studies concerning the new visibility of death (Macho/Marek) and the constancy of the dead body in its cultural significance (Laqueur).

Cultural studies of death in modern culture, then, can be related either to the narrative of disappearance or to that of constant visibility. With reference to Walter Benjamin's view of the affinity between death and story-telling, Garrett Stewart distinguishes tropes of the metaphorical depiction of death (1984), whereas Ronald Schleifer highlights the metonymic relationship of the motif of death in its relation to life (1990). The link between death and femininity has, like the link between death and war, been widely discussed. From the psychoanalytical perspective, Elisabeth Bronfen argues that the visibility of the beautiful female corpse in art is a symptom of the repression of death by the male artist. She reads this mechanism as indicative of social power relations (1992).

The opposition between the narratives of the disappearance of death in modernity and the counter-narratives of the constancy of its cultural significance is one of the premises of this chapter. This dialectic of death is a characteristic of modernity insofar as the end of life has lost some of its finitude with the Enlightenment's progress optimism concerning the abolition of age as well as death (Gruman; Roberts). In his critique of modernity, Theodor W. Adorno makes the diagnosis, with reference to Freud, that the relationship of the living to the dead is one of the "symptoms of the sickness of experience" in modern times (225). Adorno grounds the concept of individual life in its opposite, in destruction. The meanings attached to death are thus displaced into materiality. By looking at four exemplary modernist and postmodernist texts that focus on the end of life, I will illustrate this materiality of the modern experience of death and will, thus, begin to delineate a thanatological biopolitics of modern culture. The focus in these readings will be on representations of the dead body, on the one hand, and on those of the dying consciousness, on the other hand. I will argue that the concept of embodiment, which is situated between biopolitics and the neurosciences, is expressed and illuminated in the literary strategies of modernism and postmodernism.

In the twenty-first century, the paradox of the existential resistance of death to experience as a problem of representation is confronted by the biomedical definition of the end of life in a "pragmatics of dying" (Nassehi). The method of cultural criticism that is associated with Age Studies is particularly helpful when it comes to analyzing the existential and aesthetic dimensions of the end-of-life experience in all its aspects and for investigating the specific materiality of modern death. The characteristics of modern death shape the relationship between body and mind that is significant for the notion of embodiment. The chapter endeavours to explore the attributes of the material attitude towards death in the close connection between death and narrative, which will be analysed in its repercussions for representations of dying in the literary texts chosen for analysis.

In order to set the frame for the volume, the introduction has explored some of the conceptual aspects of the term embodiment. The focus in this chapter is on literary representations of the end of life from the early twentieth to the twenty-first centuries. These exemplary readings will look at Henry James's 'material' ghosts, trace Samuel Beckett's 'talking corpses', uncover Christopher Isherwood's phenomenology of the dying body and, finally, illustrate how the materialism of modern death continues its structure of recognition and denial in Julian Barnes's postmodern concern with dying and the fear of death.

HENRY JAMES'S 'MATERIAL' GHOSTS

According to Tzvetan Todorov's influential definition of the fantastic, the genre ends with the emergence of psychoanalysis, which takes over its themes (*The Fantastic* 160). In this way Todorov claims a tautological relationship between ghost story and psychoanalysis, which ignores the multiplicity of psychological approaches in literary modernism as well as the different variants of both the fantastic and the ghost story as one of its subgenres. From the perspective of embodiment, the modernist ghost story is not the endpoint of the fantastic. Rather, it can be characterized as a transitional genre, which alternates between embodiment and disembodiment. With reference to the 'ghosts' of modernism a turn towards the material can be observed, which characterizes both the literary and the psychological explorations of human consciousness.[1]

In its positioning between life and death, presence and absence, the fantastic figure of the ghost enables an exploration of the limits of human experience. In contrast to the positivist tendencies of the early nineteenth century, literature and psychology at the end of the nineteenth century have asked questions concerning the constitution of the modern subject and modern society with reference to an interest in the supernatural. Whereas the 'gothic tale' becomes popular at the end of the nineteenth century, the experimental psychology of the time is interested in spiritualism. Both Sigmund Freud and William James were members of the Society for Psychic Research. In psychological case studies of the time, for instance in investigations of the visions of mediums, a broadening of the concepts of the 'normal' and the 'real' takes place, which is also in evidence in the genre of the modern psychological ghost story. Henry James was sceptical of the genre with its reputation of triviality, and he observed the institutionalised interest in the spiritual with critical distance. Nevertheless, he was also influenced by these cultural discourses and published ghost stories himself (Lustig; Hay 161–167).

The clear focus in James's writings on the thinking processes of his characters appears to contradict a concern with the material. Current research on James, however, has shown in what ways the modern tendencies towards materiality characterise even his late work, which encompasses the most abstract of his writings. Examples are the connection between James's late work and the paradigm of the visual (Brosch) and the transformation of thinking into a physical act (Brown, *Things*). The late novels have been described in cognitive approaches as visualised "Psycho-Narration" (Cohn) and representations of the "thinking body" (Cuddy-Keane). They have also been used as illustration for the interaction of body and mind in the narrative focus of the medical humanities (Charon).

---

1 | In a more recent definition of the genre of the ghost story, the link to psychoanalysis is made explicit with reference to trauma and the unnarratable: "the ghost is something that comes back, the residue of some traumatic event that has not been dealt with and that therefore returns, the way trauma always does", and: "Ghost stories are a mode of narrating what has been unnarratable, of speaking such a history belatedly, of making narratively accessible historical events that remain in some fundamental sense inaccessible." (Hay 4)

James's later ghost stories demonstrate his ambiguous attitude toward the materiality of consciousness. The ghosts in the late stories, for instance in "The Jolly Corner" (1908), can be read as material indications of the author's coping with ageing, death and dying. The protagonist of the story, Spencer Brydon, returns to New York City after having lived for thirty-three years in Europe. At the age of fifty-six he returns to his native city "to look at his 'property'", two buildings, one of which is the family home on "the jolly corner" (307). Brydon meets an old friend from his youth in the city, Alice Staverton, with whom he visits the uninhabited and unfurnished boyhood house and discusses the meaning of the house for him: "He spoke of the value of all he read into it, into the mere sight of the walls, mere shape of the rooms, mere sound of the floors, mere feel in his hand, of the silver-plated knobs of the several mahogany doors, which suggested the pressure of the palms of the dead" (312). The materiality of the house, thus, stands for the ageing and dying of the family members who have lived in it. Brydon begins to visit the house alone in the evenings in order to encounter his ghostly American *alter ego*, insisting to his friend that the house, for him, "is lived in", since "his parents and his favourite sister, to say nothing of other kin, in numbers, had run their course and met their end there" (313). The idea of the *alter ego*, of the businessman he might have been if he had not moved to Europe to live a more leasurely life, materialises as the ghostly presence in the house: "His *alter ego* 'walked'—that was the note of his image of him, while his image of his motive for his own pastime was the desire to waylay him and meet him. He roamed, slowly, warily, but all restlessly, he himself did—[...] and the presence he watched for would roam restlessly too." (318) Brydon does not regard the notion of the ghost as frightening, rather he cherishes the idea as an extension of his consciousness. Also, he regards himself as turning "the tables and become himself, in the apparitional world, an incalculable terror" (319). Brydon's self assurance in his roaming of the empty house of his childhood falters, however, when he recognises a door closed which he had left open. The house, then, takes over the function of the ghostly encounter personified in the image of "hard firm hands":

"The house, withal, seemed immense, the scale of space again inordinate; the open rooms, to no one of which his eyes deflected, gloomed in their shuttered state like mouths of caverns [...]. But what he most felt was that now surely, with the element of impunity pulling him as *by hard firm hands*, the case was settled for what he might have seen above had he dared that last look. The closed door, blessedly remote now, was still closed—and he had only in short to reach that of the house." (327-328; emphasis added)

The description of the subtle change in Brydon's encounter with the house leads him to the awareness of the "most immediate presence of some inconceivable occult activity" (328), which prepares the reader for the next step, the vision of the ghost himself: "Rigid and conscious, spectral yet human, a man of his own substance and stature waited there to measure himself with his power to dismay" (329). Brydon encounters the ghost with an elaborate perception of details, noticing every instance of the ghost's appearance, his "grizzled bent head and white masking hands" (329), and describing his evening dress in minute detail, comparing the apparition to a society painter's portrait: "No portrait by a great modern master could have presented him with more intensity" (329).[2] A further detail is that the apparition has two fingers of one hand missing, the hands which are covering the face. Ultimately, the revealed face resembles Brydon's own face, turns out to be his own ghostly mirror image, which Brydon realises in horror: "Horror, with the sight, had leaped into Brydon's throat, gasping there in a sound he couldn't utter; for the bared identity was too hideous as *his*, and his glare was the passion of his protest" (330, emphasis original). In reaction, Brydon feels that he has been "sold" and that "the face was the face of a stranger" (330). Contemplating his *alter ego* Brydon finally loses consciousness. When he slowly recovers, Brydon notices that he has collapsed on the staircase and has been found by his housekeeper, Mrs. Muldoon and his friend, Alice Staverton, who "for a long unspeakable moment [had] not doubted he was dead" (331). Brydon's death-like state is also the subject of the concluding conversation of the story, in which Miss Staverton and Brydon discuss the material possibilities of Brydon's closeness or distance from his ghostly *alter ego*, the shrewed businessman with the two missing fingers. Miss Staverton describes her own feelings about Brydon and his potential other self, whom she pities. In conclusion, she acknowledges Brydon's difference from his ghostly double, and, thus, makes the protagonist 'real' again in response to his spectral *alter ego* and as a reaction to his encounter with death. Alice Staverton's final

---

2 | The reference that comes to mind here is the painter John Singer Sargent, who was a friend of James and who also painted the writer.

sentence focuses on this difference: "'And he isn't—no he isn't—you!' she murmured as he drew her to his breast" (334).

The ways in which objects—represented in the uninhabited house in "The Jolly Corner"—construct the relationship of the protagonist to his personal 'ghosts' gives us a glimpse of the conservative author's rejection of the materialist attitudes in American society. The society ghost Brydon encounters, his *alter ego* as businessman, is rejected, but is then transformed into Brydon's liminal experience of near death as the loss of consciousness. In contrast to the more material, bloody or cruel ghosts of the early gothic, James's ghosts are mainly located in the conciousness of the narrator, character and in the perceptions of the reader. Therefore, the transition between James's realistic writing and his ghost stories is gradual and sometimes imperceptible, it encompasses embodied as well as disembodied states. As Virginia Woolf has pointed out in her essay on James's ghost stories, "Henry James has only to take the smallest of steps and he is over the border. His characters with their extreme fineness of perception are already half-way out of the body. There is nothing violent in their release. They seem rather to have achieved at last what they have long been attempting—communication without obstacle." (322) But Woolf also draws attention to the disturbing aspects of James's ghosts. These—I think—are crucial for their effectiveness, in the example of "The Jolly Corner" the disturbing quality resides in the climactic encounter of Brydon with his ghostly *alter ego*, which casts the material reality of the protagonist into doubt.

Another attempt to define the quality of the ghostly in Henry James is given in Todorov's essay, "Tales of Henry James" (1973), in which he draws attention to a structural element of James's ghost stories:

"On the one hand, then, there is an absence (of the cause, of the essence, of the truth) but this absence determines everything; on the other hand, there is a presence (the quest) which is simply the pursuit of the absence. The secret of James's tales is, therefore, precisely this existence of an essential secret, of something which is not named, of an absent, overwhelming force which puts the whole present machinery of the narrative into motion. [...] The essential element is absent; absence is an essential element." ("Henry James" 75)

This relationship between absence and presence is then determined as the specific quality of James's ghosts: "if this ever-absent cause is to become present, it *has* to be a ghost. For, curiously enough, Henry James always speaks of ghosts as *presences*. [...] The essence is never present except when it is a ghost, that is, when it is absence *par excellence*." (82; 83) Looking at James's ghost stories, Todorov observes in James's texts "an absence which is both absolute and natural: *death*" (87).

The tendency to physically materialize the psyche in Henry James's ghost stories is closely related to the author's treatment of his own ageing process. James's experience of ageing is reflected in his late stories, in which older artists are frequently the main protagonists. His reaction to the death of people close to him is reflected in the presence of death as a topic of his late work (Cutting). Furthermore, his preoccupation with the 'afterlife' of his own writing is related to the approaching end of his life—in evidence in his editing of the New York Edition of his works. This concern with the literary 'afterlife' has been distinguished as a distinct phase in James's late work (Posnock; Stuart), with which he creates his personal thanatology.

In the short story "The Altar of the Dead" (1895), the protagonist George Stransom is more deeply involved with his memories of the dead than with the living. Whereas the story has not been included in the ghost stories, its foregrounding of death and the dead makes it interesting for the question of embodiment. According to Todorov, the story "merits first place among [James's] explorations of the life of the dead": "Nowhere else is the force of death, the presence of absence, so intensely affirmed. Stransom, the principal character of this tale, lives in the cult of the dead. All he knows is absence and he prefers it to everything else." ("Henry James" 90)

As a wealthy man, Stransom has created the altar of the title as a material site of remembrance. His special relationship to the dead is explained, first, as his keeping "the day of the year on which Mary Antrim died", his fiancé who had died before the marriage could take place (185). Nevertheless, Stransom's relationship to the dead fiancé is described as a very close and special one, which affects his whole life, which "was still ruled by a pale ghost, it was still ordered by a sovereign presence" (185–86). James, thus, as Todorov observed, describes the absent woman as a presence. Although Mary Antrim is a very special ghostly presence for Stransom, his life is devoted to the dead more generally: "There were other ghosts in his life than the ghost of Mary Antrim. He had perhaps not had more losses than most men, but he had counted his losses more; he had not seen death more closely, but he had, in a manner, felt it more deeply" (186–87). The centrality which Stransom accords to the dead is illustrated when he meets an acquaintance on the street, Paul Creston, whose wife died some months ago. Creston has met his new wife during a journey to America and introduces Stransom to her. While he keeps up appearances, Stransom feels this encounter as a shock. He feels for the dead woman much more than for the living replacement: "That new woman, that hired performer, Mrs. Creston? Mrs. Creston had been more living for him than any woman but one." (191) The death of Kate Creston, for whom he felt a deep friendship and on whose remembrance he spends time, "if the man to whom she had given everything couldn't" (192), is contrasted with the death of Acton Hague, of whom Stransom reads in the newspapers. Acton Hague had been an intimate friend of Stransom's, but this friendship had been betrayed by Hague, although the narrative does not reveal in what this betrayal consisted, constituting thus another 'absence' at the center of the story. Hague's death does not count for Stransom among his personal losses, but rather measures "exactly how much he himself could feel like a stone" (195).

When Stransom walks through the suburbs of London, he encounters a catholic church with an altar on which a lot of candles are lighted. He comes to think of this altar as an instance of remembrance for the dead, and sets into motion what is necessary to obtain the altar as "some material act, some outward worship" (197). He thinks of his altar as the possession of the dead: "Now they had really, his dead, something that was indefeasibly theirs; and he liked to think that they might, in cases, be the Dead of others, as well as that the Dead of others might be invoked there under the protection of what he had done" (200).

The central position Stransom has given to the dead is contrasted with the prospect of his own afterlife, which depends on the living. The living are represented in Stransom's encounters with an unnamed woman, whom he meets repeatedly at his altar. He gradually befriends this woman, a process which is described as very slow, since their separate worship of the dead is their most important bond: "For long ages he never knew her name, any more than she had ever pronounced his own; but it was not their names that matters, it was only their perfect practice and their common need" (209). Gradually, Stransom comes to think of this unnamed woman as "the priestess of his altar" and the guardian of his own afterlife (212). When Stransom is finally invited to the woman's lodgings, he comes to realize that she was not only acquainted with Acton Hague, but that "[i]t was all for Acton Hague that she had kneeled every day at his altar" (217). This realization brings the two into conflict, since Stransom asserts that there is no light and no place for Acton Hague at his altar, whereas the woman has focused in her remembrance exclusively on Hague. When the woman asks Stransom to give a candle to Acton Hague and he refuses, she, in consequence, says good-bye to Stransom. Although Stransom does not want to sacrifice this slowly established friendship, he understands that she can no longer come to his altar. He feels jealous of Hague and resents the change he has brought to their relationship: "She had been right about the difference—she had spoken the truth about the change; Stransom felt before long that he was perversely but definitely jealous" (227). Before the realization that Acton Hague was the central object of the woman's mourning, Stransom had reached an understanding with her that she was to become "the eventual guardian of his shrine; and it was in the name of what had so passed between them that he appealed to her not to forsake him in his old age" (232). In the course of renouncing the friendship with the woman, Stransom falls ill, and, thus, the link between physical and mental embodiment is highlighted: "His irritation took the form of melancholy, and his melancholy that of the conviction that his health had quite failed" (234). Stransom is too weak to visit the altar, so that "[a]ll the lights had gone out—all his Dead had died again" (234). During his illness the woman comes to inquire after him. After his recovery he enters the church again, prepared "for the great surrender", for allowing a candle to Acton Hague (239). He encounters the woman again at his altar and the conflict between the two is dissolved. The woman tells him that "I could come for what you yourself came for: that was enough. So here I am" (241). At the end of the story, then, Stransom accepts the candle and dies at the altar, leaning on the shoulder of the unnamed woman: "'Yes, one more,' he repeated simply, 'just one!' And with this his head dropped on her shoulder; she felt that in his weakness he had fainted. But alone with him in the dusky church a great dread was on her of what might still happen, for his face had the whiteness of death" (242).

  The story sets aside the difference between life and death, with a conclusion that focuses on the closeness of the loss of consciousness to dying. Henry James's short story opens up questions concerning the embodiment of dying. In "The Altar of the Dead" the privileged treatment of the dead is endorsed as a positive form of living. Although Stransom is not depicted as a religious man, his worship and remembrance of the dead is described as a form of spirituality. Concerning the protagonist's own afterlife, however, the remembrance of the living is at stake: he cannot influence or control the living. James's protagonist enacts a form of afterlife, which is physically linked to the altar as a space for conjuring the dead. James's work on his own writerly afterlife with the New York Edition, too, focuses on the materiality of death. In James's narrative, the gradual, almost unnoticeable shift from this world to the hereafter is confronted by the paradox that the afterlife relies on others, who bear witness to the dead. Whereas "The Jolly Corner" depicts the ghostly presence of an *alter ego* in the material setting of the family home, which is dedicated, in the protagonist's consciousness, to the familiar dead, "The Altar of the Dead" presents the close connection between narrative and the remembrance of the dead and enacts the process of dying as the conclusion of a story about absent, ghostly presences.

SAMUEL BECKETT'S LANGUAGE OF REDUCTION: MATERIALIZING DEATH AND DYING

If Henry James's material ghosts move between absence and presence, embodiment and disembodiment, Beckett's work is concerned with failure, loss and silence—as well-known plays like *Waiting for Godot* (1948–9) or novels like *Malone Dies* (1951) illustrate. He has developed his poetics of reduction in response to the modernist approach to language. More particularly, he has described his own tendency to reduce language to its 'bare bones' as an attempt to distinguish his own writing style from that of James Joyce's strategy of accumulation: "I realised that Joyce had gone as far as one could in the direction of knowing more, [being] in control of one's material. He was always adding to it; you only have to look at his proofs to see that. I realised that my own way was in impoverishment, in lack of knowledge and in taking away, in subtracting rather than in adding." (Knowlson 352)

Beckett's tendency to strategically reduce language fits with his work's focus on loss. Also, it accords with his fascination with the deviant, with, in his own words "what has always been set aside by artists as something unusable—as something by definition incompatible with art" (Knowlson 772). In 1981, at the age of seventy-five, Beckett extends this attitude towards language to the diminishing possibilities of old age, incorporating the approaching end of (his) life into his poetics of reduction: "It's a paradox, but with old age, the more the possibilities diminish, the better chance you have. With diminished concentration, loss of memory, obscured intelligence—what you, for example, might call 'brain damage'—the more chance there is for saying something closest to what one really is." (Shainberg, n. p.)

Significantly, Beckett's strategy of reducing language to its bare bones is already observable in his early work, thus providing a matrix, I would argue, for his later writing. It prefigures a characteristic topic to which Beckett will return repeatedly in his later work: the close connection between birth and death. Births and deaths, beginnings and endings, thus become part of Beckett's poetics from his first collection of poetry. The complete title of this collection—*Echo's Bones and other Precipitates*—already points to endings in two ways. By naming his poetry "precipitate", he refers to it as the end product in a chemical process, a form of waste, something unusable.[3] This negative connotation is reinforced by the reference to the narcissus myth. Recalling with his title the process of petrification the nymph Echo undergoes in her unrequited love for Narcissus, Beckett focuses once more on a process of material reduction: the transformation of life into something lifeless. In Ovid's rendering of the nymph's transformation, her body is reduced first to bone ("[t]he sounding skeleton"), then to stone ("[h]er bones are petrify'd"). Echo's disembodiment, which in her case does not mean dying, itself undergoes a transformation. The end of the nymph's body is not imagined as the end of her life but, rather, as her physical dematerialisation. Echo remains present, however, as an immortal voice. Beckett employs the beginnings and endings of birth and death in similar ways. At the time of his writing the poems that are collected in *Echo's Bones*, Beckett underwent psychoanalytic treatment after his father's sudden death in 1933. Wilfred Bion,

---

3 | According to the *Oxford English Dictionary*, precipitate has the following meanings: "1. *Chem.* Any of various solid mercury compounds formed by methods involving precipitation or separation from solution; formerly freq. *attrib.* designating pharmaceutical preparations containing such compounds. Now chiefly *hist.*; 2. a. *Chiefly Chem.* Any precipitated substance; a solid, often powdery or flocculent, which separates or is deposited from a solution as a result of chemical action, cooling, etc."

who was his analyst at the Tavistock clinic in London (1933–35), took him to a lecture by C. G. Jung. Beckett was fascinated by a phrase Jung used to illustrate his idea that "being born" was a process that both preceded and continued after the individual event of one's birth. Talking about the unusual mythological dreams of a young girl, Jung maintained, after her early death, that she "had never been born entirely". In his later novel *Watt* (1953), Beckett rewrote this phrase into the more negative "never been properly born" (Thurston 128).

Thus for Beckett both beginnings and endings, birth and death, are processes rather than points in time. In his first poetry collection, death itself is transformed into a process. The interchangeability of beginnings and endings in Beckett's poetics can be illustrated by the two short poems which frame the collection, "The Vulture" and "Echo's Bones".

"The Vulture"
dragging his hunger through the sky
of my skull shell of sky and earth
stooping to the prone who must
soon take up their life and walk
mocked by a tissue that may not serve
till hunger earth and sky be offal (Beckett 5)

In the opening poem, the 'lyric I' is associated with a vulture as a figure, which traverses the space of sky and earth. This association is achieved through the image of the skull. At the same time, the phrase "the sky/ of my skull" replaces the more traditional association of the poetic imagination with the mind. In addition, a figure for the 'others' appears: "the prone"—possibly as people in general, or readers in particular. However, "the prone" do not appear in this poem as either observers or addressed counterpart, but instead as the victims of the poet-vulture. In the allusion to Matthew, the "prone" also refers to the paralyzed Jesus Christ admonished to walk.

The short poem lacks any interpunctuation and opens its three double lines in a parallel construction with the verbs "dragging", "stooping", "mocked". The first double verse describes the movement of the vulture, arrested by hunger and/or the poet's skull. This halting beginning shifts, in the second double verse, to the quick movement of the predator out for his prey, while the mocking third double verse disrupts this movement again by dismantling the poem's material. As a reflection on poetic form, this initial poem turns its embryonic gesture of beginning to a premature and almost apocalyptic end—or, to put it in Beckett's terms, the first poem of the collection is "never properly born". In it, the poet-as-vulture is "mocked by a tissue" that feeds him with inspiration only when it is already too late: when the poem's elements introduced in the first double verse—hunger, sky, earth—have decomposed, have become waste.

If the initial poem with its focus on the vulture hints at the future process of decomposition, the last poem in the collection draws attention to organic decomposition in its reference to "[falling] flesh" and "maggots":

"Echo's Bones"
asylum under my tread all this day
their muffled revels as the flesh falls
breaking without fear or favour wind
the gantelope of sense and nonsense run
taken by the maggots for what they are (Beckett 23)

The poetic voice is drawn into the picture of organic decomposition with the reference to movement: "my tread". Whereas this movement provides an "asylum" for the poetic voice, the run—the accelerated movement—is already made oblivious with the reference to artistic creation as "the gantelope of sense and nonsense". According to the *OED*, "gantlope/gauntlet" is defined as "[a] military [...] punishment in which the culprit had to run stripped to the waist between two rows of men who struck at him with a stick or a knotted cord". While this reference opens up the poem's movement to a military connotation, the deviating writing of "gantelope", instead of "gantlope", also refers us to the association with "antelope", according to the *OED* "distinguished by extreme grace and speed of motion". The apparent dismissal of the creative process as "the gantelope of sense and nonsense" is revised, therefore, through this accentuation of formal grace.

The opening poem, like the closing one with its similar focus on the material aspects of death and dying, thus illustrates how close beginnings and endings are in Beckett's work. If the individual experience of the sudden death of his father, when Beckett was still in his twenties, provides another explanation for the overwhelming associations with death and dying in this early work, the materialist approach to this liminal experience is a specifically modernist one. In regarding birth and death as continuous processes, Beckett's poetics can be linked both with Freud's thanatology, in which the human subject is decentered by the interrelation of life and death drives and with Jung's archetypal extension of the individual experience of birth and death. Beckett thus draws on the ambiguous psychoanalytic attitude towards the materiality of death and dying. However, in characteristically modernist fashion a paradox remains: At the end of the process of dematerialisation, it is the voice—of Echo, of Beckett—which remains.

CHRISTOPHER ISHERWOOD'S MATERIAL VISION OF HOMOSEXUAL EMBODIMENT

Like Beckett's first poetry collection, Christopher Isherwood's novel *A Single Man* (1964) is concerned with loss, more specifically, with the loss of the protagonist George's partner Jim through a car accident. The novel narrates one day in the life of the bereaved English professor George. Embracing the contemporary gay liberation movement, Isherwood creates in this novel a gay character whose homosexuality is an integral part of his personality.[4] Isherwood focuses in minute detail on George's body, on the link between physical embodiment and consciousness at the beginning of the novel, and on the link between embodiment and dying at its end, thus providing a frame for the narrative. Before the reader is introduced to George by name, we witness his slow process of awakening to conscious-

---

4 | Isherwood's novel has frequently been read in the context of gay liberation in its depiction "of homosexuality as a legitimate minoritarian identity, rather than individual pathology", which was a radical political gesture in the 1960s when the novel was first published (Gonzalez 758). For a reading that focuses on the aspect of homosexual identity and sees it balanced by a transcendent religious vision, grounded in Vedanta Hinduism, see Claude Summers. In a more recent study, Octavio R. Gonzalez argues against a strong focus on homosexual identity in *A Single Man*. Instead, Gonzalez focuses on Isherwood's "aesthetic commitment to an ascetic ideal of impersonality, a queer ideal in a non-identitarian sense" (760). My reading of the surfaces of the protagonist George's body in the text agrees with Gonzalez' argument for what he describes as "the modernist impersonality" of *A Single Man* (776).

ness as he gets up in the morning: "Waking up begins with saying *am* and *now*. That which has awoken then lies for a while staring up at the ceiling and down into itself until it has recognised *I*, and therefrom deduced *I am, I am now*. *Here* comes nexts, and is at least negatively reassuring; because here, this morning, is where it had expected to find itself; what's called *at home*." (1)

The first two-and-a-half pages of the novel consist in a detailed inventory of George's body, which also includes the description of his age of "fifty-eight years". His face before the mirror registers different ages superimposed upon each other, highlighting an awareness of the material vision of ageing and using geological metaphors: "Staring and staring into the mirror, it sees many faces within its face—the face of the child, the boy, the young man, the not-so-young man—all present still, preserved like fossils on superimposed layers, and, like fossils, dead" (2). Ageing and dying are aspects of experience of which this slowly emerging consciousness is supremely aware: "Their message to this live dying creature is: Look at us—we have died—what is there to be afraid of?" (2)

The narrative turns on various encounters George has in one day of his life. In the morning, he thinks about his dead partner Jim, musing about "what exactly it is that survives": "Just suppose that the dead do revisit the living. That something approximately to be described as Jim can return to see how George is making out." (6) His morning routine encompasses a brief spell of reading, the encounter with the children of his neighbours, and a phone call by his friend Charlotte, who asks whether he wants to come for dinner in the evening. His next encounter is with the freeway system of Los Angeles on his way to work at the college. He feels invigorated by the speed of the freeways, even loves them "because he can still cope with them": "He can still get by" (20).

When he reaches the San Tomas State College campus, George thinks of his work as that of an actor: "So now George has arrived. He is not nervous in the least. As he gets out of his car, he feels an upsurge of energy, of eagerness for the play to begin. [...] He is all actor now." (29) He thinks of the students he encounters on his way to his office, as "the male and female raw material which is fed daily into this factory" (32). Then he encounters one of his own students, Russ Dreyer, who is individualised as having "gradually become George's personal attendant, executive officer, body-guard" (34). Instead of entering the classroom with Dreyer, George resorts to his office before meeting the group of his students as part of a ritual, a "deeply-rooted dramatic instinct" (39). The encounter with the students is depicted, equally, as a dramatic act, when he stands in front of the class and prepares himself for the beginning of the lesson: "George finds this frank confrontation extraordinarily exhilarating. He draws strength from these smiles, these bright young eyes. For him, this is one of the peak moments of the day. He feels brilliant, vital, challenging, slightly mysterious and, above all, *foreign*" (41). The nonverbal communication with his students is dwelt upon in some detail, and he regards his having to speak as "spoil[ing] everything" (45). The topic of the lesson is Aldous Huxley's novel *After Many a Summer Dies the Swan* (1939), a book about a millionaire who fears his impending death. Huxley, after having moved to California, examines in this novel American culture in its narcissism and its obsession with youth. George dwells in his lecture on the title of Huxley's novel, a quotation from Tennyson's poem *Tithonus*, immortalised by Zeus but not given eternal youth, so that he turns into "a repulsively immortal old man" (48). George presides "over the novel like an attendant at a carnival booth", while the students are enjoying themselves. He comes in on the discussion when it takes a turn to Huxley's potential anti-semitism, which George denies. He begins, instead, to talk about minorities in general, losing track of time until he realizes that "he must be running overtime" and his "feathers are ruffled. It's been a long time since last he forgot and let himself get up steam like this, right at the end of a period" (55). This lecture scene "employs the persistent theme of social existences as a series of performances, or as performative being" (Gonzalez 769), which links back to the narrative frame of the novel's focus on George's body as performative.

After George leaves the college, he visits a friend of his and Jim's, Doris, in a hospital. Again, George's feelings are registered on his body in his revulsion for the place: "Ah, how the poor body recoils with its every nerve from the sight, the smell, the feel of this place! Blindly it shies, rears, struggles to escape." (74) Doris is a woman with whom Jim had an affair. George regularly visits the woman, who is dying of an unnamed illness, since she represents a link to Jim. He conducts an internal dialogue with Jim, while he visits Doris: "Wouldn't you feel a crawling horror to think that maybe, even then, her body you fondled and kissed hungrily and entered with your aroused flesh already held seeds of this rottenness?" (75) George, in spite of his physical reluctance to enter the hospital, links himself to Doris by holding her hand, thus signalling that he can share her preoccupation with death: "Everything that matters to her is now right here in this room, where she is absorbed in the business of dying. [...] This preoccupation is with death, and we can all share in that, at any time, at any age, well or ill." (76)

After his visit to the hospital, George stops at his gym in order to make himself feel alive after the encounter with dying at the hospital. Again, the reference is to his embodied self: "He wants to rejoice in his own body; the tough triumphant old body of a survivor. The body that has outlived Jim and is going to outlive Doris." (82) George cherishes the "atmosphere of leisureliness" at the gym (84): "How delightful it is, to be here! If only one could spend one's entire life in this state of easy-going physical democracy!" (86) On his way home George reconsiders the dinner invitation of his friend Charlotte and calls her to confirm that he will come to see her. Charlotte provides another link to Jim, since both partners were on intimate terms with her. Charlotte's "wonderful lack of perception" has frequently brought the two lovers together again. George muses in internal monologue on this ability of Charlotte's which he sees in her lack of understanding: "How many times, when Jim and I had been quarelling and came to visit you—sulking, avoiding each other's eyes, talking to each other only through you—did you somehow bring us together again by the sheer power of your unawareness that anything was wrong?" (98) During the evening the two friends get drunk and talk about the possibility of Charlotte's returning to England. Charlotte tells George that Jim asked her to take care of him, and George argues against her going back to England, since it would be a return to the past, and, according to George, "[t]he past is just something that is over" (113). When George leaves Charlotte's house he realizes that he is very drunk. Nevertheless, he decides to run down the road toward the ocean and to a familiar bar, the Starboard Side, close by. George knows this bar since the time after the Second World War, when he frequented it to pick up sex partners. He moves to his favourite table in the corner when he sees a young man, who is one of his students, Kenny Potter. The two talk and drink together, and George sees in this dialogue a symbolism of opposites: "You and your dialogue-partner have to be somehow opposites. Why? Because you have to be symbolic figures—like, in this case, Youth and Age" (125). George regards this symbolic encounter impersonally. The conversation turns on the question of the past, too, which Kenny denies as unimportant to the young. He also refuses to acknowledge the present, and George tells him that he is "stuck with the Future" and this future, for George, is associated with death. Kenny, however, replies that he hardly ever thinks about death (127). When the two finally decide to go swimming, their relationship "is no longer symbolic" but becomes physical (131). After their swim and the encounter with an "apocalyptically great wave" (133), Kenny drags George out of the water and they go to George's house where they have some more drinks. When George passes out, Kenny puts him in his pyjamas and leaves the house to make his way home, leaving a message for George, who goes back to sleep.

Conscious and alert to embodiment, the novel fades out with a similar focus on George's sleeping body, which provides, together with the beginning focus on George's emerging consciousness, the frame for the novel. George's various encounters with different people throughout the day illuminate the material possibilities of being alive and human in the world, illustrating George's awareness of his middle age and homosexuality. His sleeping body is again compared with geological formations, "a lava reef under the cliffs", "a lot of rock pools" (149). These are identified with the persons George has encountered throughout his day. And this day in George's life is linked with the imagery of nature, connecting the ocean to consciousness:

"But that long day ends at last; yields to the night-time of the flood. And, just as the waters of the ocean come flooding, darkening over the pools, so over George and the others in sleep come the waters of that other ocean; that consciousness which is no one in particular but which contains everyone and everything, past, present and future, and extends unbroken beyond the uttermost stars." (150)

The narrator, at the end of the novel, again describes George's physical functions, while he is asleep, in medical detail. He depicts how an activity in George's coronary artery begins a slow process, of which the brain is also a part, that leads to a "melodramatic situation": "the formation of the atheromatous plague" (151): Owing to this "wildly improbable" happening, George dies in his sleep, a process which is depicted in detail. At the end of the novel, the George whose process of waking up and emerging to consciousness the reader has witnessed, turns back into "the non-entity we called George" (152). So, in this novel of embodied consciousness and physical awareness, the ending coincides with death, detailing a slow and unspectacular process of dying randomly in one's sleep and providing, thus, a phenomenology of dying.

JULIAN BARNES: FINALITY AND THE FEAR OF DEATH

If Isherwood's novel presents the awakening of consciousness in the morning as a beginning and closes with killing off its principal character during the night, constituting a phenomenology of the living and dying body, Julian Barnes's *Nothing to be Frightened Of* both indulges in and writes against an excessive remembrance of dying in the form of an extended reflection on the fear of death.

The ambiguities inherent in the acceptance of the finality of death are translated into the figure of irony by Terry Eagleton: "Human beings, too, have to live ironically. To accept the unfoundedness of our own existence is among other things to live in the shadow of death. Nothing more graphically illustrates how unneccessary we are than our mortality. To accept death would be to live more abundantly." (210) Whereas Eagleton is more concerned with human attitudes towards death, the ironic paradoxes he points out also pertain to a representational problem. Death as a limit to representation has been conceived as a major challenge to aesthetics such that the attempt to fictionalize endings entails the end of fiction (Hart Nibbrig 9). On the other hand, as Sigmund Freud has pointed out, the paradox of experiencing death in life may be undergone only in the realm of fiction, as, for instance, the dying of George at the end of Isherwood's novel: "We die with the hero with whom we have identified ourselves; yet we survive him, and are ready to die again just as safely with another hero" (291).

In terms of knowledge, death can only be approached from an external perspective, since "a self-referential system can conceive neither its own ending nor its infinite duration" (Macho, "Unsterblichkeit" 261; my translation). It thus delimits perception and knowledge as well as representation, so that Freud's assumption that we are unconsciously convinced of being immortal is logically both correct and incorrect. A further paradox concerns the distinction between death and dying: Whereas death remains outside the realm of experience and perception, the knowledge of dying is, according to Norbert Elias, a problem of the living (6). The discourse on death, then, produces the ambivalent position of knowing that one will die while being ignorant about death, or in Frank Kelleter's words: "The individual knows *of* its death but it knows nothing *about* it" (20; my translation; emphasis original).

It is difficult to determine the genre to which Julian Barnes's *Nothing to Be Frightened Of* belongs. As Barnes points out in a self-reflective passage, "[t]his is not, by the way, my 'autobiography'" (34). His concern with his parents' deaths, he asserts, is with "trying to work out how dead they are" (35). This apparently bizarre statement, concerned with a measurement for being dead, relates to his overarching concern with a secular form of immortality. Stating at the beginning his impossible longing for a spiritual way of transcending death—"I don't believe in God, but I miss him" (1)—the text is driven forward by Barnes's search for an antidote to his fear of it.

He considers the attraction of the Christian religion as a beautiful story with a happy ending and draws on the analogous powers of art as a potential remedy against existential dread. The idea that art may replace the religious notion of immortality, however, is called into doubt by his juxtaposing it with the long duration of evolutionary conceptions of time that ultimately defeat the time scope relevant for the writer's afterlife (76). Furthermore, Barnes continuously tries to adjust his intuitive sense of himself as a free individual and a writer against the contemporary evolutionary narrative of genetic determinism that he subscribes to (95). He frequently refers to Montaigne as the authority on a modern *ars moriendi*. He shares with him the belief that, "since we cannot defeat death, the best form of counter-attack is to have it constantly in mind" (41) so that we will "disarm [death] of his novelty and strangeness" (Montaigne, n. p.). Whereas Montaigne thus becomes for Barnes not only the warrantor of the art of dying but also an instructor for keeping the fear of death at bay by anticipating it to the point of "bor[ing] death itself with your attention" (181), he repeatedly places his vivid imagination of his "own eternal non-existence" against Freud's assumption that the unconscious mind is convinced of its own immortality (138, 179, 212). He rejects this idea in spite of his bargaining search for some form of personal immortality or a writer's afterlife, at one point even ironically contemplating giving up his profession as a writer in exchange for immortality: "You get rid of death and I'll give up writing. How about that for a deal?" (67) These contradictions shape the text as a form of writer's legacy, which is at the same time an artist's manual for staring down the fear of death with "pit-gazing" (95).

The main focus and motivation of the text is, thus, Barnes's fear of "NOTHING" (99), revealing the second meaning of the punning title as the fear of death as "total extinction" (95), which he discusses with reference to his biological family as well as his elected artistic family of novelists, philosophers and composers. In her review of the text, Penelope Lively describes it as "a maverick form of family memoir" that is "so bursting with voices that is seems almost to be a novel" (n. p.). She further identifies it as "an inventive and invigorating slant on what is nowadays called 'life writing'" (n. p.). Whereas "life writing" has become a popular umbrella term for the genres of autobiography, biography, memoir and diary, it has also come to designate the more specific forms of writing one's life under the conditions of illness, disability and old age (Couser 4, 5). Barbara Frey Waxman defines "autobiographies of aging" as a form of self-reflexive life writing which focuses "on the period [of a person's life] in which aging or senescence becomes central to the subject's definition of self" (10). Furthermore, this form attends "carefully to the body: the limits age imposes on mobility, the lessening of strength and endurance, the vulnerability to illness, the increasing unreliability of the senses and memory" (8).

Whereas Barnes's text blurs the distinction between autobiography and biography and focuses on the later stages of life, it self-consciously rejects the idea of older age as a period of wisdom—a claim Waxman makes for autobiographies of ageing which she regards as a form of "ripening into senescence" (11). Instead, Barnes treats the belief that old age is a period of wisdom ironically. He rejects the idea of growing into maturity as one ages as an illusion. From the perspective of this questioning stance towards notions of development as a form of progress narrative, adulthood does not feel like an achievement:

"Rather, it felt like a conspiracy: I'll pretend that you're grown up if you pretend that I am. Then, as acknowledged (or at least unrumbled) adults, we head towards some fuller, maturer condition, when the narrative has justified itself and we are expected to proclaim, or shyly admit, 'Ripeness is all!' But how often does the fruit metaphor hold? We are as likely to end up a sour windfall or dried and wizened by the sun, as we are to swell pridefully to ripeness." (190)

Julian Barnes not only rejects the optimistic idea of 'growth' or 'ripening' that frequently underwrites definitions of life writing concerned with age and illness narrative, he also questions the equation of life with a narrative as it is promoted by some narrative gerontologists. Referring to his physician's belief that life is a narrative, of which dying is the conclusion, Barnes resists this idea, arguing that mere chronology does not provide a story: "And so it is with our lives: one damn thing after another—a gutter replaced, a washing machine fixed—rather than a story. Or (since I meet my GP in concert halls) there is no proper announcement of theme, followed by development, variation, recapitulation, coda, and crunching resolution." (189) Barnes's outline of the structure of classical music may also serve as an implicit description of his own narratives, which frequently merge fictional with essayistic writing so that his essay on the fear of death reads partly like a novel. Furthermore, Barnes dismisses the idea of the life review as a "developmental task of the later years" which can "provide new insights that result in the resolution of old issues" (R. Butler, n. p.) and is "our last opportunity to find meaning in the story that is about to end" (Barnes 188), since he suspects such reviewing of one's life from the perspective of approaching death to be a confabulation, expecting "a dying person to be an unreliable narrator, because [...] what is useful at that time is a sense of having lived to some purpose and according to some comprehensible plot" (190).

If Barnes, then, rejects the prevalent definitions of life writing and the life review for narratives concerned with the end of one's life, *Nothing to Be Frightened Of* can perhaps be better understood as 'death writing'. Indeed, Barnes's text incorporates ritualized genres concerned with memorising the dead such as the obituary or necrology,[5] the epitaph, and the artist's last words. His obsessive thinking about death—which he refers to variously as "Montaignery" or "pit-gazing" and defines, in a variant of the paradoxical configuration of death, as "the attempt to make death, if not your friend, at least your familiar enemy" (181)—is linked to a search for personal immortality when he wonders "if we can somehow farewell ourselves in advance" (86–87). Julian Barnes's *Nothing to Be Frightened Of* invents different versions of the prospective farewell, the first of which concerns the perspective of the stranger: seeing "the death of 'me' through the eyes of others" (87). This version attempts, and fails, to minimize the fear of death by reducing the importance of the subject: "Unknown person dies: not many mourn. That is our certain obituary in the eyes of the rest of the world. So who are we to indulge our egotism and make a fuss?" (87)

---

5 | Apart from the meaning of "necrology" as an "obituary notice or article", the *OED* lists the meaning of "[t]he history or study of the dead", which also applies more generally to Barnes's *Nothing To Be Frightened Of*. For definitions of the genres of remembrance of the dead, such as funeral address, elegy, necrology, obituary and epitaph, see also Füger (77-79).

Next, Barnes presents the abbreviation of his life from a potential biographer's perspective: "'Got up,' his version went. 'Wrote book. Went out, bought bottle of wine. Came home, cooked dinner. Drank wine.' I immediately endorsed this Brief Life" (131). Whereas this very "Brief Life" takes an ironic position between a writer's regarding himself as an eligible subject for biography and not making "a fuss", Barnes reiterates the idea of the obituary written by himself. He rewrites these two versions into a short description of his own life and death in a self-referential necrology in newspaper style: "LONDON MAN DIES: NOT MANY HURT" (178). This final version of the prospective farewell resolves the anonymous style of the stranger's anti-obituary with the satirical abbreviation of his life by a friend into a more intimate perspective, which, however, remains a third person narrative: "He wrote books, then he died. Though a satirical friend thought his life was divided between literature and the kitchen (and the wine bottle), there were other aspects to it: love, friendship, music, art, society, travel, sport, jokes. He was happy in his own company as long as he knew when that solitude would end. He loved his wife and feared death." (178)

Switching to the third-person voice for this brief and modest obituary lessens the charge of "committing the cardinal English sin of drawing attention to oneself" which Barnes self-ironically considers after this version of prospective farewell before he returns to the prevalent first-person voice (179). Barnes further pursues the idea of a writer's posthumous fame by looking at its opposite end, at the process of being forgotten, which he imagines as an inevitable evolutionary development in which forgetful publishing houses, receding academic interest and social changes take a share. In the writer's case, however, the focus is on the "last reader" (225). Whereas he first considers this last reader as an inevitable aspect of the writer's fate, he next turns this into a scene of "sentimental" acknowledgement before reconsidering and dismissing his last reader as "by definition, someone who doesn't recommend your books to anyone else. You bastard! Not good enough, eh?" (226) In this comic address to the reader, Barnes pursues another variant of 'farewelling himself' by making his prospective 'last reader' responsible for his eventual fall into oblivion, which he has previously considered calmly in the abstract.

In thus inventing expressions of a writer's posthumous fame—however unreliable and precarious—Barnes takes up different imaginary narrative perspectives on his own death. At the end of the book, while self-reflectively referring back to his various attempts at a prospective farewell, he puts both farewell and last words off as premature, indulging instead in a meta-fictional repetition of the formal last page's "The End", until he is satisfied with the third version in capital letters. This playful and self-referential gesture displaces the obsessive concern in the text with death as "total extinction" (95), "NOTHING" (99), "total annihilation" (114), "eternal non-existence" (212), into "THE END" (250) of the book. Barnes depicts the contradictions involved in the fear of death, which illustrate modern death's structure of recognition and denial in a mixture of self-reflexively autobiographical genres concerned with narrating one's own death. *Nothing to Be Frightened Of* ultimately rejects the idea of ageing as growth by questioning the "fruit metaphor" which proclaims that "[r]ipeness is all" (90).

Conclusion

The four texts considered approach the topic of death and dying in different ways. In Henry James's texts the ghostly presences are depicted in different material settings—the family home, the altar—and are placed against the structural concern with absence. The ghost as an absent presence materializes as the protagonist's *alter ego* in "The Jolly Corner", whereas dying and the remembrance of the dead is the concern of "The Altar of the Dead". Drawing on the ambiguous attitude of Freudian and Jungian psychoanalysis, Samuel Beckett's aesthetic concern with a language of reduction determines the depiction of births and deaths, beginnings and endings, as a cultural matrix already apparent in his first poetry collection *Echo's Bones*. Christopher Isherwood's *A Single Man* is concerned with the protagonist George's embodied consciousness and physical materiality, which the novel follows throughout a single day in his life. In the frame narrative the focus on embodiment is most obvious and the story's ending, like the ending of "The Altar of the Dead", coincides with the protagonist's death. In this novel, homosexual embodiment is focused upon whereas George's dying in his sleep is depicted as a natural, even if improbable, event. In Julian Barnes's *Nothing to Be Frightened Of* we follow the author's concern with the fear of dying, which is employed in imaginative ways, detailing different forms of "death writing" as a particular, ironic form of "life writing". Barnes is sceptical of the autobiographical age narratives' concern with progress narrative and presents his own version of an ironic encounter with death. Taken together, the reading of the four modernist and postmodernist texts in their different approaches to death and dying intends to outline a first sketch of a phenomenological thanatology of modern culture.

WORKS CITED

Adorno, Theodor W., Max Horkheimer. *Dialectic of Enlightenment*. [1944] London: Verso, 1997. Print.
"Antelope." *Oxford English Dictionary Online*. Third Edition. 2014. Web. 20 August 2017. http://www.oed.com.
Ariès, Philippe. *Studien zur Geschichte des Todes im Abendland*. Übers. Hans-Horst Henschen. München: Hanser, 1976. Print.
Audoin-Rouzeau Stéphane, Annette Becker. *1914–1918. Understanding the Great War*. Trans. Catherine Temerson. London: Profile Books, 2002. Print
Barnes, Julian. *Nothing To Be Frightened Of*. London: Vintage, 2009. Print.
Beckett, Samuel. *The Collected Poems of Samuel Beckett*. Ed. Seán Lawlor, John Pilling. London: Faber and Faber, 2012. Print.
Beistegui, Miguel de, Guiseppe Bianco, Marjorie Gracieuse. Eds. *The Care of Life. Transdisciplinary Perspectives in Bioethics and Biopolitics*. London: Rowman & Littlefield, 2015. Print.
Bennett, Jane. *Vibrant Matter. A Political Ecology of Things*. Durham: Duke UP, 2010. Print.
Bourke, Joanna. *An Intimate History of Killing: Face to Face Killing in Twentieth-Century Warfare*. London: Granta Books, 1999. Print.
Braidotti, Rose. *The Posthuman*. Cambridge: Polity P, 2013. Print.
Bronfen, Elisabeth. *Over Her Dead Body. Death, Femininity and the Aesthetic*. Manchester: Manchester UP, 1992. Print.
Brosch, Renate. *Krisen des Sehens. Henry James und die Veränderung der Wahrnehmung im 19. Jahrhundert*. Tübingen: Stauffenburg, 2000. Print.
Brown, Bill. "Thing Theory." *Critical Inquiry* 28.1 (2001): 1–22.
Brown, Bill. *A Sense of Things. The Object Matter of American Literature*. Chicago: U o Chicago P, 2003. Print.

Butler, Judith. *Precarious Life. The Powers of Mourning and Violence*. London: Verso, 2004. Print.
Butler, Robert N. "Life Review." *Encyclopedia of Aging*. 2002. Encyclopedia.com. Web. 13 August 2017. http://www.encyclopedia.com/doc/1G2-3402200232.html.
Charon, Rita. "The Novelization of the Body, or, How Medicine and Stories Need One Another." *Narrative* 19.1 (2011): 33–50.
Cohn, Dorrit. "'First Shock of Complete Perception': The Opening Episode of *The Golden Bowl*, Volume 2." *The Henry James Review* 22 (2001): 1–9.
Coole, Diana, Samantha Frost. Eds. *New Materialisms: Ontology, Agency, and Politics*. Durham: Duke UP, 2010. Print.
Couser, G. Thomas. *Recovering Bodies. Illness, Disability, Life Writing*. Madison, Wisc.: U of Wisconsin P, 1997. Print.
Cuddy-Keane, Melba. "Narration, Navigation, and Non-Conscious Thought: Neuroscientific and Literary Approaches to the Thinking Body." *University of Toronto Quarterly* 79.2 (2010): 680–701.
Cutting, Andrew. *Death in Henry James*. Houndmills: Palgrave Macmillan, 2005. Print.
Derrida, Jacques. *Learning to Live Finally. The Last Interview*. Trans. Pascale-Anne Brault and Michael Naas. Hoboken, NJ: Melvillehouse Publishing, 2007. Print.
Eagleton, Terry. *After Theory*. New York: Basic Books, 2003. Print.
Elias, Norbert. *Über die Einsamkeit der Sterbenden*. [1982] Frankfurt a. M.: Suhrkamp, 2002. Print.
Freud, Sigmund. "Thoughts for the Times on War and Death." *The Standard Edition of the Complete Psychological Works of Sigmund Freud*, Vol. 14. London: Vintage, 2001. 273–300. Print.
Füger, Wilhelm. *Jonathan Swifts Autonekrolog—Die Verse auf den Tod von Dr. Swift, D. S. P. D. Übersetzung—Kommentar—Interpretation*. Hamburg: Dr. Kovac, 2006. Print.
"Gantlope/gauntlet." *Oxford English Dictionary Online*. Third edition. 2014. Web. 20 August 2017. http://www.oed.com.
Gehring, Petra. *Theorien des Todes: Zur Einführung*. Hamburg: Junius, 2010. Print.
Gonzalez, Octavio R. "Isherwood's Impersonality: Ascetic Self-Divestiture and Queer Relationality in *A Single Man*." *Modern Fiction Studies* 59.4 (2013): 758–783.

Gruman, Gerald J. "A History of Ideas about the Prolongation of Life. The Evolution of Prolongevity Hypotheses to 1800." *Transactions of the American Philosophical Society*, New Series. 56.9 (1966): 3–102.

Hart Nibbrig, Christiaan L. *Ästhetik des Todes*. Frankfurt a. M.: Insel, 1995. Print.

Hay, Simon. *A History of the Modern British Ghost Story*. London: Palgrave Macmillan, 2011. Print.

Isherwood, Christopher. *A Single Man*. London: Vintage, 2010. Print.

James, Henry. "The Jolly Corner." *Ghost Stories of Henry James*. Intr. Martin Scofield. Hertfordshire: Wordsworth Editions, 2008. 306–34. Print.

James, Henry. "The Altar of the Dead." *Terminations*. Philadelphia: U o Pennsylvania P, 2004. 185–242. Print.

Kelleter, Frank. *Die Moderne und der Tod. Das Todesmotiv in moderner Literatur, untersucht am Beispiel Edgar Allan Poes, T. S. Eliots und Samuel Becketts*. Frankfurt a. M.: Peter Lang, 1996. Print.

Knowlson, James. *Damned to Fame. A Life of Samuel Beckett*. London: Bloomsbury, 1997. Print.

Lacina, Katharina. *Tod*. Wien: facultas wuv, 2009. Print.

Laqueur, Thomas. *The Work of the Dead. A Cultural History of Mortal Remains*. Princeton, N. J.: Princeton UP, 2015. Print.

Lively, Penelope. "Before Darkness Falls." Rev. of *Nothing to Be Frightened Of* by Julian Barnes. *Financial Times* 1 March 2008. Web. 10 August 2017. http://www.ft.com.

Lustig, T. J. *Henry James and the Ghostly*. Cambridge: Cambridge UP, 1994. Print.

Macho, Thomas, H. *Todesmetaphern: Zur Logik der Grenzerfahrung*. Frankfurt a. M.: Suhrkamp, 1987. Print.

Macho, Thomas, H. "Religion, Unsterblichkeit und der Glaube an die Wissenschaft." *Ruhm, Tod und Unsterblichkeit. Über den Umgang mit der Endlichkeit*. Ed. Konrad Paul Liessmann. Wien: Zolnay, 2004. 261–77.

Macho, Thomas, Kristin Marek. Ed. *Die neue Sichtbarkeit des Todes*. München: Fink, 2007. Print.

Mbembe, Achille. "Necropolitics." Trans. Libby Meintjes. *Public Culture* 15.1 (2003): 11–40.

Montaigne, Michel de. *Essays of Michel de Montaigne*. Ed. William C. Hazlitt. Trans. Charles Cotton. [1877] Project Gutenberg. 17 September 2007. Web. 10 August 2017. http://www.gutenberg.org/files/3600/3600-h/3600-h.htm#2HCH0019.

Nassehi, Armin, Georg Weber. *Tod, Modernität und Gesellschaft: Entwurf einer Theorie der Todesverdrängung.* Opladen: Westdeutscher Verlag, 1989. Print.

Nassehi, Armin. *Geschlossenheit und Offenheit.* Frankfurt a. M.: Suhrkamp, 2003. Print.

Offizier, Frederike. "Death of the Other: Dying, Alterity, and Appropriation." *The Morbidity of Culture. Melancholy, Trauma, Illness and Dying in Literature and Film.* Ed. Stephanie Siewert, Antonia Mehnert. Frankfurt a. M.: Peter Lang, 2011. 119–38. Print.

Ovid, *Metamorphoses.* Trans. Sir Samuel Garth, John Dryden. *The Internet Classics Archive.* Web. 14 August 2017. http://classics.mit.edu/Ovid/metam.html.

Posnock, Ross. *The Trial of Curiosity: Henry James, William James, and the Challenge of Modernity.* New York: Oxford UP, 1991. Print.

"Precipitate." *Oxford English Dictionary Online.* Third edition. 2014. Web. 15 August 2017. http://www.oed.com.

Roberts, Marie Mulvey. "'A Physic Against Death': Eternal Life and the Enlightenment—Gender and Gerontology." *Literature and Medicine During the Eighteenth Century.* Ed. Mary Mulvey Roberts, Roy Porter. London: Routledge, 1993. 151–67. Print.

Schleifer, Ronald. *Rhetoric and Death: The Language of Modernism and Postmodern Discourse Theory.* Urbana: U o Illinois P, 1990. Print.

Shainberg, Lawrence. "Exorcising Beckett." *The Paris Review* 104 (1987). Web. 13 August 2017. http://www.samuel-beckett.net/ShainExor1.html.

Stewart, Garrett. *Death Sentences: Styles of Dying in British Fiction.* Cambridge, MA: Harvard UP, 1984. Print.

Stuart, Christopher. "'Is There a Life after Death?': Henry James's Response to the New York Edition." *Colby Quarterly* 35.2 (1999): 90–101.

Summers, Claude. "Foreword." Christopher Isherwood. *Isherwood on Writing.* Ed. James J. Berg. Minneapolis: U of Minnesota P, 2007. vii–xv. Print.

Thurston, Luke. "Outselves: Beckett, Bion and Beyond." *Journal of Modern Literature* 32.3 (2009): 121–43.

Todorov, Tzvetan. *The Fantastic. A Structural Approach to a Literary Genre.* Trans. by Richard Howard. Ithaca, New York: Cornell UP, 1975. Print.

—. "The Structural Analysis of Literature: The Tales of Henry James." *Structuralism: An Introduction*. Ed. David Robey. Oxford: Clarendon P, 1973. 73–104. Print.

Waxman, Barbara Frey. *To Live in the Center of the Moment. Literary Autobiographies of Aging*. Charlottesville: UP of Virginia, 1997. Print.

Woolf, Virginia. "Henry James's Ghost Stories." [1921] *The Essays of Virginia Woolf*. Vol. 3. 1919–1924. Ed. Andrew McNeillie. Orlando, FL: Harcourt Brace Jovanovich, 1988. 319–26. Print.

'About Suffering They Were Never Wrong, The Old Masters'
Human Pain and the Crucible of Representation

Rüdiger Kunow

SUFFERING AS MATERIAL AND MATERIALITY

This paper starts from the assumption that relations between bodies and words, even more so between bodies and stories, are and have always been more complicated, more difficult, than the current infatuation with linguistic or cultural constructivism leads us to believe. Talk is cheap, words, even stories come by easily, but not always can they do the trick, as Judith Butler reminds us: "although the body depends on language to be known, the body also exceeds every possible linguistic effort at capture" (Butler 2). Such moments of excess, when the materiality of the body outstrips the resources of language, when words are failing us, are oftentimes moments of acute corporeal sensation, pleasurable or painful. French poststructuralism has exhibited a penchant for the pleasurable ones, for bodily desires, indulgences, "jouissance," while the following argument will address the most somber fields of somato-sensory experiences. Here, too, "[w]ords do badly at bodies" (Terdiman 173; emphasis deleted). How badly, will be the thematic focus on the pages to come.

More specifically, I will argue that human suffering is and has always been a strategic, even a contested site, where the powers of representation, pictorial, textual or otherwise, assert themselves—or fail to do so. The title quote from W. H. Auden's poem "Musée des Beaux Arts" (1939)[1] is

---

1 | The references in the Auden poem are to Pieter Bruegel the Elder (c. 1530-1569) and his painting "Landscape with the Fall of Icarus" (date unknown). Since the 1990s, questions concerning the authenticity of the painting hanging in the

a useful introduction for such an argument because of its emphatic, but at the same time also ironic assertion that the old masters "got it right" about suffering, that they found a way to turn suffering into material for art. The overall perspective of the poem is then one that suggests there is no simple, straightforward way to give expression to extreme states of somato-sensory experience, and that oftentimes these states remain unarticulated or unnoticed.

Auden's irony runs counter to a long line of artistic endeavors, from the days of Greco-Roman antiquity to the present, from Sophocles and the anonymous Hellenistic sculptor of the Laocoon Group, all the way to Virginia Woolf and Joseph Beuys, to turn to somato-sensory extremities, always testing new ways of representation for human life as distressed object. This long history, to which the gruesome atrocities of the previous century have added a new chapter, may have been the reason for Theodor Adorno's astute but somewhat inconclusive declaration that "[a]ll expression is the trace left by suffering" (208; emphasis added).

I take from this the idea that representations of suffering might well be seen not as incidental, isolated special cases but as central to the processes and powers of representation itself.[2] What this phrase also suggests is this: if bodily anguish leaves traces, not more, in the available cultural archives, giving it full expression would have to be deferred to the realm of a somato-semantic utopia. As I will argue later on, we seem by now to have arrived at such a utopia, a techno-utopia to be sure. Moreover, by speaking of "traces," Adorno makes room for the possibility that the presence of human suffering in practices of representation need not be direct, "in your face," as it were, but may require some analytical, if not archeological effort[3], to restore a sense of the material, palpable, sensory site called "the body" in conditions of individual or collective anguish.

Royal Museum of Fine Arts in Brussels have been discussed, but they do not play a role for the present argument.
2 | For an elaborate and judicious reading of Adorno's argument about representation and suffering cf. Marder.
3 | From the position of an African American women writer Toni Morrison has developed the notion of "the archeological site" which empowers recollection and marks the beginning of "[her] route to a reconstruction of a world, to an exploration of an interior life that was not written." (192, 195)

One can discover literary efforts along this line in the archives of U. S. literature, especially in the domain of so-called "minority" writing; Toni Morrison's novels, such as *Beloved* (1987), being prominent instances of archeological representations of collective suffering. My own example here will be Ernest Hemingway's "The Snows of Kilimanjaro." First published in 1938, this story is a perhaps unlikely example of what cultural critique, following Arthur Kleinman, has codified as "illness narratives." It is unambiguously about the traces of pain in literary representation. One might even say that pain and painful experiences are here seen as a necessary prerequisite for such representation. The very opening words are "about" pain and situate the narrative squarely within suffering, including ways to avoid it: "'The marvelous thing is that it's painless,' he said, 'That's how you know when it starts.'" (52) The talk is about the narrator/protagonist Harry's wound that is slowly filling with gangrene and from which he will die unless outside help arrives in time at his safari camp. As the story progresses, it becomes clear that there is a *double entendre* to these words, for there is another, equally painless process festering in Harry: his betrayal of the arduous job of writing in favor of social and creature comforts: "He had destroyed his talent by not using it, by betrayals of himself and what he believed in [...] he had traded on it. [...] And he had chosen to make his living with something else instead of a pen and a pencil." (60) In his feverish thoughts all those moments of human suffering are coming to him—mostly moments of war and violence—that he should have written about will now not be written because he is dying. Realizing this is as painful for Harry as the gangrenous wound: "He could stand pain as well as any man, until it went on too long, and wore him out, but here he had something that had hurt frightfully and just when he had felt it breaking him, the pain had stopped," stopped because he had given up finding the right words for it (73). Physical pain functions in this narrative as a conceptual allegory for the agonizing process of writing, of searching for *le mot juste*.[4]

Musing on the unlikely parallel between Adorno's reflections and Hemingway's narrative does not mean that I see simple correspondences at work here. Rather, Hemingway is approaching the problematic relation-

---

4 | The idea that Harry's physical decay is in this narrative analogous to his professional decay has been discussed in criticism, most prominently perhaps in Carlos Baker's reading.

ship of words and wounds from the other end of the issue, as it were. Like Adorno, he is concerned with the "traces" of suffering in writing, but understands them as necessary precondition for honest writing, for a writing the times demand, a writing that is not making it easy for itself but deliberately and purposively courts experiences of pain, physical and mental.

THE BODY AS DISTRESSED OBJECT

Before entering into a more detailed debate about the place of human anguish in the crucible of representation, however, a note on terminology is in order. "Suffering," the expression used so far, is a rather broad, encompassing term spanning a broad range of phenomena and experiences that go well beyond the ambitions of the present paper. What humans can suffer from and under, includes a variety of conditions of the individual body but also those that have their origin in the body politic. People can suffer from illnesses just as much as from social injustices. For this reason, and in order to retain a manageable focus, the following argument will limit itself to a set of somato-sensory phenomena which the English language addresses under the term "pain."

Such a choice suggests itself from a variety of standpoints. First, the biosciences, and here especially the International Association for the Study of Pain (IASP), have over the decades consolidated a research-based, operational understanding of pain. They proposed a definition that has become widely accepted throughout the scientific community and which can thus serve as a starting point for the following argument: "Pain: An unpleasant sensory and emotional experience associated with actual or potential tissue damage, or described in such damage" (210). Secondly, "pain" has long been the object of philosophical reflections, from Aristotle, via Nietzsche all the way to Wittgenstein, and contemporary analytical philosophy[5]—reflections which link states of pain to some fundamental questions concerning the relationship between body and mind, self and other, language and world, even art and life.

---

5 | A comprehensive discussion of relevant material can be found in David Morris and Elaine Scarry; within a German context, cf. Hans-Georg Gadamer's reflections and Iris Hermann's comprehensive study.

Let me enter into my own argument by suggesting that representations of extreme states of physical distress and anguish are inherently transgressive. Pain marks an emphatic Now in the cadences of bodily temporality, one that negotiates the borderlines between the normal and the pathological (theorized by Canguilhem); they also negotiate the borderlines between the somatic and the semantic. Most often, this latter transgression has been theorized in epistemological terms, as a question of conviction and certitude. Elaine Scarry's phrasing succinctly captures the issues at hand: "To have pain is to have certainty, to hear about pain is to have doubt" (13).

Much of this view goes back to Wittgenstein. In his *Philosophical Investigations* (1953) and other writings, he took pain and its (linguistic) representations as occasion for a stringent epistemological skepticism concerning their referential content. In his view, a statement such as "he is in pain" (86) does not offer conclusive evidence that it actually corresponds to anything going on inside that person's body: "there is something Inner here which can be inferred only inconclusively from the Outer" (*Last Writings* § 951a). Even if a given statement is semantically and grammatically correct and thus not "getting into conflict with the way other people use this word [pain]" (83), and even if the person making it will support it gesturally, by crying or pointing to a body part, this will not suffice to produce epistemological certainty: "since it is the expression of a perception, it can also be called the expression of thought" (*Investigations* 168). On this basis, there can be no epistemologically unambiguous way to communicate a person's pain to another person. The next best thing to certainty for Wittgenstein is analogy: "if I suppose that someone has a pain, then I am simply supposing that he has just the same as I have so often had" (94).[6] Hence, as Wittgenstein argues, "I can only believe that someone else is in pain, but I know it if I am." (203) This position (echoed in Scarry's phrase above) has been widely shared in analytic philosophy, as the following quote from one of its most celebrated American representatives might illustrate: "To be in the same epistemic situation that would

---

6 | Cf. also Wittgenstein's repeated objections to a correspondence theory of linguistic representation, most of them phrased in terms of a grammar of expression: "if we construct the grammar of the expression of sensation on the model of 'object and designation' the object drops out of consideration as irrelevant" (*Last Writings* § 293).

obtain if one had a pain *is* to have a pain; to be in the same epistemic situation that would obtain in the absence of pain *is* not to have a pain [...]." (Kripke 152) If one is willing to be guided by such epistemological skepticism, one is also bound to concede that the pain of others must remain ultimately and fundamentally inaccessible, except, perhaps, for the one and rather special case noted by Jean Améry (who from his concentration camp experience knew what he was talking about): "If someone wanted to impart his physical pain, he would be forced to inflict it and thereby become a torturer himself." (32–33)

Whatever its merits from a strictly philosophical point of view, from the perspective of cultural critique, the point to be made about analytic philosophy's position on pain is that it is ultimately Pyrrhonic, denying not only that human life, especially in moments of extreme physical distress and anguish[7], can in any way find representation but in the last resort denying even that we can meaningfully say it exists. More importantly, for the interests of cultural critique analytic philosophy's reading of pain has little to offer besides reasserting one more time the assumption that the distressed body is an individualistic pathology and its suffering essentially individual or personal.[8] A person's pain thus seen is then private matter, or perhaps, a form of *private enterprise*, if one takes into account the troubles and travails caused by the pain experience and by the efforts to mitigate or avoid it. In any case, there is in this theoretical perspective no "We" of pain, no sociality of suffering, while it is essentially this "We," the shared intersubjective experiences, the collective presences and practices of the pain experience, that define its interest for cultural critique, and that will for this reason form the main body of the following argument. And so, my argument tries to re-locate pain and the pain experience from the inside of the human body to the social-cultural manifold. I am therefore

---

7 | Formations of physical distress are of course as varied as the experiences they are intended to designate. For reasons of convenience I will in my argument use a variety of terms such as anguish, ague, pain, often together with the term suffering. By this conceptual shorthand I do not wish to conflate these terms and suggest that pain and suffering are somehow the same; the variety of terms simply allows me to express at one and the same time the experiential and the performative side of physical hurting.

8 | For an extended version of this argument on pain as "private practice" cf. my *Material Bodies: Biology and Culture in the United States* (385-390).

deeply sympathetic to Canguilhem's observation that human life "is lived in the discretion of social [and I might add cultural] relations" (49). In the meantime, the question of representational content which so obsessed analytic philosophy is in this context more or less secondary in importance—even a person who simulates pain enters the circuits of communication and in doing so relies on the available cultural archives of pain representation.

PAIN AS COMMUNICATIVE ACTION

When a person speaks about his or her pain, their body in distress enters the public domain, the shared world of human beings where people coordinate their actions and assumptions on the basis of a broadly shared understanding of given topics or objectives. Illness, just as life, is "lived in the discretion of social relations" (Canguilhem 49). Acknowledgments of this kind might take us to the Habermasian model of discourse ethics (which is well-known and shall for this reason not be unfolded here). To connect suffering with his concept of "communicative action" is particularly helpful because it allows us to move beyond an individualistic and idiosyncratic understanding of the distressed body by situating it in the exchanges where "people come together to form a public [...] dealing with matters of general interest" (*Society and Politics* 231). It goes without saying that pain is such a matter of general interest.[9] In recent years, the ascendency of genetics and the sloganeering around the "book of life" have given new prestige and popularity to the nexus between body and story.

"Communicative" in Habermas' understanding (*Moral Consciousness* 116–194) oftentimes means discursive, which means that pain can be understood as discursively realized among people. Not all discourses about pain are narrative, of course, but many are, and as Arthur Frank, Elaine Scarry, or, more recently, Javier Moscoso have shown, narrative is indeed one of the principle conduits through which pain can find "its" representation—however inchoate, incomplete or even ideological this representation might be. Rita Charon and the project of "Narrative Medicine" have consolidated this nexus between bodily suffering and narrative rep-

---

9 | One of Habermas's examples in his discussions of communicative action is, interestingly enough, a person's call for help (*Moral Consciousness* 26).

resentation into a conceptual system and method of inquiry, more particularly in the field of medical care. The groundwork for this project was laid by Rita Charon, M. D., founder and director of the program, in a 2001 article for the Journal of the American Medical Association and later in her book *Narrative Medicine: Honoring the Stories of Illness* (2008). As the name might suggest, "Narrative Medicine" proceeds from the assumption of "the centrality of storytelling" for all forms of medical practice, including healing and care-giving. Narratives are thus seen as ways of "bearing witness [...] and helping patients navigate the moral channels of illness" (203). What is empowering about this concept is the possibility that narrative can thus lead us (back) to the suffering human body, resisting clinical abstractions and the objectification of the suffering body. Instead, narrative medicine focuses on narrative content as more or less direct, not to say mimetic, representation of a pathological medical condition.

In accordance with this line of thought one might well read language and more specifically narrative as a mediator, at times even a buffer, between the sensate body's acute condition ("being in pain") and the shared world of human beings ("speaking about one's pain"). The word "buffer" seems particularly à propos here, because by insisting on the seamless fit between "the world *in* which one tells and the world *of* which one tells" (Genette 236) in moments of pain, proponents of narrative medicine run the risk of working with a referentially and formally naïve concept of narrative. Another way of saying the same thing would be to insist on a moment of a-synchronicity involved in projects harnessing narrative for the communication of pain and more generally, illness. It seems as if the interrogations of narrative in High Modernism, its postmodern deconstruction, or contemporary cyber writing, have never happened. Instead, claims for narrative are being made—claims of truth-in-representation among them—which both in narrative theory and in literary practice have long been cast aside as outdated and epistemologically dubious. Hayden White, himself a central figure in the "narrative turn" in the Humanities, warns of the ideological uses to which narrative can be put: in the world of the narrative, "reality wears the mask of meaning [...]" (20–21). It would be wise, therefore, not to accept uncritically narrative's warrant for the representation of bodily suffering.[10]

---

10 | Such a distancing attitude takes us back one more time to Adorno who wanted to protect the sinister realities of human suffering from clichéd expres-

PAIN'S PUBLIC LIFE: SETH KAUFMAN'S *KING OF PAIN*

The marriage of body and story is thus not always or necessarily a happy one. In fact, one might argue that there is a price to be paid for the project of narrativizing pain. What price shall here be discussed with the help of a recent fictional narrative which made pain its central donné. Seth Kaufman's novel *The King of Pain* (2012) is a satirical, at times farcical example of the Hollywood novel. Its central character, "Rick 'the Prick' Salter" (12), is a media mogul, both producer of pain and its object. As the novel opens, he finds himself trapped under a wall of entertainment gadgets which have fallen over him so that he is suffering from "pain so intense my body doesn't really know what to do with it" (7). He also doesn't know how to talk about it, as "searing jolts of pain travel" through his body (17). In his professional life preceding this accident, Salter is much more at ease with pain—the pain of others. He is the creator and producer of the nation's number one TV program, "*The King of Pain*, the greatest reality TV show of all time" (79). In this format, eight contestants undergo a series of grueling trials, including a "starvathon" (a variant of the *Hunger Games*, 139), and even branding with a red coal fire iron (167–171). They are all volunteers, meeting the requirement of "past pain exposure and endurance" (93) and having signed contractual agreements not to avoid but actively court pain, physical and psychic. The cast, not accidentally perhaps all from the West Coast, includes "a gay marathoner," an army sergeant who is "a total beast," and "a professional masochist" (96–99).

In one of the sequels, the contestants receive news that loved ones have died, are dying from cancer, or that a contestant's children have suffered severe burns when their home went up in flames (242–253). All this information is false, fake news, deliberately planted by the show's makers in order to drive the ratings and thus profits up even higher, because psychic pain may be even more intense—and thus more titillating for the audience, than physical pain. The show's director calls Salter, appreciatively "an evil genius" (243), the media "a master torturer" (249). And that "genius" himself clearly knows what it takes to make pain happen, being "Hollywood's preferred family entertainment guy" (74). Even critical attacks against his show are fine with its creator "because

---

sions. For him, the exposure of "the inadequacy of [...] language" was the condition of possibility "to say what [somebody] suffered" (83).

what does it say about a country that plans its nights around a show about torture?" (170–171)

Kaufman's decision to let Salter tell his story while he himself is in acute pain establishes a narrative balance of sorts between the producer and the victim of bodily anguish. For some readers, this may amount to apportioning a form of fictional justice. The pain Salter has inflicted on others is now visited upon him. More importantly, perhaps, this arrangement puts us as readers in a position not unlike the viewers which relished *The King of Pain* show, being pain voyeurs as much as the fictional TV audience. Salter's autobiographical narrative alternates with vignettes, ostensibly from a book, *A History of Prisons*, given to Salter by one of his associates. The purported author of this book with its various instances of institutionalized violence is Seth Kaufman. Gesturing in this way at Paul Auster's metafictional plays is not really successful, and the vignettes are certainly the weaker part of a narrative that is not simply "about" pain but about its instrumentalization for viewer pleasure and entertainment. The idea that all narratives tell essentially two stories, one being their material content, the other their condition of possibility (Terdiman 235) is helpful here, because it reminds us that *The King of Pain*, both the inner-fictional show and the fictional narrative as a whole, are most successful when and because they rigorously orchestrate what happens when human suffering is media-ted, inserted into the public channels of representation.[11] Salter's comment offers a sobering thought on this issue: "Americans watch other people suffer and die all the time on the news and in movies. Only we've turned it into a pure spectacle, without pretending it ever was anything else." (15)

Kaufman's novel, by offering a series of examples of successful pain representation, both inside its fictional world and as a reading experience, invites multiple readings and reflections; I would like to focus on two of them. The most obvious choice here would be an updated Frankfurt School argument about how the human body, even in its most vulnerable moments, is being ruthlessly commodified and subjected to the commercial calculus of the "society of the spectacle" (Debord). Nancy Tomes

---

11 | The fictional narrative repeatedly brings into play the genealogy of such shows as *King of Pain*: "All those other shows—*Survivor, The Great Race, Fear Factor, The Biggest Loser*—they're all about suffering, sadism, and voyeurism [...]". (75; cf. 15, 69)

and her work on "epidemic entertainments" and the "disease sell" (628) is extremely useful here because she offers a historical account of how human suffering entered the circuits of mass communication. What she has to say about the usefulness of medical emergencies for increasing the circulation of newspapers is basically true also of today's mass media, as the fictional narrative persuasively argues. Kaufman, who was or is himself part of the Hollywood media circus, goes to some lengths to show the collusion between the deliberate violation of mass media ethics practiced by *King of Pain* and its massive media resonance.[12] The second reading takes us back one more time to Adorno and the traces of suffering he is trying to shore up in a culture's practices of representation. This reading is one which involves questions of an ethics of representation, and it is also one with which I would like to conclude this paper.

PAIN PORN?

Since the 1980s, a debate has developed about how best to represent (groups of) human beings who are materially disadvantaged, who live in dire poverty, who suffer from noxious environmental conditions or who are mentally or physically challenged. The term "poverty porn" has attained wide currency in this context, but there are also other "porns," all of them serving as a critique of representational practices, often-meaning intentions, for example well in the context of charity campaigns.

These practices, in order to solicit sympathy or sometimes merely attention, use hard-hitting, often stereotypical images, such as starving children with big eyes behind barbed-wire fences. While in some ways effective in eliciting emotional responses, these representations might well be considered pornographic because, as Jorgen Lissner who coined the term in 1981 wrote, they "expose something in human life that is as delicate and deeply personal as sexuality, that is, suffering [...]. It puts people's bodies, their misery, their grief and their fear on display with all the details and all the indiscretion that a telescopic lens will allow." (Hirsch n. p.)

---

12 | "The show kept feeding the nation's op-ed columns and blogs a never-ending supply of subjects and plotlines. Fodder to attack the show or me or the network or the nation itself." (170)

This describes exactly what is happening inside the fictional world of *King of Pain* and also highlights its satiric potential. Rick Salter and his team on the TV program are "never wrong about suffering" (to echo Auden here), because as the new virtuosos of mass communication they know how to fully realize its potential for drama and entertainment: "Pain is boring. Unless you're watching others experience it. Which is why *The King of Pain* became such a hit." (241) Such a resolute positioning of human suffering as "for show" might well be called "pain porn." Representations which solicit the pleasure of onlookers are not restricted to the fictional case the novel presents. "Pain porn"—as the novel also makes clear (15, 69, 75)—has already become a staple item in the popular media. This emphatically includes also the new digital media: A site like "Pain Doctor" (https://paindoctor.com) offers a list of 25 of its "Favorite Chronic Pain Blogs." Thus, one can say that in our time the balance of power between the body in pain and the body in representation seems to have shifted for good (or bad) toward the latter.

So the issue is no longer that which had troubled Adorno in the immediate post-Shoah period: reconstructive, archeological work is no longer necessary as the "traces" he was speaking of have meanwhile mushroomed into a veritable surfeit of media-ted suffering: "it's just pain and more pain. And sometimes one pain replaces another." (*King* 198) This oversupply together with the relative ease with which pain and suffering are now inserted into the circuits of (mass) communication effectively re-sets the terms for any critical debate about bodily distress and "its" representation. One might frame this as a "damned if you do, damned if you don't"-situation: either bodily sufferings get represented according to the prevailing cultural standards and in the available media conduits, or they must remain voiceless, unspoken, and mute.

There is no obvious solution to this quandary which is in fact older than the present conjuncture, as the examples named at the beginning of this paper remind us. My own preference is for reading this quandary dialectically, meaning that the seemingly absolute dichotomy between muteness and media-tion, silence and representation, marks in fact one, continuous field at the limit of human abilities. Pain in representation is thus both a necessary practice and one that must remain incomplete, unfinished. It is neither the Other of representation (as deconstructionists might be tempted to define it), nor its latest triumph, but both. It demands representation, in the body, in language, in text, but this representation always falls short of capturing its realities, whatever they may be. Reading this simultaneous absence and presence (Adorno's "trace") of pain can make us aware that what is a gain—removing the sensate body's sufferings from the isolation of the sick chamber—is at the same time a loss, by turning pain into a spectacle like so many others, "a sanitized spectator sport" (*King* 76) on the way to what might perhaps be called a CNN of suffering.

WORKS CITED

Adorno, Theodor W. "Heine the Wound." *Can One Live After Auschwitz? A Philosophical Reader.* Ed. Rolf Tiedemann. Trans. Rodney Livingstone et al. Stanford: Stanford UP, 2003. Print.

Améry, Jean. *At the Mind's Limits: Contemplations by a Survivor on Auschwitz and its Realities.* Trans. Sidney Rosenfeld. Bloomington, Indiana: Indiana UP, 1980. Print.

Auden, W. H. *Modern Poetry.* Vol. 7. Ed. Maynard Mack, Leonard Dean, and William Frost. Second Edition. Englewood Cliffs: Prentice-Hall, 1950. 198. Print.

Baker, Carlos. *Hemingway: The Writer as Artist.* Princeton: Princeton UP, 1972, 191–96. Print.

Butler, Judith. "How Can I Deny That These Hands and This Body Are Mine?" *Qui Parle* 11.1 (1997): 1–20.

Canguilhem, Georges. *Writings on Medicine.* Trans. Stefanos Geroulanos and Todd Meyers. New York: Fordham UP, 2012. Print.

Charon, Rita. *Narrative Medicine: Honoring the Stories of Illness.* Oxford: Oxford UP, 2006. Print.

Debord, Guy. *Society of the Spectacle.* Trans. Donald Nicholson-Smith. New York: Zone Books, 1995. Print.

Frank, Arthur W. *The Wounded Storyteller: Body, Illness, and Ethics.* Chicago: U of Chicago P, 1995. Print.

Gadamer, Hans-Georg. *Schmerz: Einschätzungen aus medizinischer, philosophischer und therapeutischer Sicht.* Heidelberg: Winter, 2003. Print.

Genette, Gerard. *Narrative Discourse: An Essay in Method.* Trans. Jane E. Lewin. Ithaca: Cornell UP, 1980. Print.

Habermas, Jürgen. *Moral Consciousness and Communicative Action.* Trans. Christian Lenhardt and Shierry Weber Nicholsen. Cambridge: MIT Press, 1990. Print.

———. *On Society and Politics: A Reader.* Boston: Beacon Press, 1989. Print.

Hemingway, Ernest. "The Snows of Kilimanjaro." *The Short Stories of Ernest Hemingway.* New York: Scribner's, 1966. 52–77. Print.

Hermann, Iris. *Schmerzarten: Prolegomena einer Ästhetik des Schmerzes in Literatur, Musik und Psychoanalyse.* Heidelberg: Winter, 2003. Print.

Hirsch, Afua. "Ed Sheeran means well but this poverty porn has to stop." *Guardian* Web. 5 Dec 2017. https://www.theguardian.com/commentis free/2017/dec/05/ed-sheeran-poverty-porn-activism-aid-yemen-liberia.

International Association for the Study of Pain (IASP). *Classification of Chronic Pain: Descriptions of Chronic Pain Symptoms and Definition of Pain Terms.* Second Edition. Seattle: IASP Press, 1994. Print.

Kaufman, Seth. *The King of Pain: a novel with stories.* N. p.: Sukuma Books, 2012. Print.

Kleinman, Arthur. *The Illness Narratives: Suffering, Healing, and the Human Condition.* New York: Basic Books, 1988. Print.

Kripke, Saul A. *Naming and Necessity.* Cambridge: Harvard UP, 1980. Print.

Kunow, Rüdiger. *Material Bodies: Biology and Culture in the United States.* Heidelberg: Winter, 2018. Print.

Marder, Michael. "Minimal Patientia: Reflections on the Subject of Suffering." *New German Critique* 33,1 (2006): 53–72.

Morris, David B. *The Culture of Pain.* Berkeley: University of California Press, 1991. Print.

Morrison, Toni. "The Site of Memory." *Inventing the Truth: The Art and Craft of Memoir.* Ed. William Zinsser. Boston: Houghton Mifflin, 1998. 185–200. Print.

Moscoso, Javier. *Pain: A Cultural History.* Trans. Sarah Thomas and Paul House. Hampshire: Palgrave, 2012. Print.

Scarry, Elaine. *The Body in Pain: The Making and Unmaking of the World.* Oxford: Oxford UP, 1985. Print.

Terdiman, Richard. *Body and Story: The Ethics and Practice of Theoretical Conflict.* 2005; Baltimore: Johns Hopkins UP, 2006. Print.

Tomes, Nancy. "Epidemic Entertainments: Disease and Popular Culture in Early-Twentieth-Century America." *American Literary History* 14.4 (2002): 625–52.

White, Hayden. "The Value of Narrativity in the Representation of Reality." *On Narrative.* Ed. W. J. T. Mitchell. Chicago: U of Chicago P, 1981. 1–23. Print.

Wittgenstein, Ludwig. *Last Writings on the Philosophy of Psychology.* Vol. 1. Ed. G. H. von Wright. Oxford: Blackwell, 1982. Print.
——. *Philosophical Investigations.* The German Text with a Revised English Translation. Trans. Gertrude E. M. Anscombe. Oxford: Blackwell Publishing, 2003. Print.

How We Imagine Living with Dying

Margaret Morganroth Gullette

> I see in you the estuary that enlarges and spreads
> itself grandly as it pours in the great sea.
> WALT WHITMAN, "TO OLD AGE"

DYING IN NONFICTION: THEY DON'T HAVE TO IMAGINE IT

Dying seems the most mysterious of human activities.[1] Although the whole life course from childhood on, Milan Kundera wrote, is a "planet of inexperience" (24), in the earlier parts we learn in advance about parenting or adultery or being an astronaut, prospectively, through the story-telling of others with experience. Living-with-dying is more opaque. What we "know" (an overstatement) emerges from reading vicariously or is deduced from watching the dying of others. And dying itself is totally occluded. Despite the caregivers' observation of another person's death, even the close watchers are excluded from that subjective experience.

Some say "People fear dying" as if it were universally true, but in fact not everyone fears dying or death equally. When statements vary so widely, every single one is a projection and a provocation—from Philip Larkin, terrified in "Aubade" of "the sure extinction that we travel to. [...] nothing more terrible, nothing more true," to George Bernard Shaw at ninety-two calling the concept of immortality "an unimaginable horror."[2] In his late novel *Ravelstein*, Saul Bellow has a character named Chick say to his dying

---

1 | An earlier version of this essay was published with the same title in *Salmagundi* (2016). My warm thanks to Peg and Robert Boyers.
2 | George Bernard Shaw's comment about immortality can be found on the first page of any edition of the Preface to the plays and is also quoted by John Updike in "Late Works."

friend, "my amateur survey shows that nine people out of ten expect to see their parents in the life to come. But am I prepared to spend eternity with them? I suspect I'm not" (138). Gerontological surveys report that many older people fear dying *less* than younger people do. This outcome might prove to be another alleviation for growing old if we didn't know how much people differ in their aging-into-old age.

Cultural history—the contexts in which people learn about this and then imagine it—influences representation. Intent on telling us what we don't know about how we live now, Slavoj Žižek points out that "[t]hings which once seemed self-evident—how to feed and educate a child, how to proceed in sexual seduction, how and what to eat, how to relax and amuse oneself—have now been 'colonised' by reflexivity, and are experienced as something to be learned and decided on." (n. p.) In the American milieu, I add, dying too has been emerging as "something to be learned."

Living with dying, at any age, is also a singular experience. The term itself indicates a fact that has yet to be fully thought through: that people hear or intuit what may be called their "death sentence" and find there is a lot of life left after that. Everyone whose life-world is mediated by medicine, science, technology, punditry, and TV specials finds the abject aspects of illnesses (incontinence, vomiting, delirium, radiation, chemo, disability, dependency, pain, and of course memory loss) widely described as fearful, even disgusting, preliminaries, which are usually associated with old age. Unfortunately for the millions of older people living with chronic illnesses, chronic disabilities, or terminal diagnoses, mediation derived from the medical model too often creates aversion from *them*, who most need attentive closeness (while this decline model simultaneously obscures all the people who age-into-old-age in good health). People can be inundated with millions of words of illness and dying discourse and remain ignorant about much that matters. For a vast audience that includes the post-war Boomers and extends to adolescents, long before illness strikes any of them, this is a plausible new curriculum. It's almost unavoidable.

As grim bodily details percolate, dread of aging and fear of dying are probably worsening. Dying now appears under the heading of choice, at least about *when* and *how*. Jenni Diski, a British novelist and journalist, wrote installments in the *London Review of Books*, one of whose recurrent themes is her medical decision-making. In "Who'll be Last?" Diski writes, channeling the voice of a jaunty reader, that cancer "has that something, that je ne sais quoi, not just death, but how long known beforehand: how will she die, should she choose to try for a longer life by accepting treatment, or settle for palliative care which at its best is a comfortable death without pain." (n. p.) Experiential literary nonfiction often honestly provides facts about the writer's physiological trials, but this genre differs even from startlingly revealing interviews (like those Roger Ebert gave Steve James for the documentary *Life Itself*) by portraying private selfhood from within, in detail. The emphases are those the author chooses to publish, including his or her decisions about what feelings to disclose, in what order. People live with dying, it appears, in ways that may swing wildly—from moment to moment, from person to person. And behind the words there may be unconscious matters.

People have been dying forever. But nonfiction that involves dying— or *autothanatographies*, as some literary critics call them—used to be rare, the province of religious writers like Anne Bradstreet, in the seventeenth century. In the past thirty years, however, this rather specialized genre, autobiography written in the knowledge that one is living with a terminal diagnosis, has seen an enormous surge in popular interest, from AIDS memoirs to cancer journals like Audre Lorde's (1980), to books by people with Alzheimer's. Many are self-published, but one of the latter sold 30,000 copies. The last essays of Harold Brodkey, an under-appreciated American writer, collected as *This Wild Darkness* (1996), form an audacious, poetic, vigorous and riveting account of his living with AIDS. In the English-speaking world the latest include Christopher Hitchens' *Mortality* (2012), Oliver Sacks' essays in *Gratitude* (2015), Clive James' interviews and essays, Tony Judt's *The Memory Chalet* (2010). The better known Americans include Edward Said *(Out of Place)*, Morrie Schwartz *(Letting Go)*, Art Buchwald *(Too Soon to Say Goodbye)*. (So far, public dying is dominated by men.) Some writers—Randy Pausch on Oprah Winfrey, Art Buchwald on TV shows like "60 Minutes"—become media "stars" of dying. In 2012 a competition for a book to be called *Final Chapters* attracted some 1,400 entries.[3]

Whatever your youth, and precisely because you expect to live longer than you once thought—you too may be reading as a way to bring the Last Events vicariously closer. Many people seem curious about what goes

---

3 | Other memoirs of living with dying are mentioned and discussed in Jeffrey Berman's *Dying in Character: Memoirs on the End of Life*.

on in the embodied psyche, in culture, over time, at a time when time is running out.

A kind of eagerness to learn the particulars of dying, or more accurately, living-with-dying, seems to me an epochal change in life-course culture from the time not so long ago when there was a taboo about mentioning death, or taking children to funerals. Richard Howard could charge in 1993 that Brodkey's discussion of his AIDS in the *New Yorker* was "a matter of manipulative hucksterism, of mendacious self-propaganda and cruel assertion of artistic privilege, whereby death is made a matter of public relations."[4] *Memento mori*—"Remember you must die"—was then a prank call or Catholic medievalism, as in Muriel Spark's eponymous novel, not a nonfiction genre making its way onto the best-seller lists.

Now even children are supposed to want to know. In a play I saw in November 2015 at the prestigious Public Theater in New York City, seven child actors from nine to fourteen started what turns out to be a rapid tour of their future life courses by saying, neutrally, as if it were a subject like geography, "We're all interested in dying." "We are all speeding toward death," one adds. A grown British woman's voice-over says, calm and cool as can be, "You're here to live and then die." Living for the children "here" is decline from then on—from druggie adolescence through to the disappointments of being forty-five [sic]; and then finally, wearing powdered hair or gray wigs, they do all but one drop to the floor performing stereotyped dying. The name of the play? *Before Your Very Eyes*. I'll agree that children must be told something age-appropriate about terrorist killings in the news or the illness and death of a relative, but exposing these youngsters to a personalized Decline-and-Death Curriculum? Is that necessary? Should it start so young? Does it not smack of child abuse? Adults, of course, set the agenda of the young, for their own reasons. And American audiences attend, learning—if they didn't get it already—how very very young decline ideology starts these days.

Editors who publish dying-memoirs believe readers want attested information, in a compact form, about all this. Writers believe they can provide it. Brodkey first feared that he was neither the hero nor the narrator of his experience, but he reassures himself. "You will have the real material and it will arise from this new-to-you, dense memory of

---

4 | Richard Howard's critique is quoted in Dinitia Smith's *New York Times'* obituary of Brodkey.

being jostled by medical and natural violence to the edge of life" (26). What of viewers of movies about dying, which Hollywood now provides? Their wishes, opinions, and feelings about the new dying curriculum may be different from those of readers, as witnessed by a cinematic emphasis on older celebrity actors shown crossing diverting items off their characters' "bucket list." That meme implies a terminal rush toward strenuous activity (and enough time and health left to be active) that may be what viewers prefer to imagine.

In an essay asking "Can You Imagine Dying?" Jenni Diski assumes that we can't. She reports that "the excruciating terror of the fact that I am in the early stages of dying comes regularly and settles on my solar plexus directly beneath my ribcage." (n. p.) Some nonfiction asserts that dying can be "fun"—one book with that message has sold 4 million copies. Some convey dread of a particular kind of dying. (Tony Judt, the historian, unforgettably dictated to a daylight amanuensis his horrifying night-time experiences of being paralyzed and alone with Amyotrophic Lateral Sclerosis, ALS.) One thing many writers want when they know they are dying—and who can blame them, when writing about their one and only life has often been their life?—is to go on writing well about this experience too, their one and only death. Asked what he valued most about life, the author of *Death in Venice*, Thomas Mann, responded, "transitoriness. But is not transitoriness—the perishableness of life—something very sad? No! It is the very soul of existence. It imparts value, dignity, interest to life. [...] Timelessness—in the sense of time never ending, never beginning—is a stagnant nothing. It is absolutely uninteresting." (n. p.) Dying—the prospect, consciously considered—certainly imparts interest and dignity to one's writing.

All these memoirs—some of them classics, some mediocre—do important cultural work, for those who can stand back a bit to see them together. They prove that people do truly *live with dying*, and sometimes with intermissions and remissions for a rather long time. By purveying missing subjectivities, the best of them undo the rabid strangeness of illness and disability. They humanize the authors. Most expand the curriculum so that the suffering body doesn't take up all the available space. They replace our ignorance and mediated aversion with knowledge of individual experience, and compassion, more successfully than experts can. They may make dying itself seems less horrifying—something ordinary people can handle better than we might have thought.

Yet to the common reader, relevance may be diminished by the writers' characterological urgencies. Perhaps for self-soothing and hiding; or for representing only what might be termed "successful dying" or "death education"; or for self-pity at dying prematurely, as Keats wrote, "When I have fears that I may cease to be/ Before my pen has glean'd my teeming brain." (297). These are understandable and touching pitfalls; yet the works may still seem to be, as it were, case studies. A reader may feel empathy for the circumstances and still find an account of the course of AIDS, a particular cancer, or Alzheimer's too particular, identification with the protagonist too difficult. *Not my case.*

Readers like me turn to novels in any case, curious about what fiction can accomplish when it deploys not the experience but the illusion of transitoriness. (Some critics like to say how little difference there is between literary fiction and nonfiction, and I often agree, but with any fiction about dying, the difference would seem obvious. We are not all dying. We do not all have "the real material.") Still. As creative illusion, the theme of dying might give a narrator's first-person situation unlabored poignancy. Certain nonfiction demands can be evaded: The long form of the novel is hampered by no autobiographical pact to provide awkward personal truths or actual symptomology. A serious novelist may insinuate the ethics of having lived a particular life in a given place and historical period, which depends on a certain sociological or philosophical detachment. And novels provide something obvious that most dying-memoirs can't: *plot.* Writing anything structured while one is ill, weak, and preoccupied draws down mightily what might well be intermittent or limited creative energy. Devising a present-tense plot rather than reminiscing about the past requires also the optimism to imagine current desiring. Desire in turn triggers literary intensities—for portraying effort, conflict, frustration—at a time when serenity may be what writers want most from their engagement with prose. Novels that can make temporal urgency plausible while managing all the high-strung demands of plotting and characterization would seem to have off-setting advantages, creatively, over nonfiction.

Given the tools of illusion and invented plots, it is surprising to discover that a first-person account of living-with-dying is an uncommon donnée for novelists. Perhaps Samuel Beckett's *Malone Dies* (in English, 1956) scared them off. A very few do have characters sicken and die in the third person-personal point of view, as Philip Roth does in *Everyman*

(2006). But novelists seem to avoid imagining it as happening to a closer surrogate for self. John Updike may have explained this in "Late Works," contemplating the question of how real death is to people in health, when he concluded that "Death was real" to very few (59). Saul Bellow, at the end of *Ravelstein*, gives his first-person narrator, Chick, a few pages that describe *nearly* dying from eating toxic fish, as Bellow in fact nearly did, and coming back to describe it. Chick recalls "preposterous" hallucinations. The Lazarus plot move is joke-worthy. "Unconscious, I had no more idea of death than the dead have." (208) "Life would soon be back. [...] Death would shrink into its former place at the margin of the landscape." (230)

IMAGINING IT: JOHN AMES'S "AUTOBIOGRAPHY" OF LIVING WITH DYING IN MARILYNNE ROBINSON'S *GILEAD*

In the midst of this absence in American fiction, Marilynne Robinson sat down every day, to write in the first person an entire novel, *Gilead*, claiming to be the autobiography of a man who is dying and who knows he is dying.[5] Of the fictions I find most interesting about dying in later life—two canonical short stories, "The Death of Ivan Ilych" by Leo Tolstoy and "The Bishop" by Anton Chekhov, and a few pages by Willa Cather in *Death Comes for the Archbishop*—Robinson's *Gilead* is by far my favorite. It takes on the challenge of greater length.

Dare I add that great novels can maximize experiences of empathy more imperceptibly, lyrically, innocently, and deeply, than short stories or nonfiction? Robinson's gifts to her readers begin with her imagining what it is like to be dying of something for which there are no medical interventions, to be not a woman but a man; and not a lonely old man—as in all the writers I have named, Beckett, Tolstoy, Chekhov, Cather—but the husband of an adored much younger wife, a minister important in his community, who is about to leave behind a much-loved son of about seven, without enough savings to help them go on. What other resources did

---

5 | Her own dying was not at issue. Nor was she old. Born in 1943, she was barely sixty when she published *Gilead* in 2004, and she went on to write *Home* and *Lila*. Unlike her protagonist, John Ames, she raised two sons at a more ordinary age for child-rearing.

Robinson bring together to make this bearable to write, and wonderful—and believable—to read?

To understand creativity, one needs not just a work's current ideological context (the odd curiosity I mentioned: the blunt and subtle pressures to read and write about terminal illness, disability, and dying in later life). We benefit also from surmising the development of an artist's own productive life—the needs it served for her. Notoriously, in 2004, Robinson had not written a novel for twenty years, and had produced only two collections of sometimes rebarbative essays. Through this protagonist, John Ames, who is writing a journal to his seven-year-old son Robby, Robinson found an authorial tone that was less censorious, defensive, and isolated. The careful sweetness of *Gilead*, its humorous meditativeness, suggest to me that for Robinson it was precisely producing the voice of a story-telling older father and husband, living with dying, and writing to his son, that enabled a fresh creative spurt, or rather waterfall. The illuminating first sentence came to her whole, a surprise, as she says in conversation with President Barack Obama in the *New York Review of Books*. Ames is addressing the boy, who will be reading this journal only years hence as an adult. "I told you last night that I might be gone sometime, and you said Where, and I said, To be with the Good Lord, and you said, Why, and I said, Because I'm old, and you said, I don't think you're old." (3)

An early reviewer of "this splendidly realized novel," William Deresiewicz thinks Robinson meets "one of the most difficult challenges of narrative art: she not only makes goodness believable; she also makes it interesting." (n.p.) True. And moreover, at the level of characterization and plot, *Gilead* suggests that what we readers want to know are the *full* and *generalizable* parts of the endgame. How a likeable persona manages to do it, how hard or easy it is. Must thoughts of dying be all-engrossing? What do we still want and worry about? First of all—I deduce this from the popular success of this novel, its winning the double crown of the Pulitzer Prize and the National Book Critics Circle Award, and its effects on me—we need reassurance of how much living goes on in that supposedly liminal space of time.

To manage this, Robinson had to make Ames' terminal prospect gentle. Not cancer, considered so dreadful in the 1950s, when the novel is set, that it was unnameable or semi-disguised as "the Big C." She didn't give him a disease full of pain, nor the declensions into disabilities of Parkinson's, ALS, or Alzheimer's, which we are now being encouraged to avoid through preemptive suicide if necessary.[6] His disease is angina pectoris; with no invasive surgery available, Ames will live and die at home. Like some people whose diseases become chronic or go into remission, Ames is lucky. Clive James, the British poet, essayist, and novelist, who has been living for years with terminal leukemia, has written a poem addressed to himself about his own luck so far.

> "Your death, near now, is of an easy sort.
> So slow a fading out brings no real pain.
> Breath growing short
> Is just uncomfortable. You feel the drain
> Of energy, but thought and sight remain:
> Enhanced, in fact." (n. p.)

And we are spared Ames' dying. The writing simply stops. "Enhanced" is precisely the right word for Ames' creative way of being as he waits for his heart to fail. Writing *is* being, in such a novel. Robinson justifies the journal form by making Ames' son too young to be *told* these stories; and Ames, a writer who is discarding his 225 volumes of sermons, needs the occupation of exploring this epistolary genre. Writing gives him both a present action and an afterlife—envisioning his son reading his journal years hence. Imagining his adult son's comforting interest is the thought that keeps him company. Kathleen Woodward, an eclectic and imaginative age critic, has pointed out how important "the figure of companionship" and the atmosphere of "companionableness" can be to reminiscence (2A-4b). She distinguishes between reminiscence and life review, but her language is very apt for *Gilead*. And Ames' dead—his father, his mother, his grandfather—are both the material of his backward look and his other companions as he writes. Everyone needs an audience, and even in *Gilead* it isn't only God in his heaven.

In many writings, Dr. Robert N. Butler, a Pulitzer Prize winner for his book *Why Survive?: Being Old in America*, developed his concept of the "life review" as a reckoning of one's whole life course. Unlike the pundits instructing us that midlife is the time we start pecking at the shortness of life, Butler thought that only the proximity of death made

---

6 | See Gullette, "Our Frightened World: Fantasies of Euthanasia and Preemptive Suicide," *Ending Ageism*, 139-162.

such summations possible and desirable. If so, might not dying in one's teens pressure a person into a mindful life review just as much? Not so much. Like Butler, Robinson valued both *the long look back* from old age and close proximity. Both. People who are growing old do not necessarily think more about dying than they did when younger, nor do they necessarily become philosophical, or indeed, *different*. Diana Athill's memoir is called *Somewhere Towards the End* (2009), but at 92, she was as healthy and as busy recounting her past work-life, sex-life, etc., as if she had been 65, or 45. Aging-into-old-age had given her only *more* of these entertaining items to cover. Merely being old—with "the natural stupidity of a sound, healthy" person (Saul Bellow again, in *Ravelstein*, 208)—does not seem to offer the same opportunities to fictional autobiography as being ill unto death.

Before young Jack, his godson, appears, Ames is simply a family man reminiscing about long-past conflicts between his father and grandfather against the backdrop of terrible wars. His goodness is unproblematic and soothing. But Robinson realized that what writers need for novels—burning elements of emotional life, painful inner struggle—can flame up from precisely this calm territory of mere reminiscent and appreciatively observant old age.

At first, neither his white hair nor his heart disease makes Ames different from himself. He is normally old, not troublingly ill. (Robinson makes this distinction—between what belongs to old age and what to illness—that age theorists wish we were more aware of, these days when the two are often taken to be synonymous.) In magazine nonfiction, older autobiographers who are far from their last gasp seem to be automatically required to describe their bio-creaks and quirks before going on to anything else. They dutifully *tell* (like Roger Angell beginning his essay, "This Old Man" in the *New Yorker*, with his arthritic fingers, because he's ninety). Ames doesn't. He's had "trouble" remembering his body might fail (73). Before Jack appears, vigorously hoisting Ames up out of the porch swing, being old with a vital younger wife has been a minor identity, not a totalizing one. *Aging*, with its typical demotions, enters with the rival man. As he sees Robby and Lila view this tableau on the porch, Ames becomes "old"—frail, smaller, less noticeable, more silent. Jack returns, playing baseball, moving furniture. Ames decides to tell his son "I was trim and fit into my sixties. [...] very strong, very sound" (141). No more disabled than he was the day before, he turns *defensively old*. After Jack, ageism too suddenly compels Ames' attention:

"[...] I have felt a certain change in the way people act toward me. [...] I really feel as though I'm failing, and not primarily in the medical sense. And I feel as if I am being left out, as though I'm some straggler and people quite can't remember to stay back for me. [...] It could be true that my interest in abstractions, which would have been forgiven first on grounds of youth and then on grounds of eccentricity, is now being forgiven on grounds of senility, which would mean people have stopped trying to see the sense in the things I say the way they once did. That would be by far the worst form of forgiveness." (141, 142, 143-44)

It's worth pausing over the complaints he's supplied with, and the misery and the loss of community he experiences, because novelists so rarely convey that it's how we are treated rather than aging itself, or even illness, that hurts. Even gerontologists who study "successful" aging can forget to ask about ageism. Robinson was not so famous before 2004: such micro-aggressions might have befallen her as a woman of sixty.

Ageism appears here not only for our guidance with others, whose old age we readers might otherwise embitter, but because Jack's performances of strength and hyper-respectfulness rankle Ames' desire—to think "graciously" about Jack when Ames sees him ingratiating himself with Lila and his son, and as he worries about their problematic future without him. Transitoriness certainly matters here, giving his ethical conflict urgency. The striving and failing worsen Ames' heart condition. "It is a strange thing to feel illness and grief in the same organ." (179)

Watching Ames' difficult persistence in this ethical task empathetically might be precious to us as human beings who are hoping, as Walt Whitman hoped for us, to enlarge and spread ourselves, before or despite physiological crisis. President Obama in his Charleston, South Carolina Eulogy for the African Americans murdered in the church in July 2015, spoke about the need for "an open heart" to achieve grace. He said,

"That, more than any particular policy or analysis, is what's called upon right now, I think—what a friend of mine, the writer Marilynne Robinson, calls 'that reservoir of goodness, beyond, and of another kind, [than] that we are able to do [for] each other in the ordinary cause of things.'" (n. p.)

In Chekhov's short story, "The Bishop," on his deathbed, Pyotr after rejoicing at seeing his mother and niece, wishes one thing more important. "If only there were one person to whom he could have talked, have opened his heart!" (356) This heart-opening aspect of terminal illness makes sense only if one is well enough to communicate some of what is concealed within. While his inner conflict grows, about whether to warn Lila about Jack's past untrustworthiness, Ames hides it except in his journal. He considers burning those bits of it, but finally trusts that his son will understand Jack's and his father's complex characters.

Ames is lucky in many ways. He has had an unexpectedly blessed later life with wife and child, and he knows it, which is as much happiness in your skull as anyone is allowed. In *To the Lighthouse*, Virginia Woolf wrote, "It is enough, it is enough" (100), about a moment when a character becomes conscious of the enhanced beauty of the world. Ames' frequent loving observations have an unexpected luminosity in the midst of his outwardly dull, settled life as a preacher in a dusty Iowa town. Ames intends to show his son the depth of his paternal love: his current delight in the child, the magic of merely living even when life itself is in jeopardy; family history and its personal/political conflicts going back to before the Civil War. Readers who think his life is narrow might still wish to emulate his deep powers. And write a journal for their children modelled on his.

Indeed, in *Gilead* dying is far from the worst grief. Family relations are. The other family Ames knows best—his old friend and preaching confrère Boughton, and Boughton's adult children, Jack and Glory—suffer from unchangeable dysfunction in relation to Jack. Robinson's own unusual definition of creativity from the essay "Family" in *The Death of Adam* fits here: it is the persistent mutual work of making family life good, generous, inclusive. "The antidote to fear, distrust, self-interest is always loyalty." Is love enough? "[L]ove is loyalty. [...] The real issue is, will people shelter and nourish and humanize one another? This is creative work, requiring discipline and imagination" (89). Some would say this is a female definition of creativity. It is arduous in practice for anyone. It is her "good" protagonist, Ames, who will need to control his imagination and rein in his speech.

To be about to die at some unknown moment makes this task more pressing. For Ames, the greatest test is this troubled, newly returned namesake. (Various critics see the Return of the Prodigal as Robinson's chosen literary topos.) Jack's return is her source for the grave conflict that drives the plot of Ames's present-tense narration. Ames fears that his once-vagabond young wife has more in common with Jack than with him; "covetise," as he calls it (141), exacerbates his anxiety that he never treated this other "son" properly. Jeffrey Gonzalez, a professor of English, says Ames struggles "to encounter Jack ethically in order to square with the example he wants to be to his son" (376). Proclaiming the need for forgiving and liberating, he struggles, under the watchful eyes of Lila his wife. Robinson endowed Lila and Glory, here and in *Home* as well, with a dispassion and pity, an "emollient" tongue, that contrast with masculine rigidities. These qualities fit the women to see verbal harm coming and evade it, or warn the men to mend their speech. For Robinson, speech is behavior. It is *speech* that requires discipline and imagination, speech that succors or destroys. "The tongue is a fire" is the New Testament metaphor that Robinson burned into many dialogues. She shows Ames' words searing Jack, and Jack's searing his.

Jack's secret backstory is the means by which the evil of American racism comes into a novel that Robinson (inconspicuously) set during the Montgomery bus boycott in the run-up to the 1956 election. Deresiewicz rightly described Ames' spiritual autobiography as "as sweet-tempered a book as one can imagine" (25). But racism is the "fire next time" that Robinson planted in the town's ethos. It was not nostalgia, as some critics assert, that motivated her decision to set the novel (and the next, *Home*), in 1950s America. It was hard judgment. Robinson said in an interview with the *Nation*,

"[w]hen I wrote *Gilead*, I was very aware that I wanted to make John Ames old enough, and to make his life occur early enough, so that I could give him an abolitionist ancestry [...] and at the same time put him in the period when the civil-rights movement was becoming important. And that did establish the time frame for all these books that are related to each other" ("Talking" 31).

The structure of *Gilead* depends on that two-period contrast. In the first third of the novel, Robinson invented Ames' ambivalent but calm stories of his grandfather's abolitionist activism before and during the Civil War. "I believe the old reverend's errors [sic] were mainly the consequence of a sort of strenuousness in ethical matters that was to be admired finally" (90). But, as Jeffrey Gonzalez points out, such strenuousness, "though it should be admired, is not to be emulated in the moral universe of these novels. Ames's father and Ames each seem wary of the eldest Ames's involvement with John Brown, and the profound pacifism of Ames and his father would seem to argue against something like the Civil War." (383) Robinson needs *male* protagonists in this novel because only men could be ministers, and only ministers brought religion and race, abolitionist John Brown and the American Civil War, Jim Crow and lynching, into the public pulpit, *or failed to*.

Even in rural places with a distinguished anti-slavery past—like Gilead, Iowa—white Americans in the 1950s did not take responsibility for their racism. In a long monologue that shows lessened wariness toward his godfather, Jack reveals that he is in love with a black woman: "we have considered ourselves man and wife" (225). They can't marry, and they can't live together in "lewd" cohabitation (225); their son is illegitimate and mostly lives apart from him. In most ways, including Della's father's hostility to him as a white atheist, their family life is destroyed by racism. All Jack is literally asking of Ames is an estimate of the hostility his family would face if he moved them there: "Would people leave us alone?" (231) "Ames's reluctant admission that he doesn't know," constitutes Robinson's most damning indictment of Gilead's—and, by implication, America's— moral decline," Deresiewicz concludes (28). And Ames' tongue? Readers can imagine Jack's pain when he hears Ames call the conflagration set behind the Negro church "a little nuisance fire" (231), yet they both know the congregation left never to return.

Weary and downhearted, this preacher is unable to convey to his fragile namesake that he knows racism is a cause of unending anguish to him. Speech fails him. *Gilead* is structured to makes this sadly, bitterly disappointing. In the high-minded representations of one of our greatest living novelists, conscience and considerate language are not too much to ask, even of a man who is dying in a benighted era. But he recognizes that his "old dread" (233) of Jack was about as far from the mark as could be. Robinson gives him the grace to bless Jack as he leaves a town that, in Ames' bitter self-judgment, unspoken but written down in his journal, "might as well be standing on the absolute floor of hell for all the truth there is in it, and the fault is mine as much as anyone's" (233).

Robinson patched onto Ames' kindness and humor and failures all the concerns of her best heart. Using transitoriness to propel the narrative, she made her deep disappointment over the persistence of American racism one subtext, the love of the visible world a source of poetry, the history of a religious family over three generations a repository of values in conflict, with Ames' attempt to be open finally to Jack's wary, needy otherness personalizing the political and tying together the whole. The old body in extremis turns out be the least of it. This novel rarely portrays Ames' body. A film, by showing an actor's body, would necessarily make more of his slow walk, naps, the porch swing episode. In another kind of novel, too, Ames' ailing body might loom larger. Here, what surmounts all are moral speech and behavior, or what Robinson would call "Christian" ethics, amidst grave lack. Ethically, for her protagonist, Robinson made *Gilead* a novel of hard-won progress. The slowness of Ames' arc is closely allied to the long blindnesses and belated self-revelations of classic tragedy. It is best perhaps to consider it a literary accomplishment, her being able to convey both spiritual progress and disappointment toward the end of such a reflective life.

Telling people about the book, however, as I often do, I find myself recounting Ames' stories about the heroic past (his grandfather's "one" lost eye, the horse that sank in the tunnel meant for the Underground Railroad; the escaped slave's chuckle in the dark) and praising Ames' careful, kind narrative voice and the "moments of being" (as Virginia Woolf called them in "A Sketch of the Past") that he describes when overtaken by the beauty of his son, his wife, or the natural world. Maybe the painful, equivocal moral arc of Ames' life review becomes in re-reading even less important than his failing body, and it is his steady living voice that remains a comforting hum in one's mind.

However differently people read *Gilead*, this is not a decline novel, as readers inured to the common stereotypes about later life and frailty might expect any novel about living with dying to be. Life—desire, observations, feelings, hard-won reflections, human relations, spiritual questions, secrets, the possibility of change—all can be intact, or even more intense and absorbing, until the end. Some goods that accumulate for the protagonist, and perhaps – but who knows?—for us, come not *despite* the nearness of death, but *because* of it.

WORKS CITED

Angell, Roger. "This Old Man." *The New Yorker* 17 Feb 2014. Web. 4 January 2018. https://www.newyorker.com/magazine/2014/02/17/old-man-3.
Athill, Diana. *Somewhere Towards the End: A Memoir.* New York: W.W. Norton, 2008. Print.
Bellow, Saul. *Ravelstein.* New York: Penguin, 2000. Print.
Berman, Jeffrey. *Dying in Character: Memoirs on the End of Life.* Amherst, Mass.: U of Massachusetts P, 2012. Print.
Brodkey, Harold. *This Wild Darkness: The Story of My Death.* New York: Metropolitan Books: 1997. Print.
Butler, Robert N. *Why Survive?: Being Old in America.* New York: Harper & Row, 1975. Print.
Chekhov, Anton. "The Bishop." *Ward No. 6 and Other Stories.* Trans. Constance Garnett. New York: Barnes and Noble, 2003. 343–358. Print.
Deresiewicz, William. "Homing Patterns," *The Nation*, 13 October 2008: 25–30.
Diski, Jenny. "Like a Lullaby: Can You Imagine Dying?" *London Review of Books* 37.7 (9 April 2015): 23–24. Web. 29 December 2017. https://www.lrb.co.uk/v37/n07/jenny-diski/like-a-lullaby.
Diski, Jenny. "Who'll be Last?" *London Review of Books* 37.22 (19 Nov 2015): 13–14. Web. 29 December 2017. https://www.lrb.co.uk/v37/n22/jenny-diski/wholl-be-last.
Gonzalez, Jeffrey, "Ontologies of Interdependence, the Sacred, and Health Care: Marilynne Robinson's *Gilead* and *Home*." *Critique: Studies in Contemporary Fiction* 55.4 (2014): 373–388.
Gullette, Margaret Morganroth. *Ending Ageism, or How Not to Shoot Old People.* New Brunswick, N.J.: Rutgers UP, 2017.
James, Clive. "Japanese Maple, Clive James' Farewell Poem," *The New Yorker* 15 Sep 2014. Web. 4 January 2018. http://www.dyingmatters.org/page/clive-james-japanese-maple.
Keats, John. *John Keats: A Selection of His Poetry.* Ed. J.E. Morpurgo. Melbourne: Penguin, 1953. Print.
Kundera, Milan. "Key Words, Problem Words, Words I Love." *New York Times*, March 6, 1998: 1, 24.
Larkin, Philip "Aubade." Web. 4 January 2018. https://www.poetryfoundation.org/poems/48422/aubade-56d229a6e2f07.
Mann, Thomas. ([1952] 2007) "Life Grows in the Soil of Time." *This I Believe: The Personal Philosophies of Remarkable Men and Women.* Ed.

Jay Allison and Dan Gediman. New York: Henry Holt & Company, 2007. Web. 27 December 2017. http://thisibelieve.org/essay/16783.

Obama, Barack. "Eulogy for the Honorable Reverend Clementa Pinckney." Charleston, S.C., July 2015. Web. 27 December 2017. https://www.whitehouse.gov/the-press-office/2015/06/26/remarks-president-eulogy-honorable-reverend-clementa-pinckney.

Obama, Barack and Marilynne Robinson. "President Obama & Marilynne Robinson: A Conversation in Iowa." *New York Review of Books* 5 Nov 2015. Web 17 Dec 2017. http://www.nybooks.com/articles/2015/11/05/president-obama-marilynne-robinson-conversation.

Robinson, Marilynne. "Family." *The Death of Adam: Essays on Modern Thought*. Boston: Houghton Mifflin, 1998. Print.

——. *Gilead*. New York: Ferrar Straus Giroux, 2004. Print.

——. "Talking with Marilynne Robinson," *The Nation*, January 26, 2015: 31.

Smith, Dinitia. "Harold Brodkey, 65, New Yorker Writer And Novelist, Dies of Illness He Wrote About." *New York Times* 27 Jan 1996. Web. 20 November 2015. www.nytimes.com/1996/01/27/us/harold-brodkey-65-new-yorker-writer-and-novelist-dies-of-illness-hewrote-about.html?pagewanted=all.

Updike, John. "Late Works." *Due Considerations: Essays and Criticism*. New York: Knopf, 2007: 49–67. Print.

Whitman, Walt. "To Old Age." *Complete Poetry and Collected Prose*. New York: Literary Classics of the United States, 1982: 414. Print.

Woolf, Virginia. "A Sketch of the Past." *Moments of Being: Unpublished Autobiographical Writings*. New York: Harcourt Brace Jovanovich, 1976. Print.

Woolf, Virginia. *To the Lighthouse*. New York: Harcourt, Brace & World, 1927. Print.

Woodward, Kathleen. "Aging, Reminiscence, and the Life Review." *Telling Stories*, 1a-9b. Web. 29 December 2017. http://depts.washington.edu/uwch/documents/articles/Telling_Stories.pdf.

Žižek, Slavoj. "You May!" *London Review of Books* 21.6 (18 March 1999). Web. 29 December 2017. https://www.lrb.co.uk/v21/n06/slavoj-zizek/you-may.

Disgust in Samuel Beckett's *Molloy*

Sarah J. Ablett

> "[T]hat tone I know, compounded of pity, of fear, of disgust."
> BECKETT 12

Samuel Beckett wrote *Molloy* (1955) during his time in Paris in the late 1940s. The novel is structured into two associatively linked parts, which are both told from a first-person perspective. In part one, an old man named Molloy remembers his troublesome journey to visit his mother and to "finish dying" (3). In part two, we learn about the narrator Moran, who is sent out on a mysterious mission to find a man called Molloy. At the core of Molloy's narration in the first part of the novel lies the protagonist's experience of existential crisis. In face of his own ageing body's ailments as well as his fading memory and cognitive abilities, Molloy struggles to locate himself in space and time and to find meaning in his existence. In this liminal mental and physical state, the desire to get to his mother's house is the only certainty that remains, and it is both the cause and the drive of his narration. The aesthetic representation of Molloy's crisis demands a specific mode of expression, a tone of voice that is able to transport his particular state of mind, and Beckett masterfully creates such a tone—a tone that navigates in the liminal spaces of body and mind, and which is best described with a quote from the text, as one "compounded of pity, of fear, of disgust" (12).

In this passage, Molloy not only mentions the well-known aesthetic sensations of pity and fear, which have dominated the literary discourse on emotional effects ever since Aristotle named them in his seminal *Poetics* (cf. 1449b), but adds disgust as a third emotion. And any reader of *Molloy* will hardly deny that the sensation of disgust not only accompanies the evocation of pity and fear in Beckett's narration, but to a large degree dominates the discourse. Like many of Beckett's other characters and protagonists, Molloy "leaves no stone unturned and no maggot lonely" (Pinter 86) as he investigates, probes, and struggles with his existence. In the novel we find an "entire compendium of sources of disgust" as Linda Ben-Zvi notes (684). She illustrates this point with a list of physical disgust-elicitors which are all present in *Molloy*: "excrement; vomit; bodily fluids and emissions, soft, runny, slimy substances; bad smells, decaying bodies; illness; deformities; grotesque copulations; corpses; and death" (684). While Ben-Zvi focuses on the comical potential of disgust in Beckett's *Molloy* (681–98), the ensuing analysis will look at the tragic component of aesthetic disgust in the novel, its specific forms, functions, and effects.

Before proceeding to the tragic core of disgust and its manifestation in Beckett's writing, I will first offer a contextualizing overview of what disgust means and how it has been approached by artists and scholars in the past, especially with regard to its aesthetic function. It is necessary to attend in some detail to the complexity of the seemingly unambiguous emotion of disgust, because it has until recently received comparably little attention in literary research. Disgust, furthermore, stands at particular risk of being misconstrued as a simple physiological defence mechanism. The following survey of relevant theoretical approaches includes a brief explanation of Julia Kristeva's psychoanalytical conceptualisation of the disgust-related notion of the abject as "death infecting life" (4)—a universal stage of crisis. Using Kristeva's notion of the abject, I will then look at the different manifestations of disgust in content and form in *Molloy*. The focus of the analysis will be on the protagonist's ambiguous relationship to his mother, his "Ma, Mag, [...] Countess Caca" (13), which can be argued to lie at the core of Molloy's narration of disgust. With the exemplary study of Beckett's novel I aim to demonstrate the potential of a 'narrative-of-disgust' in mediating and offering insight into the complex concept of abjection. I thereby wish to establish disgust as an equal counterpart to the much researched and well-established sensations of pity and fear as desired emotional responses to works of art, and to determine its specific narrative potential to aesthetically communicate liminal physical and mental experiences. After all, disgust is capable, more than any other emotion, of expressing the core of human conflict as being caught up in dualistic struggles of life and death, body and mind, nature and culture, as well as attraction and repulsion.

Disgust, Literature, and Theory

At first sight, disgust seems to be an unambiguous sensation denoting, as its linguistic roots suggest "something offensive to the taste" (Darwin 259). Charles Darwin was the first to systematically define 'disgust' as one of the six basic emotions in *The Expressions of Emotions in Man and Animals* (1872). He conceives of disgust as a universal, yet uniquely human reaction that is "readily excited by anything unusual in the appearance, odour, or nature of our food" (257). What is special about disgust for Darwin is that it does not require actual contact with the seemingly appalling substance, but can be induced even by "the mere idea of having partaken of any unusual food" (259). Darwin's definition of disgust as an aversive reaction to certain foods to a large degree still dominates our understanding of the sensation today. Yet, disgust is much more than a mere physical reaction to 'unusual' food, as one of the pioneers of research on disgust, Paul Rozin, notes. Rozin expands the "range of disgust elicitors" to include: "stimuli that remind humans of their animal origins (e. g., body boundary violations, inappropriate sex, poor hygiene, and death), a variety of aversive interpersonal contacts, and certain moral offences" (870). Like Darwin, Rozin conceives of disgust and all its different manifestations to have evolutionarily developed from a "response to bad tastes", which was later "map[ped] onto a moral emotion" (870). In *Disgust. The Gatekeeper Emotion* (2004), Susan Miller summarizes the main contemporary scientific approaches that predominantly understand disgust as an instinctive response functioning to protect us from four main areas of potential harm: food, infection/contagion, animals, and waste (2). What these approaches generally do not address is the questions of *why* disgust should have developed from an animalistic aversion (=distaste) against health-harming foods in the first place. Both animals and small children display distaste and aversion against specific foods, but they do not feature disgust in their emotional register, which means that it must, at least to some degree, be a cultural (learned) emotion—an emotion that has something to do with what makes us human.

Another facet of disgust that is rarely addressed in psychological and scientific studies is that objects, people, and behaviours that are deemed disgusting, commonly not only evoke repulsion, but also some kind of fascination or even attraction. It is surprising that this essential feature has received so little attention in current research since Plato already discussed the inherently paradox reaction to disgusting objects in his analysis of the different parts of the soul in the *Republic*. Plato's Socrates tells the story of a man called Leontius who walks passed recently executed bodies and at their sight feels utter disgust *(dyschéreia)*. What Leontius experiences, however is not simply aversion, but are contradictory sensations: the desire to look and the urge to cover his eyes and turn away (439e-440a). From this observation, Socrates concludes that Leontius' reaction can be neither a purely desirous/animalistic/physical drive, nor a purely rational command, but must be something *in-between*, some kind of embodied moral response. He allocates this to a so-called 'spirited' part of the soul (439e), which he claims protects the just state of the soul (442a) from "injustice, licentiousness, cowardice, lack of learning, and, in sum, vice entire" (444a-b). Even though empirical research rarely addresses disgust's two-sidedness, findings from these fields nevertheless implicitly confirm Plato's observation of an inherent ambiguity in disgust reactions. Scientists have found that when subjects are confronted with typical disgust-elicitors, their whole body seems to tune us into staying close to that which causes repulsion: heart-rate, blood pressure, and respiration rate decrease; our mouths open and we experience increased salivation (cf. Olatunji and Sawchuk 936). These reactions have been commonly explained to indicate the initial stages of nausea and vomiting (cf. ibid.), as Darwin poetically describes it: "the mouth being widely opened, as if to let an offensive morsel drop out" (258). The opened mouth can, however, just as well be read to indicate the opposite: an invitation to incorporation. These findings indicate that disgust even in its most basic function cannot be construed as a clear-cut aversive emotion which protects us from incorporating harm; seeing as the 'logical' thing to do, if we were to avoid health-harming contacts, would be to first and foremost keep our mouths shut and safe and establish some distance to the source of danger. This brief sketch of historical and current scientific approaches to disgust should suffice to show that: a) disgust cannot be understood as a simple aversive physical reaction to health-harming incorporation, b) disgust-elicitors cover a range of objects and behaviours that exceed items related to food and incorporation, c) disgust reactions are often paradoxical, causing not only aversion, but also attraction. Further dichotomies that disgust reactions address, which can be deducted from the discussion so far, are the pairings of body/mind as well as of nature/culture.

The most insightful research regarding the two-sidedness of disgust comes from psychoanalytic theory. Already Sigmund Freud emphasizes the importance of disgust in *Totem and Taboo* (1913) and *Civilisation and its Discontents* (1930). He regards disgust as a socially constructed mechanism of the civilisation process which functions to repress libidinal (i.e. animalistic/natural) drives in order to distinguish us from our animalistic ancestry. The most elaborate study on disgusting phenomena and their meaning, however, is Julia Kristeva's *Powers of Horror. An Essay on Abjection* (1980), in which she introduces the notion of the *abject*—"a vortex of summons and repulsion" (1). In this 'essay' Kristeva relates the notion of *abjection* back to our first relationship with our mother and marks it out as an essential component for our development as human subjects, which she sees accomplished through the infant's acquisition of language. Like her predecessor, Jacques Lacan, Kristeva locates the emergence of subjectivity within the intrinsically connected orders of the pre-verbal stage (semiotic) and the verbal stage (symbolic) of the psychosexual development, which is realised in the child's separation from the symbiotic relationship with its mother. Kristeva comes to the conclusion that the infant's motivation to initiate the traumatic experience of separation can only be caused by (while at the same time leading to) the experience of rejection. She poetically defines this experience (i.e. *abjection*), as: "[A] 'something' that I do not recognize as a thing. A weight of meaninglessness, about which there is nothing insignificant, and which crushes me. On the edge of non-existence and hallucination, of a reality that, if I acknowledge it, annihilates me." (2)

Abjection is thus first experienced physically at the pre-verbal semiotic stage—against "'something'" that is "not recognize[d] as a thing" (2). The child rejects or *abjects* that which is other from itself, because it is experienced as a threat—"The abject has only one quality of the object—that of being opposed to *I*" (1). At the same time Kristeva conceives of *abjection* as the experience of a lack of something (that which is not I) and "[a]ll abjection is in fact recognition of the *want* on which any being, meaning, language, or desire is founded" (5). The subject's attempts to repress the threat of *abjection*, which it recognises as a lack, initiates not only its wants and desires, but also results in the creation of an *Ersatz* (=substitute) for what is experienced as lacking. This substitute is established by symbolic means (=language), which are able to provide a world of meaning and order. Because the experience of *abjection* is thus not only the cause of establishing language, but in fact of all systems of rules and order that structure society (i.e. symbolic order), Kristeva holds this experience to be also the "primer of [our] culture" (2).

According to Kristeva's theory, the experience of *abjection* is not left behind with the successful entry into the symbolic order, but stays with us in the form of a memory of the body in the state of separation, which continues to confront the human subject at all stages of life. *Abjection* haunts us whenever we experience states of unresolvable ambiguity, of in-betweenness. Kristeva regards "food loathing [a]s perhaps the most elementary and most archaic form of abjection" (2), which she illustrates with her famous example of loathing the skin of milk: the skin, being neither part of nor clearly different from the milk, brings up embodied memories of separation from the mother (cf. 2). Physiologically, she relates phenomena of in-betweenness to the orifices—excretion, vomiting, or bodily wounds, as they are simultaneously part of the inside and the outside of the body.

"[W]hat goes out of the body, out of its pores and openings, points to the infinitude of the body proper and gives rise to abjection. Faecal matter signifies [...] what never ceases to separate from a body in a state of permanent loss in order to become *autonomous, distinct* from the mixtures, alterations, and decay that run through it." (108)

In Kristeva's theory, it is not only physiological states, like the ones listed above, that give rise to *abjection* and thus disgust, but because *abjection* is intrinsically linked to the child's entry into the symbolic order, on a more abstract level, anything that "disturbs identity, system, order" is able to cause repulsion (4). Kristeva gives the example of "the traitor, the liar, the criminal with a good conscience, the shameless rapist, the killer who claims he is a savior" to illustrate this point (4). For Kristeva, the most identity-threatening encounter in life is death, or more specifically "death infecting life" (4), which she argues to manifest the essence of *abjection*; an in-between that shows itself in many forms in life; a fact that cannot be adequately expressed by means of language and thus be grasped (controlled) by rational means of understanding.

"A wound with blood and pus, or the sickly, acrid smell of sweat, of decay, does not *signify* death. In the presence of signified death—a flat encephalograph, for instance—I would understand, react, or accept. No, as in true theater, without makeup or masks, refuse and corpses *show me* what I permanently thrust aside in order to live. These body fluids, this defilement, this shit are what life withstands, hardly and with difficulty, on the part of death. There, I am at the border of my condition as a living being." (3)

Kristeva here convincingly argues against the *abject* being a direct 'signifier of death' and thereby part of an 'understandable' symbolic order. For Kristeva, it is the human corpse "seen without God and outside of science, [that] is the utmost of abjection. It is death infecting life. Abject." (4) However, as mentioned above, *abjection* poses not only a threat to the subject, but is also expressive of its needs and the development of desires, whereby *abjection*, just like disgust, is ultimately governed by ambiguity. According to Kristeva, the *abject* is not only a source of revulsion, but also of a specific kind of pleasure which she refers to as: *jouissance* (= 'unspeakable bliss'): "One does not know it, one does not desire it, one joys in it *[on en jouit]*. Violently and painfully" (9). This 'pleasurable' component of *abjection* explains why the subject should be motivated to enter a process of separation from the mother in the first place. For Kristeva, the pleasure of *jouissance* is realised in 'joyful' transgressions of the law or other forms of embracing the in-between and the ambiguous (cf. 9). Her notion of *jouissance* closely resembles Nietzsche's construct of the Dionysian principle in *The Birth of Tragedy* (1872), which destroys the "usual barriers and limits of existence", leading to ecstasy and oblivion and insight into "the true essence of things", insights into the reality beneath appearances (40). Nietzsche argues that "[under] the mystical, jubilant shout of Dionysus the spell of individuation is broken, and the path to the Mothers of Being, to the innermost core of things, is laid open" (76). Kristeva, like Nietzsche, claims that by means of art the "true essence of things" (= 'death infecting life') can be expressed and thereby helped to be endured or in fact purified.

Kristeva regards modernist writing as the most successful mode of responding to the social and psychological crises experienced by the subjects of twentieth-century Western culture. She claims that by confronting *abjection*, art is able to function as a form of sublimation, which can even defer the eruption of 'real' psychosis (cf. Kristeva in Morgan and Morris 27). For her the "aesthetic task" of modernist writing is thus to "descend into the foundations of the symbolic construct" which "amounts to retracing the fragile limits of the speaking being, closest to its dawn"

(18). This task, however, demands a particular form of writing, a "perversion" or "corruption" of language: "The writer, fascinated by the abject, imagines its logic, projects himself into it, introjects it, and as a consequence perverts language—style and content" (16). In Kristeva's view the crisis of *abjection* cannot be expressed in a clear-cut narrative, or 'story' as we know it: "[W]hen even the limit between inside and outside becomes uncertain, the narrative is what is challenged first. If it continues nevertheless, its make-up changes; its linearity is shattered, it proceeds in flashes, enigmas, short cuts, incompletion, tangles, and cuts." (14)

Because *abjection* takes place in-between a pre-verbal (semiotic) and a verbal (symbolic) state, it is expressive of experiences which defy the logic of language (as we know it), which in its artistic manifestation causes a "recasting of syntax and vocabulary" (141). Not only the words and contents express the abject, but also the particular tone of the narrative voice, which re-connects author and recipient with the semiotic realm of signification: "The abject lies beyond the themes, [...] in *the way one speaks*; it is verbal communication, it is the Word that discloses the abject." (23; my emphasis)

Kristeva's notion of the *abject* helps us to understand not only the ambiguity of our disgust reactions, but also why it might play such a dominant role in works of art. It can hardly be denied that even the briefest look at the literary canon will convey numerous examples across the centuries and genres that are deeply engaged with topics relating to disgust. Examples range from Seneca's Thyestes being served his sons' heads for dinner (*Thyestes* IV) to Hamlet's preoccupation with "things rank and gross" (I.ii, 136), Gregor Samsa's transformation into a monstrous insect-like creature in Kafka's *Metamorphosis* (1915), or the present day fascination with 'gross-out' movies. More than any other emotion, the experience of disgust is an experience of paradoxes encountered physically and/or cognitively. The sensation of disgust holds a unique place in-between contradictory pairs and is thus the prime reaction to liminal embodied experiences, such as illness, decay, and dying, which are located precisely in-between the dichotomous positions of: life/death, body/mind, etc. Disgust's ambiguous quality makes it a crucial (if not essential) component of the aesthetic effect that results from representing universal human conflicts, as I hope to demonstrate with the exemplary analysis of the narrative voice in Beckett's *Molloy*.

SAMUEL BECKETT'S NARRATIVE OF DISGUST IN *MOLLOY*

Beckett, who was living in Paris at the time of writing *Molloy*, is clearly influenced by the existentialist and psychoanalytic approaches of contemporaries like Jean-Paul Sartre, Georges Bataille, and many others that dominate the cultural life of post-World-War-II Paris. Like other avant-garde writing of his time, Beckett's literary style is expressive of a 'new' 'structure of feeling' in Western European society after the tremendous industrial and technological changes and the traumata of two world wars in the first half of the twentieth century. Disgust plays an eminent role in a majority of works at the time: Sartre's novel *La Nausée* (1938) addresses a disgust at existence; Bataille, *enfant terrible* of the time, not only writes highly disturbing literary pieces like *L'Anus Solaire* (1931), but also develops a philosophical theory called 'scatology' ("the science of excrements") in his essay on the "Value of de Sade" (cf. 102 f.), and Antonin Artaud sets his aesthetic task to "break through the language in order to touch life" (13) in a theatre that is as radical as the plague. Winfried Menninghaus claims that Western European artists and intellectuals thereby establish an "affirmative aesthetic of the repellent" (343). And even though Menninghaus does not mention Beckett in his *Disgust. History of a Strong Sensation* (2003), Beckett's writing can be viewed as a prime example of this category. Not only do his works contain basically all the typical physical disgust elicitors Ben-Zvi lists (excrement, wounds, bad smells, decaying bodies, etc.; cf. 684), but they also explicitly address issues of disgust that are more complex, such as the dichotomous relations between: nature/culture, animal/man, body/mind, life/death, etc. Beckett furthermore investigates the intricate relation between disgust and the use of language, which culminates in a questioning of the meaning of human life *per se*.

With *Molloy* Beckett goes particular far in reaching down to the core of existence, and he does so by literally letting his protagonist embark on "the path to the Mother of Being, to the innermost core of things" (Nietzsche 76). The narrative voice demonstrates what Kristeva calls *abject* writing; a voice that is in search of the "true essence of things": the fact that our existence is being determined by the *abject*, by "death infecting life" (4), and expressive of the wish to come to terms with this fact. As Kristina Czarnecki states: "The principle elements of abjection—the mother, the body, language, and narrative—comprise Molloy's experience" (53). In *Molloy*, the mother-figure relates to the universal experience each living human has made, as having been born by a mother, and thus *qua* life, having been born to die. From the relation to the mother—the embodiment of our paradoxical living-situation between life and death—all other incidents or experiences of *abjection* are mere derivatives. The mother also functions as a current reminder of our first experience of *abjection* in our separation from her body.

BIRTH, DEATH, AND EXCREMENTS

Molloy repeatedly informs us about the need to see and tell us about his mother. He begins with a 'recollection' of the circumstances of his birth: "I have to speak, [...] of her who brought me into the world, through hole in her arse if my memory is correct. First taste of shit" (12). This account is appalling and disturbing in multiple ways. First of all, the mentioning of bodily orifices and excrement, each in itself, unsettles what we understand as a symbolic order (i.e. rules of social life, behavioural conduct, etc.). Defecation is considered as defilement and needs to be "jettisoned from the '*symbolic system*'. It is what escapes the social rationality, that logical order on which a social aggregate is based." (Kristeva 65) Disgust at excrements functions as a distinctive human marker of difference from our animalistic ancestors (cf. Menninghaus 189 f.). Molloy is aware of the fact that his *parlé* of excrements is not in line with rules of etiquette, as another passage demonstrates, where he ponders on his mother's potential incontinence: "I think she was quite incontinent, both of faeces and water, but a kind of prudishness made us avoid the subject when we met, and I could never be certain of it." (13) However, the next sentence also demonstrates his fascination with the topic, as he gives a visceral account of what he imagines his mother's digestive products to be like: "a few niggardly wetted goat-dropping every two or three days" (13). By calling the avoidance of the subject "prudish", he displays a critical stance towards "the disavowal of [...] modes of corporeality, especially those representing what is considered unacceptable, unclean or anti-social" (Grosz 86). It is easy to regard Molloy's interest in his mother's digestive apparatus as 'perverse'. We should, however, be aware of the fact, that this judgement results to a large degree from our 'intuitive' disgust-reaction, which is in fact no more than an embodied social rule and should not be misunderstood as a rational or objective assessment of the situation. It would also be quite possible to ascribe Molloy's descriptions of his mother's troublesome bowel movements and incontinence (which are not uncommon ailments of the ageing body) to a genuine interest in her health. Chances for such an evaluation are scarce though, because Molloy's mentioning of his mother's incontinence represents a violent break with the symbolic order of Western society, where ageing bodies with their illnesses and symptoms of decay (leading to their ultimate death), are to a large degree banned from everyday life via our disgust reactions. Ageing and dying could even be argued to happen outside of, or at least in some kind of liminal space on the borders of society. And excrement does not even need to be directly linked to illness as in the example above to evoke disgust on at least three levels: a) by association to animality, b) by being a product of in-between (inside and outside of the body), and c) by being linked to the dualism of life and death—they are utmost *abject*: "These body fluids, this difficulty on part of death. [...]. Such wastes drop so that I might live, until, from loss to loss, nothing remains in me and my entire body falls beyond the limit—*cadere*, cadaver." (3)

The third aspect is especially emphasized in the above quoted reference Molloy makes to his birth, as Molloy's image of the circumstances of his birth invert the 'classical story' of being born on all levels. Instead of coming into the world through the mother's vagina, as a pure and innocent new being, he claims to have been born "from a hole in her arse" (12), which equates him to other waste products departing from there: a 'piece of shit'. This is further heightened by the following metonymic sentence where Molloy describes his "[f]irst taste of shit", because with the simple word 'taste', the faecal products that most likely accompanied his birth are directly associated with eating. Thereby this phrase once again alludes to the ambiguous relation of life and death in the *abject*, seeing as excrements, which should be transported out of the body "so that I might live" (3), are linked to incorporation instead. Of course Molloy cannot have been born from his mother's anus—a disruption of system and order, which in itself already causes disgust, but Molloy does in fact admit to his 'story of birth' being fictional by making reference to memory, ("If I remember correctly"), which he of course cannot have of his birth. However, not only is the orifice of the anus so closely located behind the opening of the vagina that a confusion of both is not entirely unthinkable (depending on perspective, anatomical knowledge, attention, etc.), as Molloy himself declares in a later passage, where he cannot remember whether he had vaginal or anal sex with a former lover (cf. 52); with the image of a birth among excrements, Beckett actually openly depicts a common side effect of 'real' childbirths (seeing as the muscles used for defecation are the same used to push out the baby), a topic of social taboo that is generally barred from being discussed in public. For Molloy birth and life are ultimately linked to excrements and death and thus deemed disgusting. For this attitude he holds his mother responsible: "[I]f ever I'm reduced to looking for a meaning to my life, you never can tell, it's in that old mess I'll stick my nose to begin with, the mess of that poor old uniparous whore and myself the last of my foul brood, neither man nor beast." (14f.) This phrase can be read in two ways and is probably meant in both: a) as an accusation against Molloy's mother for having born him into the 'mess' he finds his existence to be, and b) in reference to the psychoanalytical stance that children's later psychological issues result from their early parental relationships, which Molloy regards as 'mess[y]' or 'mess[ed up]'.

MOTHER NURTURE: ATTRACTION, AVERSION, ACCEPTANCE

Molloy's relationship to his mother is not purely aversive, but also expressive of a great need. The plot is solely driven by his desire to see her and the need to "go and see my mother" throughout the novel actually remains the only certainty, the one fact that is never questioned. This ambiguity also comes clear in Molloy's naming of his mother. He has different names for her, one establishing her relation to excrements as "Countess Caca", the other one, even more interesting in being expressive of his ambiguous feelings towards her being "Mag", because as Molloy explains:

"I called her Mag, because for me, without my knowing why, the letter g abolished the syllable Ma, and as it were spat on it, better than any other letter would have done. At the same time I satisfied a deep and doubtless unacknowledged need, the need to have a Ma, that is a mother, and to proclaim it, audibly. For before you say mag, you say ma, inevitably." (13)

The letter 'g' being added to the normally used 'Ma' to form 'Mag' is not at all arbitrary, as Molloy explains: no "other letter would have done" (13). In this description we once again find the ambiguity of *abjection* on multiple levels (the Kristevan semiotic and symbolic). On the level of content (the symbolic), the passage can be regarded as a re-enactment of the embodied memory of the subject's first experience of *abjection* in its psycho-social development: Molloy here expresses his "need to have a Ma", concurrent with his desire to separate from this bond "the letter g abolished the syllable Ma". Molloy's ambiguous sentiments are mirrored in the onomatopoetic charge of the three-letter word (semiotic): the guttural sound of the 'g' evokes a gagging movement in the speaker's throat (=disgust reaction), which brings the softness and infinite openness of the 'Ma' to an abrupt end, signifying at once closure (of the air flow; nothing can enter the body) and rejection, a readiness for expulsion in the form of vomiting. ("Countess Caca" works similarly). The process of vomiting itself once again mirrors the infant's state of separation via rejective gestures from its dependence on the mother's nurturing body—"The abject confronts us [...] with our earliest attempts to release the hold of the maternal entity" (Kristeva 13).

According to Kristeva, "food loathing is perhaps the most elementary and most archaic form of abjection"(2). In *Molloy*, food loathing plays an elementary role in the protagonist's relation to his mother, himself, and the way he perceives the world around him. Eating is directly linked to nurturing and necessity, and thereby to the mother's body, the first source of nurture, which guarantees existence and growth, but also symbolizes dependency. Molloy is most of the time disgusted by food, as it is an affirmative action to living which is oppositional to his wish to "finish dying" (3). The emphasis in this expression must be laid on "finish" and not on "dying", seeing as nutrition will in fact prolong the painful existence of his decaying body. He thus describes his mother's attitude towards him as a form of "charity that kept me dying" (18). An assessment that is mirrored shortly after, when he describes his first encounter with a woman on his journey to his mother's house, during his short stay in prison. "[A] woman rose up before me, a big fat woman dressed in black or rather in mauve. I still wonder today if it wasn't the social worker. She was holding out to me, on an odd saucer, a mug full of greyish concoction." (19) His ambiguous relation to the "big fat" woman that brings him food already becomes apparent in his unclear memory of the colour of her dress: black being associatively linked to death, whereas the colour mauve generally represents positive, specifically female and life-affirming qualities. The mashed-up food ("concoction") highly disgusts him, especially when he sees the contents on the plate mixing up even further in his trembling hands into a "pile of tottering disparates, in which the hard, the liquid, and the soft were joined" (19), which he experiences as some kind of existential threat filling him with fear, anguish, panic, and above all disgust. For Molloy, the repulsive "vomitory" (20) quality of the food forces him to violently reject it, throw it "to the ground, [...] or against the wall, [...] with all [his] strength" (20). In her role of providing food, the 'social worker' is like the mother associated with "charity", which Molloy regards as a way of prolonging death: "when social workers offer you [...] something to hinder you from swooning, [...] it is useless to recoil, they will pursue you to the ends of the earth, the vomitory in their hands.[...] Against the charitable gesture there is no defence." (19) Molloy's ambiguity towards food also becomes clear in a passage later in the novel, where he is provided with food by the motherly figure of Sophie/Lousse (whom he also associates with the colour mauve: lavender): "[T]he little I did eat I devoured [...]. I flung myself at the mess, gulped down the half or the quarter of it in two mouthfuls without chewing [...], then pushed it from me with loathing. One would have thought I ate to live!" (49) Molloy's wish to, on the one hand, overcome his dependency on food/life/his mother is symbolized by another imagery that relates to the existential disgust described in Sartre's *La Nausée*, where the protagonist suddenly comes to realize his nausea at existence by contemplating the materiality of a stone (the "In-Itself") he finds at the beach. Molloy has a habit of sucking stones in order to overcome hunger, which is a double-entendre of Sartre's 'nausea', as the sucking of stones is at once an incorporation of materiality (the In-Itself, which causes Roquentin's disgust), and a method employed to overcome the material component of his existence (the fact that he has a body in need of nourishment), which is also mirrored in his desperate attempts to create a mathematical system (symbolic: order, control) for his stone-sucking procedures.

    The most interesting passage relating to Molloy's ambiguous relation to food and the feminine is his recalling of his first encounter with love to an elderly woman, called Ruth/Edith, whom he meets "at a rubbish dump", where he was "poking about the garbage [...] in the hope of finding something that would disgust [him] forever with eating" (52). Beckett's narrative here delves in almost all imaginable elicitors of disgust. They become prevalent in the uncomfortable dichotomous pairings of concepts such as: eating/waste, human/animal ("I would have made love to a goat to know what love was"), man/woman ("perhaps she too was a man"), anus/

vagina ("perhaps after all she put me in the rectum"), love/prostitution ("she gave me money"), life-affirmation/death ("she might have expired in my arms"), (52 f.).

Molloy's relation to Ruth/Edith, however, also displays the possibility of an overcoming of disgust by love (= mother dealing with baby's faeces, spouses caring for their elderly or ill family members without being disgusted, etc.). This is shown in a statement of Molloy which demonstrates the caring attitude the couple displays towards each other: "Our commerce was not without tenderness, with trembling hands she cut my toe nails and I rubbed her rump with winter cream." (52) The described moment of a care and tenderness is not the only instance where a loving attitude is shown to be able of overcoming of disgust. The character of Lousse had also demonstrated this ability in her offer to give Molloy a home: "If I did not choose to be clean, to wear nice clothes, to wash and so on, I need not. [...] All she asked was to feel me near her." (43) In Molloy's final and brief description of encounters with women at the seaside, he also marks that while most of them "turned away" at the sight of the "wretchedly clothed" vagabond living in a cave, "one of them [...] came and offered [him] something to eat", an act of "charity" which he does not reject, but instead "looked at her in silence, until she went away" (69). In the order of the appearances of nurturing women in Molloy's narration one can thus observe a development in his attitude towards them, mirrored in his reaction to the food they provide. This development moves from pure aversion ("social worker") to silent acceptance (woman at the beach), which in turn seems to indicate that Molloy's stance towards having to live, which he initially aggressively rejected, seems to have shifted, maybe not a life-affirming or embracing attitude, but at least to some kind of 'neutral' position.

Conclusion

Beckett's *Molloy* defies any form of satisfactory interpretive closure: not only because the present analysis only deals with the first half of the novel, itself part of a trilogy, of which all parts are seemingly infinitely linked to other works of classical literature, as well as Beckett's own writings; but also because, even with the focus on the single aspect of disgust in Molloy's narrative voice, it feels like the topics discussed present no more than a thimble-sized tip of the iceberg. However, what I hope to have demonstrated with this exemplary analysis of disgust in the narrative voice of Molloy, is how potent and 'worthy' this highly ambiguous sensation is of incorporation in literary theory. By embarking literally on the "path to the Mother of Being" (Nietzsche 76), Molloy delves into all matters of disgust, which are, if we agree with Kristeva's approach on *abjection*, all manifestations of the tragic core of existence "death infecting life" (4). By exposing both sides of disgust-elicitors, their repulsiveness as well as their attraction in all detail, these opposites seem to neutralize each other towards the end of Molloy's narrative. In a state of comparable calm and peacefulness Molloy stoically asserts: "There seemed to be rain, then sunshine, turn about. [...] Molloy could stay, where he happened to be" (85). One maybe would not expect a highly hermetic narrative voice like Beckett's Molloy's senile and apparently depressive ramblings to convey universal insight into life to a broader readership. But it is precisely that specific tone "compounded of pity, of fear, of disgust" (12), which functions at a physical and cognitive level to turn the reader to the paradoxes of life that are uncomfortable to address: ageing, illness, dying. In the twenty-first century, where we invest much effort into keeping the non-permanence of life at bay, not only as individuals, but also as a society, Beckett offers those who dare a view of a reality deeply buried under layers of protective conditioning.

Works Cited

Aristotle. *Poetics*. Trans. Joe Sachs. Newburyport: Focus Publishing, 2006. Print.
Artaud, Antonin. *The Theatre and Its Double*. New York: Grove Press, 1994. Print.
Bataille, Georges. "The Use Value of D. A. F. de Sade." *Visions of Excess: Selected Writings, 1927–1939*. Ed. Allan Stoekl. Minneapolis: University of Minnesota P, 1985. 91–105. Print.
Beckett, Samuel. *Three Novels: Molloy, Malone Dies, The Unnamable*. New York: Grove Press, 2010. Print.
Ben-Zvi, Linda. "Beckett and Disgust: The Body as 'Laughing Matter'". *Modernism/Modernity* 18.4 (2011): 681–698. Web. 27 September 2016.

Czarnecki, Kristin. "'Signs I Don't Understand': Language and Abjection in Molloy." *Journal of Beckett Studies (Journal of Beckett Studies)* 2007: 52–77.
Darwin, Charles. *The Expression of the Emotions in Man and Animals*. New York: Appleton & Company, 1872. Print.
Freud, Sigmund. *New Introductory Lectures on Psychoanalysis*. New York: Norton & Company, 1989. Print.
Grosz, Elizabeth. "The Body of Signification." *Abjection, Melancholia, and Love: The Work of Julia Kristeva*. Ed. John Fletcher, Andrew Benjamin. London: Routledge, 1990. 80–103. Print.
Kristeva, Julia. *Powers of Horror: An Essay on Abjection*. New York: Columbia UP, 1982. Print.
Menninghaus, Winfried. *Disgust: The Theory and History of a Strong Sensation*. Albany: State U of New York P, 2003. Print.
Miller, Susan B. *Disgust: The Gatekeeper Emotion*. Hillsdale: Analytic P, 2004. Print.
Morgan, Stuart, and Frances Morris. *Rites of Passage: Art for the End of the Century*. London: Tate Gallery Publications, 1995. Print.
Nietzsche, Friedrich W. *The Birth of Tragedy And Other Writings*. Ed. Raymond Geuss and Ronald Speirs. Cambridge: Cambridge UP, 2007. Print.
Olatunji, Bunmi O., and Craig N. Sawchuk. "Disgust: Characteristic Features, Social Manifestations, and Clinical Implications." *Journal of Social and Clinical Psychology* 24.7 (2005): 932–962.
Pinter, Harold. "Beckett." *Beckett at 60: A Festschrift*. Ed. W. J. McCormack. London: Calder & Boyars, 1967. 86. Print.
Plato. *The Republic*. Ed. Allan Bloom. Second Edition. New York: Basic Books, 1991. Print.
Rozin, Paul, Laura Lowery, and Rhonda Ebert. "Varieties of Disgust Faces and the Structure of Disgust." *Journal of Personality and Social Psychology* 66.5 (1994): 870–881.
Sartre, Jean-Paul. *La Nausée*. Paris: Gallimard, 1938. Print.

'Blue with Age'
Dis- and Dys-appearance of the Body
in Eudora Welty's "A Worn Path"

Ellen Matlok-Ziemann

INTRODUCTION

In recent decades, aging has been prominently addressed in literary texts not only to shed light on ageist discourse in so-called "decline narratives" but also to open up positive possibilities of representations of old women and men and to gain a better understanding of aging. Numerous authors have discussed and reflected on the aging process and old age in, for instance, "Reifungsromanen" to explore what it means to grow and be old. These scholars have rightly questioned and criticized stereotypes of aging that have been prevalent in Western societies.[1]

As the stereotypes of aging often were characterized by bodily deterioration and decay, gerontologists, such as Moody, Neugarten, Rowe and Kahn[2], drew with their studies more positive pictures of aging. These revealed that a large proportion of people over 75 years are not constrained or limited by old age or even that almost no one in that age group shows signs of physical deterioration (Deats and Lenker 3). Indeed, many studies and reports seem to suggest that, since aging is socially constructed, it is possible to age "successfully" without any physical debility. However, while the aging body is always a social construct, it is also at the same time a biological organism, something that often has been overlooked.

---

1 | See Sara Munson Deats's and Lagretta Tallent Lenker's "Introduction" to *Aging and Identity* (9).
2 | In Deats's and Lenker's "Introduction" to *Aging and Identity* (3). See also John W. Rowe's and Robert L. Kahn's "Successful Aging."

This paper addresses, on the one hand, the failure to take into account the biological body as this seems to corroborate ageist discourse, and, on the other hand, the opportunity that a taking into account of the specificities of the aging body offers for a more nuanced understanding of representations of old women. My analysis of Eudora Welty's short story "A Worn Path" illustrates how the inclusion of the material body in the investigation of representations of aging can overcome the binary of decline narratives and narratives of "successful aging". Drawing on Maurice Merleau-Ponty, Simone de Beauvoir, and Drew Leder's phenomenological investigations, my reading of Welty's short story provides a different and more fruitful understanding of representations of aging and old women.

BINARY OF SUCCESS AND DECLINE

While it has been necessary, and still is, to counter and question negative stereotypes of aging, the emphasis on the possibility of aging without physical and/or mental decline helped contribute to establishing another stereotype, that of successful aging.[3] The assertion of "successful aging" also implies that anyone who has not been able to do that has "failed". Interestingly, in the public, aging stereotypes have been increasingly questioned as well and the same binary pattern, that of successful aging or aging as decline, can be discerned in the discussion of aging and old age in the media. While the media have become more aware of the growing number of "senior citizens" and warned the public of the financial burden for society, the media also depict active and agile old people, usually middle-class and urban people, who frequently travel and take an interest in culture.[4]

---

[3] | See, for instance, Anne Bowling's and Paul Dieppe's critical discussion of successful aging in "What is successful ageing and who should define it?"

[4] | The article "Cost of ageing population 'needs re-calculating'" published in *BBC News* claims that the fact that the number of ageing people increases does not necessarily imply that people over 65 are in medical need. However, the article also notes that while life expectancy is increasing, "people are living with disabilities for longer than before". (n. p.) This claim, on the one hand, that old age does not necessarily imply debility, and on the other, the fear of increasing costs because of old age-related diseases, mirrors the binary of two prevalent positions of decline and success in aging studies.

What is common to the stereotypes of decline and success is perhaps the assumption that the biological[5] body precludes agency. The aging body as a deteriorating body and thus in decline has been problematized in medical sciences as this body hinders the subject from interacting with others or even makes this impossible. Diseases "typical" for aging, such as coronary diseases, high blood pressure and dementia, have been categorized and medicalized. Furthermore, recently efforts have been undertaken to postpone this inevitable decline and to re-design and engineer the body. Even death is no longer regarded as certain by, for instance, biomedical gerontologist Aubrey de Grey.[6]

In narratives of "successful aging", on the other hand, there is a conspicuous absence of the aging, frail body, something that may suggest that "everybody can age successfully". It seems that if one only identifies and challenges negative representations as ageism, the "battle" is won. The underlying assumption may be that, if there are negative representations of aging, then they must be based on socially constructed views and prejudices. However, the fact that, in narratives of "successful aging", the body does not appear—there is no material aging body—may indicate an underlying fear that if the biological body were acknowledged then this biologically aging body would preclude agency as claimed in medical sciences.[7]

AWAY FROM DECLINE AND SUCCESS

The need to move away from this binary of decline and success has been discussed by several scholars[8]. As Linn Sandberg rightly points out, discourses of successful aging do "not ultimately challenge the age hierarchy

---

5 | Some scholars find it controversial to claim that there is a biological body but accept the notion of the specificity of the material body. See, for instance, Elizabeth Grosz's *Volatile Bodies* (41).
6 | See Yuval Noah Harari's discussion in *Homo Deus*.
7 | In *What Is A Woman?*, Toril Moi criticizes the fear of many feminists that acknowledging a biological, natural, body would imply essentialism, "that sex, unlike gender, is outside history, discourse, and politics" (36). The evident absence of the aging body suggests that there may be a similar fear in aging studies.
8 | See, for instance, Margaret Morganroth Gullette's *Agewise* and Linn Sandberg's essay "Affirmative Old Age—the Ageing Body and Feminist Theories on Difference."

and ageism [...]. Rather it retains youth and the characteristics of youth as desirable [...]. [S]uccessful ageing should perhaps more rightfully be termed non-ageing or agelessness" (13). To overcome this binary some scholars propose to draw on Elizabeth Grosz's *Volatile Bodies* to take into account the facticity of the material body. In *Volatile Bodies*, Grosz likens the material body to paper onto/into which a text is "edged". According to Grosz, the body is not simply a passive—smooth—surface onto which social norms and values are inscribed. The body is characterized by its specificities and this, Grosz argues, affects the way a message is edged onto the body. Even the content of the message may be influenced by the very material of the body.[9]

Yet, even when taking into account the specificities of the material body, it still appears very difficult to overcome the binary of success and decline. Sandberg, too, despite her criticism of this binary, does not quite succeed in moving away from success and decline. Although her concept of "affirmative aging" includes the material body, as Grosz suggests in *Volatile Bodies*, the cases she presents in her study seem to be, once again, narratives of successful aging. Sandberg herself admits that "there is a *slight* overemphasis on the positive and joyful experiences of embodied ageing" (34, emphasis mine).[10] I would therefore like to present the usefulness of the phenomenological concept of aging based on Maurice Merleau-Ponty and Simone de Beauvoir and developed further by Drew Leder.[11] This approach explains, on the one hand, why the denial of the body is so dominant in the Western world, and, on the other hand, how changes of the aging body can be negotiated without judgment or demands for success. My reading of Welty's short story "A Worn Path" demonstrates the usefulness of this concept.

---

9 | See also Toril Moi's discussion of poststructuralists and their failure, including Grosz's, to realize that Beauvoir's concept of the body overcomes the binary of sex and gender (30-43).

10 | It should be pointed out that Sandberg's study is a gerontological one and not an analysis of a literary text.

11 | Drew Leder's *The Absent Body* is one of the first attempts "to understand the ways of the body in illness from a phenomenological perspective". See Fredrik Svenaeus's essay "The Body as Alien, Unhomelike, and Uncanny".

DIS- AND DYS-APPEARANCE OF THE BODY

One of the key elements of Merleau-Ponty's and Beauvoir's theory is that it is not possible to differentiate between the object, the body, and the subject, the mind. "The lived body can never be a fully explicit thing" (Leder 17), the body is both object and subject. One is one's body. As Drew Leder states in *The Absent Body*, "the lived body is [...] first and foremost not a located thing but a path of access, being-in-the-world" (21). Every body part and organ make possible the access to the world, to project outward from its place of standing. My body is a situation and as such brings into being, as Toril Moi explains it, "experiences of myself and the world" (63). At the same time, my lived experiences through my interactions with the world become part of my body, sedimented, and thus influence my body as a situation. As we will see, in Welty's story, the protagonist Phoenix Jackson's lived experiences have very much influenced her body, as well as her body as a situation influences her way of interacting with the world.

Another key element of this concept is that the phenomenological body is not fixed but changes constantly; it is a living process and a habitual body, able to incorporate tools and other objects into one's own body scheme. Merleau-Ponty mentions, for instance, the wearing of an object, a hat, or the use of a tool, a car, as examples for such an incorporation. In both examples the hat and the car become part of the body and enable me to go through a door without bumping into the door frame or to drive my car as if it were part of my body. Usually we do not notice our bodies, we are our bodies, and the body, as Drew Leder puts it, does not appear, and in that sense it "dis-appears" (25, 26). I am not aware of my eyes reading a text or my fingers typing it. Nerves and organs that enable my bodily actions are even less noticeable. This is the "normal" functioning body. Ironically, these experiences reinforce the binary of body and mind, a Cartesian paradigm. Western life style and modern technology have further contributed to this dualism. As Leder argues, "[o]nly because the body has intrinsic tendencies toward self-concealment could such tendencies be exaggerated by linguistic and technical extensions" (3). The body is absent.

Yet, there are also other examples that give evidence of a disturbed body scheme, where the interaction with the world and being-in-the world is disrupted. This may have physical reasons, such as a sudden change of the body caused by diseases or, as discussed by Iris Marion Young, pregnancy.[12] When we then fail to interact or perform, or when we feel unwanted pain, we suddenly become aware of this failing body part; it seems "foreign" to us and we are no longer our bodies. The body becomes "it" and we tend to objectify and separate "it" from "us" (Leder 76).[13] The body now *dys-appears*. Leder uses the Greek prefix *dys* signifying 'bad', 'hard', or 'ill' to indicate that the *dys*-appearing body is a "body in a *dys* state" (Leder 84). However, we also notice our body when it is not sick. Our bodies change constantly during growth, puberty, menstruation, pregnancy, menopause, and aging.[14] Despite the fact that modern medicine tends to consider menstruation, menopause and aging diseases and treats them accordingly, these bodily dys-appearances do not necessarily imply a dys-function of the body. These changes can show a heightened body awareness and possibly the need to incorporate them into the habitual body.[15]

Bodily changes and diseases are not the only reason that we notice our bodies, that the body dys-appears or even dysfunctions. The gaze of others in society, in particular the male gaze, may contribute to social dys-appearances of the body. Referring to Beauvoir, Leder argues that "one incorporates an alien gaze, away, apart, asunder, from one's own, which provokes an explicit thematization of the body" (99).[16] Social dys-appearance may lead to biological dysfunction (anorexia may serve as such an example), and biological dysfunction of, for instance, the disabled, handicapped, may effect social dys-appearance (Leder 99). As we will see, Welty's protagonist Phoenix also is an example of social dys-appearance because of her age and race.

---

12 | See Young's essay "Pregnant Embodiment".
13 | See chapter 2 in Leder's detailed discussion of how every body organ operates outward and enables us to interact with the world.
14 | Young argues that only men in middle years experience their (healthy) bodies as unchanging (in Leder 89).
15 | Leder differentiates between dys-appearance that may require volitional attention and dys-appearance (such as pain) that demands immediate attention (92).
16 | Beauvoir's *The Second Sex* discusses in detail how the othering of women causes women's social dys-appearance. See also Toril Moi's discussion of *The Second Sex* in *What is a Woman?*

'Blue with Age': Dis- and Dys-appearances of Phoenix's Body

In Eudora Welty's short story "A Worn Path," published in 1941 and much discussed, a very old black woman, Phoenix Jackson, sets out to walk to town to get medicine for her grandson. Her walk is long and lonely; only once, before she reaches town and arrives at the doctor's office, does she meet another person, a white hunter. Scholars, such as Roland Bartels, Jim Owen, Mae Miller Claxton,[17] have mostly focused on Phoenix's interaction with the hunter and the white nurses and discussed themes, such as racism, social injustice, poverty, and mythology. Very few take notice of her age as such or analyze the role of age and her aged body in this story.

Yet, right from the beginning the narrator lets the reader know that this woman is "very old and small," her "eyes [are] blue with age" and her forehead is marked with "numberless branching wrinkles" that form the pattern of a tree (Welty 142). Even though we do not know in what ways Phoenix experiences her body, the narrator's emphasis on her old body makes clear that this body does not dis-appear. It is very much present. Not only is Phoenix forced to take notice of her old body but so is also the reader. This can be seen when early on her long way to town Phoenix's dress gets caught in a thorny bush. The more Phoenix tries with her old stiff fingers to pull herself away from the bush the more she gets trapped; she cries. While she nonetheless succeeds in disentangling the cloth from the thorns, she trembles from exhaustion. As Leder would put it, she is not her body, her body is not absent; it dys-appears. For her it takes an extra physical and mental effort to free her dress from the thorns.

Although her body dys-appears, demands attention, it is not dysfunctional. Her body is also a situation in a particular situation with lived experiences that have become part of her habitual body. As scholar Jean Sheperd Hamm states, Phoenix is "a black [old] woman in the Jim Crow South" (226), probably a former slave, since she is, so Sheperd Hamm notes, "too old at Reconstruction to be required to attend school" (228). Her poverty is appalling; she does not own a winter coat and despite the cold in December she is clothed only in rags and bleached sugar sacks. All these lived experiences have become sedimented and are part of her

---

17 | Their analyses of these themes will be discussed in my reading of Welty's text below.

body as a situation. She has experienced many difficult and dangerous situations in her life, as she later tells the hunter, and yet she is not easily deterred from reaching her goal. Time and again, she encounters problems, these "thorns", and Phoenix cries that they "do their appointed work. Never want to let folks pass, no sir" (Welty 143). During her life she has learned to master situations where she as a black woman was threatened and stopped. She is, as Timothy K. Nixon puts it, a "survivor" (951) and rather than destroying her chances of moving on by impatiently tearing away or even giving up, she persistently and very carefully removes every single thorn from her dress. She is exhausted and frustrated but despite the fact that her body dys-appears, her habitual body enables her to go on. Her body is not dysfunctional but rather her body's dys-appearance forces the reader to take notice of Phoenix's situation.

There are several instances that reveal the dys-appearance of Phoenix's body and signs of her body awareness. As before, these dys-appearances are caused by racist Southern society. Shortly before her dress gets caught in the thorn bush a steep path leads her up to a hill. She stops and complains: "Seem like there is *chains about my feet*, time I get this far [...]. Something always take a hold of me on this hill-pleads I should stay" (Welty 143; emphasis mine). As scholar Dennis J Sykes notes, this is a clear reference to slavery and sheds light on Phoenix's situation. Her experiences of the South have become part of her body, sedimented. Again and again, something "always take a hold of" her and forces her body to dys-appear. Yet, this dys-appearance demands not only from Phoenix to notice her body. Phoenix's body awareness renders this injustice and crime distinctly visible to the reader. Her "going on," living her life, requires for a black woman in the deep South extreme (physical) effort.

Another case of dys-appearance can be discerned a little later when Phoenix, after crossing a creek, needs to rest. While she sits down under a tree, she sees a little boy approaching her with a plate of cake. However, when she reaches out and speaks to him, she realizes that this boy and the cake only existed in her imagination. Some critics[18] have read this passage as evidence for age-related dementia, but they fail to understand that Phoenix does not have the means to provide for herself. These critics further miss to take into account that after a long and tedious journey Phoenix is simply extremely hungry. The fact that she imagines a delicious

---

18 | See, for instance, Roland Bartels.

cake does not indicate a disease caused by old age but her suffering from lack of food. This dys-appearance is yet another example that demands from the reader to pay attention to her dire situation.

There are, however, also several scenes in the story that illustrate the *dis*-appearance of Phoenix's body despite a severe bodily dysfunction, her failing eyesight. "Her eyes [are] blue with age," the narrator lets us know. When Phoenix gets caught in the bush she is annoyed about not having noticed the thorns and says:"Old eyes thought you was a pretty little *green* bush" (Welty 143). Yet, despite being almost blind she regularly walks into town. The incident with the bush is one of numerous challenges she has to face and crossing a creek is a particular test, a "trial" (Welty 145). A log laid across the creek serves as a bridge and even for a person with normal eyesight it is not an easy task to walk on a log. Phoenix manages this without problems—not by opening her eyes wider to see more but by closing her eyes. She focuses on her feet and relies on them to take the right steps. Only when she reaches the other side does she open her eyes again. Her crossing the creek clearly demonstrates that her body is "a path of access", that her body dis-appears.

Two more times Phoenix deliberately closes her eyes and relies on her tactile senses. In fact, as her encounter with the bush earlier showed, her eyesight is not only poor but it also deceives her. When she goes into a corn field she believes she sees a man moving before her. As she cannot hear any sounds from him, she is convinced that he must be a ghost and asks him whose ghost he is, for she has heard of "nary death close by" (Welty 144). When the man still does not say anything she shuts her eyes and touches a sleeve. Relieved she realizes that she mistook the scarecrow for a man. Although she reprimands herself for being "too old" that her senses are "gone", she knows that her senses work well. Later, when she reaches town and enters a building, she again relies on her feet; she walks "around and around until her feet kn[o]w to stop" (Welty 147). Phoenix is her body.

Yet, at one occasion her eyes, though otherwise failing her, help her seize the opportunity to take advantage of a situation. This scene illustrates again Phoenix's dis-appearing and well-functioning body, a dis-appearance that makes painfully visible racist Southern society, and thus, at a meta-level, the dys-appearing and dysfunctional body of the South. After the white hunter helped her out of the ditch she had fallen into, he asks her a few questions and when hearing that she intends to go to town, he advises her to return home; "[w]hy, that's too far!" he says.

Phoenix, however, insists that she is "bound to go to town [...] [t]he time come round" (Welty 145). The young hunter condescendingly laughs at Phoenix. Although he does not know her, nor the reason she wants to go town, he claims: "I know you old colored people! Wouldn't miss going to town to see Santa Claus!" (Welty 145). Yet, Phoenix's reaction to this remark seems peculiar. Apparently, his insulting words mean nothing to her but, as we will see, she skillfully uses the white hunter's racist prejudice of "old colored people" to deceive him. Only her wrinkles indicate that she has noticed something unforeseen and that she quickly needs to distract the hunter. There is "something [that holds] Phoenix very still. The deep lines in her face [go] into a fierce and different radiation" because she has seen "with her own eyes" that a "flashing nickel" had fallen out of the hunter's pocket to the ground (Welty 145). Again, this experience, a flashing nickel falling down, is part of her lived experiences, in her eyes' memory. Phoenix knows at once what this flash means. Slyly she distracts the hunter so that she can obtain the nickel. Very slowly she bends down and, relying on her tactile senses, her fingers "with grace and care" find and pocket the nickel.[19] While this is part of her habitual body, Phoenix is her body, she bitterly complains about her lived experiences in Southern society, that she is forced to steal. When a bird flies by at the moment she pockets the nickel, she whispers: "God watching me the whole time. I come to stealing" (Welty 146). Her dis-appearing body renders visible the dys-appearing and dysfunctional "body" of the South.

While Phoenix is bitter, she nonetheless skillfully uses, performs, her age and race, has her body dys-appear and dysfunction, to get away with expressing her anger at Southern society. When she reaches the doctor's office in town, an attendant, briefly glancing at her, addresses her with: "A charity case, I suppose" (Welty 147). Instead of answering the attendant Phoenix just looks *above* her head, not responding. Again her wrinkles in her face react. "There [is] sweat on her face, the wrinkles in her skin sh[ine] like a bright net" (Welty 147), almost as if to warn the attendant of her disrespectful, to say the least, manner. However, the attendant does not see a person in front of her but only an old black woman and continues in the same manner: "Speak up, Grandma!" Phoenix is clearly annoyed, does

---

19 | I agree with scholar Elaine Orr that "no careful reader will believe Phoenix could not tie her own shoes" and yet she asks a white woman in town to do that. Orr argues that Phoenix wants to see "what her talk will do" (63).

not answer and only gives a "twitch to her face as if a fly were bothering her" (Welty 147). This twitch indicates that Phoenix finds the white attendant bothersome but merely like a fly that can be swatted. By regarding the white attendant as an irritating but meaningless fly, Phoenix clearly reverses racial power positions in the deep South.[20]

When a second nurse enters the room and repeatedly asks Phoenix questions about her grandson, she still does not respond. She is "silent erect and motionless, just as if she were in armor" (Welty 148). As scholar Elaine Orr argues, "Phoenix refuses to answer in the way that the attendant requires [...] Phoenix provokes the nurse" (67). But Phoenix knows that she can provoke the nurse only to a certain extent and before she goes too far she responds and maintains that she "forgot why [she] made [her] long trip" (Welty 148). She suddenly is "*like* an old woman begging a dignified forgiveness for waking up frightened in the night" (Welty 148; emphasis mine). The nurse finds this very peculiar, since her walk to town is very long and difficult for an old woman like Phoenix. Indeed, some scholars, as does Jim Owen[21], either find it normal that after her strenuous and heroic path she forgets why she sets out or, that she loses her ability to speak because she has no education and is in a white setting.[22] However, as Shepherd Hamm argues, Phoenix "knows and tells the story the nurse and the attendant want to hear and already believe" (229), that she is an old, uneducated, and forgetful woman.

Phoenix does not stop talking, continues speaking unasked about her grandson's condition and insists that she will not ever forget her grandson. It is clear that Phoenix does not only know what they want to hear at the doctor's office, she also knows how to perform the old forgetful black woman, a performance that cannot harm her as it repeats the expected script.[23] However, she exaggerates her performance to the point that the nurse sees herself forced to silence her by getting the medicine and handing it to Phoenix. While it may seem that Phoenix suffers from old age—on the one hand, she cannot speak, seems to be deaf, is forgetful and

---

20 | Some critics have explained Phoenix's silence with her inability to speak in a white context. See, for instance, Mae Miller Claxton and Dean Bethea.
21 | He compares Phoenix's path to town to Ulysses's trials in Homer's *Odyssey*.
22 | See Mae Miller Claxton.
23 | As Orr argues, Phoenix "actually overanswers [...] and fulfills the image the nurse has of her" (68).

on the other, she does not stop speaking—that her body is not only dys-appearing but also dysfunctioning, her behavior suggests the opposite: Phoenix is her body. Yet, her body makes visible the dysfunction of the deep South in the 1940s.

Phoenix's old body expresses a striking dis- and dys-appearance. While both are used to criticize racist society, Phoenix also illustrates, despite a severe impairment, her failing eyesight, how to be one's body. Her lived experiences and habitual body enable her to distrust her eyes and to rely on her body. The fact that she at times is her body and at others displays a dys-appearence or even dysfunction, is emphasized right in the beginning of the story and creates a tension in the text.[24] The narrator describes how Phoenix walks slowly "with a balanced *heaviness* and *lightness* of a pendulum in a grandfather clock." Her cane is "thin and small" yet it makes a "grave and persistent noise," a noise that is compared to a meditative "chirping of a solitary little bird" (Welty 142). Phoenix's skin is marked by countless wrinkles that form a "little tree" on her forehead. Yet her hair visible below her red rag is "the frailest of ringlets, still black." Phoenix laughingly finds herself too old, that she "ought to be shut for good" because she was frightened of a scarecrow but she then tells it to dance with her (Welty 144). Phoenix's fingers explore the dirt like a baby while she slowly creeps and crawls through a barbed-wire fence (Welty 143). All these contrasts illuminate that Phoenix is both "young" and "old," that at any age she is her body, as well as she is not. Her body is constantly changing and as such she is continuously acquiring a habitual body that is formed by her lived experiences. Her failing eyesight is a serious dysfunction yet her body's experiences complement this impediment. Phoenix is not an example of "successful aging." She is miserable, poor, and almost blind. However, her habitual body and her lived experiences enable her to go on.

---

24 | A similar tension can be discerned in another short story by Welty, "The Purple Hat." Although the main protagonist is only middle-aged, she seems young and, at other times, very old. The binary of "young" and "old" is further undermined in the story, as the protagonist is killed several times but nonetheless always re-appears unharmed. See my discussion of the story in *Alive and Kicking at All Ages*. It would be worth investigating if this tension and the refusal to be categorized occur in other texts by Welty.

Phoenix's ability to go on is something that many scholars have commented on. Various scholars find that the protagonist's name "Phoenix" emphasizes such an extraordinary ability of endurance. Like the mythical bird, some scholars maintain, Phoenix seems to be able to rise and continue her walk after numerous trials.[25] Yet, critic Roland Bartels, drawing on this myth, believes that her falling into the ditch indicates her senility and thus her ultimate demise to ashes (290). Another critic, James Robert Saunders, finds that apart from the similarity of the color of Phoenix's rag and the bird's plume, she, like the bird, constantly recreates herself (64) and thus overcomes death. Orr, on the other hand, finds that naming the old woman "after the mythical phoenix [...] and having her appear in December [...] complicates" a comparison with the ancient myth, since, according to folk tradition, in December the "Witch Destroyer and Regenatrix appears" (61). She regards Phoenix as "simple and wise." I would rather like to suggest that the tensions and contradictions in the text indicate that Phoenix and her body refuse to be categorized, since it is a habitual body in constant change. Her lived experiences, the sediment of her habitual body, evoke both the lightness (her young age) and heaviness (her old age) of her walk. She is at once both young and old, enjoying a dance and miserably suffering pain and hunger.

Utilizing Merleau-Ponty, Beauvoir and Leder's concept of the habitual body with its lived experiences and the body as a situation in a situation in "A Worn Path" demonstrates how representations of aging can be more fruitfully understood. Not only does a phenomenological approach overcome the binary of subject and object but it also moves away from the binary of decline stories and successful aging. On the one hand, Phoenix's experiences, her old body and her failing eyesight, evince clearly that she suffers, that her story is hardly a story of "successful aging." Her way of interacting with the world with a body as a situation in a situation, on the other hand, also makes visible how every new situation she encounters becomes part of her lived experiences and that she, because of her lived experiences, is able to deal with these situations in the ways possible for her. It is because of this ability that many readers find her "dignified"[26] and that "A Worn Path," despite Phoenix's suffering and misery, is not another example of decline stories.

---

25 | See Jean Shepherd Hamm (225-226).
26 | See Ralph M. Cline's "Aging and the Public Schools: Visits of Charity-The Young Look at the Old" (172).

WORKS CITED

Bartels, Roland. "Life and Death in Eudora Welty's 'A Worn Path'." *Studies in Short Fiction* 14:3 (Spring 1977): 288–290.
BBC News. "Cost of Ageing Population 'Needs Re-Calculating'." Web. 5 Feb 2017. http://www.bbc.com/news/health-11243976.
Beauvoir, Simone de. [1949] *The Second Sex*. London: Vintage, 1997. Print.
Bethea, Dean. "Phoenix Has No Coat: Historicity, Eschatology, and Sins of Omission in Eudora Welty's 'A Worn Path'." *International Fiction Review* 28:1–2 (January 2001): 32.
Bowling, Ann and Paul Dieppe. "What is Successful Ageing and Who Should Define It?" *British Medical Journal* 331 (December 24–31, 2005): 1548–51.
Claxton, Mae Miller. "Migrations and Transformations: Human and Nonhuman Nature in Eudora Welty's 'A Worn Path'." *The Southern Literary Journal*. 47.2 (Spring 2015): 73–88.
Cline, Ralph M. "Aging and the Public Schools: Visits of Charity—The Young Look at the Old." *Aging and Identity: A Humanities Perspective*. Eds. Deats, Sara Munson and Lagretta Tallent Lenker. Westport, CT: Praeger P, 1999: 169–180. Print.
Deats, Sara Munson and Lagretta Tallent Lenker (eds). "Introduction." *Aging and Identity: A Humanities Perspective*. Westport, CT: Praeger, 1999: 1–20. Print.
Grosz, Elizabeth. *Volatile Bodies: Toward a Corporeal Feminism*. Bloomington: Indiana UP, 1994. Print.
Gullette, Margaret Morganroth. *Agewise: Fighting the New Agism in America*. Chicago and London: U of Chicago P, 2011. Print.
Hamm, Jean Sheperd. "'The Worn Path' and the Hero's Journey." *Bloom's Literary Themes: The Hero's Journey*. Ed. Harold Bloom. New York: Blake Hobby, 2009: 225–232. Web. 29 June 2016. http://ezproxy.its.uu.se/login?url=https://search-proquest-com.ezproxy.its.uu.se/docview/741832586?accountid=14715.
Harari, Yuval Noah. *Homo Deus: A Brief History of Tomorrow*. London: Harvill Secker, 2016. Print.
Leder, Drew. *The Absent Body*. Chicago: U of Chicago P, 1990. Print.
Matlok-Ziemann, Ellen. "'Old Women that will not be kept away': Undermining Ageist Discourse with Invisibility." *Alive and Kicking At All Ages: Cultural Constructions of Health and Life Course Identity*. Eds. Ulla

Kriebernegg, Roberta Maierhofer and Barbara Ratzenböck. Bielefeld: transcript, 2014: 259–273. Print.

Merleau-Ponty, Maurice. [1945] *Phenomenology of Perception.* London and New York: Routledge, 2002. Print.

Moi, Toril. *What Is a Woman? And Other Essays.* Oxford: Oxford UP, 1999. Print.

Ngovo, Bernard L. "Historical Approach to Eudora Welty's 'A Worn Path' in a College Reading Course." *Eureka Studies in Teaching Short Fiction.* 9.1 (2008): 118–126.

Nixon, Timothy K. "Same Path, Different Purpose: Chopin's La Folle and Welty's Phoenix Jackson." *Women's Studies.*32:8 (2003): 937–956.

Orr, Elaine. "'Unsettling Every Definition of Otherness': Another Reading of Eudora Welty's 'A Worn Path'." *South Atlantic Review.*57: 2 (May, 1992): 57–72.

Owen, Jim. "Phoenix Jackson, William Wallace, and King MacLain: Welty's Mythic Travelers." *The Southern Literary Journal* 34: 1 (Fall 2001): 29–43.

Rowe, John W., and Robert L. Kahn. "Successful Aging." *The Gerontologist.* 37. 4 (1997): 433–440.

Sandberg, Linn. "Affirmative Old Age—the Ageing Body and Feminist Theories on Difference." *International Journal of Ageing and Later Life* 8:1 (2013): 11–40.

Saunders, James Robert. "'A Worn Path': The Eternal Quest of Welty's Phoenix Jackson." *The Southern Literary Journal.* 25:1 (Fall 1992): 62–73.

Sykes, Dennnis J. "Welty's 'A Worn Path.'" *The Explicator* 56.3 (1998): 151–153.

Svenaeus, Fredrik. "The Body as Alien, Unhomelike, and Uncanny: Some Further Clarifications." *Philosophy, Psychiatry, & Philosophy* 20: 1 (March 2013): 99–101.

Welty, Eudora. [1941] "A Worn Path." *The Collected Stories of Eudora Welty.* New York: Harcourt Brace Jovanovich, 1980: 142–149. Print.

Young, Iris Marion. "Pregnant Embodiment." *Body and Flesh: A Philosophical Reader.* Ed. Donn Welton. Oxford: Blackwell P, 1998: 274–285. Print.

Growing Bodies
Narrating Death and Sexuality in Contemporary Young Adult Fiction

Mirjam Grewe-Salfeld

"Moments. All gathering towards this one."[1]—with this fragment a fictive life is ended; death becomes the last one of a collection of moments that make up a life, given meaning and coherence through narrative. Literary representations of death face the challenge of narrating this unknown and unknowable event, of introducing readers to such an existential embodied experience. Despite the often-cited avoidance of death in Western societies, many authors have tried their hand at this difficult task. It is no surprise, therefore, that this topic is also taken up in popular Children's and Young Adult (YA) novels ranging from the mystical-magical sphere—the *Harry Potter* series with its many deaths comes to mind—to dystopian science fiction—such as the *Hunger Games* franchise with its framework of killing for entertainment.

The focus in this analysis, however, is on narratives with a broadly realistic framework, more precisely, on some of their most popular representatives: Alice Sebold's *The Lovely Bones* (2002), Gayle Forman's *If I Stay* (2009), Jenny Downham's *Before I Die* (2007), and John Green's *The Fault in Our Stars* (2012).[2] These novels use different but also remarkably similar

---

1 | This quote consists of the last two lines of Jenny Downham's *Before I Die* (2007). This line is representative of the fragmented narration used to convey the protagonists' death, but also reminds of common end-of-life tropes such as a life "review" through memories.

2 | A few words about the choice of books: Even though *The Lovely Bones*, in contrast to the other novels, was not originally targeted at young adults, it resonated highly with this age group and is also recommended for mature teenage

ways of narrating death. They will be grouped in pairs of two, with one narrative being a "precursor" of the other with similar thematic foci and narrative structures. Sebold's *The Lovely Bones* and Forman's *If I Stay* share a basic plot line: Both open with drastic bodily experiences—sexual assault leading up to murder and a car accident, respectively—after which the female protagonists narrate their story and contemplate their lives and loved ones from 'out-of-their-body', one in heaven, one in a liminal world between life and death. These two rather disembodied narrations of death and dying stand in contrast to two narratives that put a lot of emphasis on the body in illness and death: Downham's *Before I Die* and Green's *The Fault in Our Stars* both center around teenage girls with terminal cancer that try to come to terms with their impending death while desperately trying to live.

These narratives illustrate, as I will argue, that in YA fiction the body—even in death—becomes a process and site of growth, most pervasively realized in its concern with development and sexuality. This narrative approach provides the reader with a viable—in the most literal sense—counterpart to the harsh and drastic realities of their main topic and thus might facilitate better identification and understanding. The analysis, therefore, centers on the bodies that populate the narratives: living bodies, sick bodies, dying bodies, dead bodies, yearning bodies, sexual bodies, material bodies and those that are actually no longer bodies at all. After a brief general theorization of death, dying and embodiment, I will turn to the specifics of Young Adult fiction's narrativization and representation of these topics. On this basis, I will look at the aforementioned novels and show how these narratives employ bodies and bodily experiences, mainly death and sexuality, as catalysts for growth. My method will be primarily text driven, taking its cues from the literature itself. A brief conclusion will take up the relevance and function of embodiment for YA fiction.

THEORIZING DEATH—BETWEEN AVOIDANCE AND OBSESSION

How narrative represents the moment of death and the experience of dying is always also molded by the general attitudes towards death in a given society. With his historical studies Philippe Ariés provided valuable

---

readers. All the books examined were highly successful in but also outside of their target groups and have been turned into equally successful movies.

insights into the reading and understanding of death in Western culture. He portrays the changing attitudes towards death over centuries: Death changed from a natural, inevitable, tame, familiar and public experience to an increasingly individualized, medicalized, traumatic and unfamiliar event, until death became something unnamable—a social taboo—in the 20th century (Davies 17; James 11). What caused this cultural uneasiness, even anxiety, about death?

Ariés traces Western attitudes towards death during the past centuries and finds a gradual disappearance of the dead from the world of the living. Modernity, especially the eighteenth and nineteenth centuries, saw important changes in the relationship between the living and the dead: On the one hand, an increasing personal relationship with the dead—a cult of the dead expressed for example through regular visitations to burial sites as individualized places of grief—brought them closer together in remembrance; on the other hand, they physically moved further apart with the displacement of cemeteries from city centers (Ariés 70). With the evidence of death removed from public view, also the act of dying slowly but increasingly moved to the hidden spheres of hospitals, nursing homes, and professional facilities (Wood and Williamson 17)—death became a condition to be medically managed. This changing attitude is also visible in responses to death that turned from traditional approaches where death is religious, communal and frequent, to a more and more hidden and private experience dominated by medical authority, characterized by fear, anxiety, and reluctance about the dying (James 23; Wood and Williamson 21). Even though such a historically broad trajectory of death is prone to generalization and does not take into account regional, cultural, attitudinal specificity, what is true for Western societies is that from the seventeenth century onwards death moved away from its traditional religious and social roles towards individualized, secularized, commercialized views (Wood and Williamson 18). However, contrary to the perceived taboo, the past few decades have seen a revival of death. It is being critically examined in its connection to culture, meaning making and representation in almost all fields of academia but also in public discourse (James 2): The emergence of the hospice movements to counteract the impersonal nature of institutionalized death, the explicit inclusion of death and its evidence in cultural productions as well as public discourses around physician-assisted suicide, a good life and a self-determined death are a case in point.

But death is not just a theoretical concept or social and cultural phenomenon, it also is a fundamentally embodied experience. Keeping embodiment in mind means foregrounding lived experiences, passion, pain, suffering, emotions—in short, the physical, sexual and psychological consequences of having a material body. The embodied identities of the living and the identities of the dead are seen as profoundly different—or as Douglas J. Davies puts it: "The dead are too still for the comfort of the living," their inertness marks them as out of place among the living (48). The increasing invisibility of death resulted in an uneasiness over the boundaries between the corporeal bodies of the living and the dead (Shilling 196). With the changing attitudes towards death, also dead bodies were seen differently: they were removed from the home and neighborhood, put into special places, relegated to the care and handling of experts and specialists. Nowadays, dead and dying bodies are avoided because they force people to confront the reality of their own mortality. Contemporary Western death culture is defined by reluctance about and distance to death and dying bodies, a sanitization of dying and, especially in American funeral culture, the beautification—the vitalization—of dead bodies. However, at the same time postmodern culture is also saturated with images of the dead, wallows in their presence: Dead bodies, whether real, famous or fictional, populate television, film and literature in ways never seen before—zombies, vampires, corpses, autopsies, crime—dead is the new sexy.[3] The body is central to death and it is through bodily enactment and "performance" of dying—of pain, fear, suffering, panic, even hope—that death is communicated and bestowed with meaning (Offizier 127).

Narrating Death in Young Adult Literature

Because death is ultimately unknowable, narrations of death and dying typically face some limitations. The only way we can experience and communicate death is the death of the Other: We can never narrate (our) death itself. Autobiography and death, usually, are mutually exclusive.

---

3 | For a discussion of how death and dying have become the "new sexy" see Foltyn, who argues that, especially in the case of celebrities, the corpse has become the new object of a voyeuristic exploration in popular culture.

These limits of narration also have implications for the process of giving meaning to death: It is always an Other, a person, cultural scripts, society's perception, that makes meaning of an individual's death.[4] Personal agency, here, naturally is limited. Death is beyond the point of self-representation, which in literature also becomes a question of voice and perspective, of who narrates, who focalizes, which perspective is taken (Offizier 125). But death is not, in itself, beyond the point of narration. In fact, the impossibility of experiencing death means that it is always only represented. This attempt of representation of the unknown—and often scary—means that death has held a special place in literature, art and music. The aim of such structuring, ordering, and narrativizing is to come to know and understand death and to create sense and meaning out of the end of life (James 25). Fiction can transcend the limits of representation inherent in the experience of death and thus can make death and dying perceptible. However, death fiction also means that there remains an element of wonder and doubt; especially realist narratives need to create strategies that do not violate common notions of death but at the same time allow for its rendition.

Even though Young Adult (YA) fiction is a rather new and controversial field of literature, its high presence in popular culture—visible in the tremendous commercial success of YA novels as both books and films—makes it all the more relevant. According to YA fiction scholar Kathryn James, confronting "serious" issues and problems and being willing to engage with traumatic and harsh aspects of life is one of its defining features (73). Death and dying seem to appeal to YA audiences especially, which can be seen in the varied and numerous ways in which authors engage with these topics. This success of 'dark' themes is often traced back to Sebold's *The Lovely Bones* and its premise of a dead teenage narrator, which at the time of its publication was something like a novelty.

---

4 | As Friederike Offizier argues, witnessing the death of an Other is inherently connected to the process of making meaning from death: The witness is the ultimate source of giving meaning to the Other's death by interpreting death but also the embodiment of the process of dying (124, 126). That cultures create meaning from death is also visible in popular attitudes towards good deaths and useless, bad, deaths (Davies 150). Good deaths are connected to old age and a peaceful, sleeplike end of life, while bad and distressing deaths are sudden and often involve accidents, children or young people.

After Sebold's success many publishers and authors took up morbid and emotionally extreme themes, which lead to a plethora of novels published about rape, murder, suicide, self-harm and (terminal) illness.[5] These are weaved into—sometimes more, sometimes less—complex stories of growing up, that include issues relevant to young adults and teenagers.

In fact, one of the most widespread themes in YA fiction is that of growth and development, of coming-of-age. This growth is shown as a consequence of coming into contact with social issues and problems. These experiences "teach protagonists (and, by extension, readers) about life and about how to 'grow up'" (James 7). James argues that in such a "literature of becoming," representations of death—of the inevitable end of life and becoming—can have a special relevance (2). She contends that often YA texts frame mortality through this theme of growth, portraying death as a catalyst that alters the protagonist's perspective or a signifier of transformation and change (96). In doing so most YA fiction is optimistic, or at least hopeful. In novels that deal with the brutal realities of life, characters must face and overcome adversities, which helps them mature, learn new values and gain a deeper understanding of self (Owen 13).

Learning about their sexuality, their (changing) bodies, romance and romantic relationships is a fundamental experience for adolescents—one deeply connected with growth and maturation—and therefore also a typical topic of YA fiction. James highlights that, indeed, oftentimes awareness of mortality and exploration of sexuality are part of the same narrative (4). This, I would argue, draws on the inherent connection between sex(uality) and death as opposing poles in human life: Sexuality, the touching, caressing, penetrating of bodies, is sensual, pleasurable, physical, even ecstatic and thus a fundamentally embodied experience—signaling vitality and the creation of life. At the same time, sex is inextricably linked to mortality, which is poetically depicted in Sigmund Freud's

---

5 | The success of and controversy sparked by the *Netflix* release of the serial adaptation of the YA novel *13 Reasons Why* in 2017—told from the perspective of a dead teenage girl who had committed suicide after experiencing severe bullying and sexual assault—is another case in point. *13 Reasons Why* was not included in this analysis due to its widely different premise of suicide. Still, one needs to contend that sexuality, both forced and voluntary, and romantic love play an important role in this narrative as well. Furthermore, the theme of growth through death is embodied in this case in the emotional journey of the characters.

notion of Eros and Thanatos, life instinct and death instinct.[6] In Freudian psychoanalysis reproductive (Eros) and destructive (the death drive, or Thanatos) urges exist in a state of tension (James 18). Sexuality fights death by affirming life, but in the end death always wins. But sex can also transcend death through its generative power; it creates life, relationships, creativity. Sex, therefore, becomes a ritual of death and rebirth, a reminder of their inseparability (Diamond). As such sexuality is imbued with potentiality and future—a stance that counters the bleakness of death. Also in YA fiction, sex and death are linked to depict the carnality of the human body: experiencing sexuality is as important to maturation as the understanding that humans are mortals who will die (Seelinger Trites 478). As Roberta Seelinger Trites argues, sexuality becomes a rite of passage between childhood and adulthood, a fundamental experience on the way to becoming an adult, but also towards the realization of an adolescents' own awareness of mortality, the limitations set to their bodies, the inescapability of death (478). Two fundamentally embodied experiences, sexuality and mortality, thus, become themes that represent personal growth for characters and, by extension, young readers.

AN EMBODIED MIND?
YEARNING FOR AND RECLAIMING A BODY

Alice Sebold's *The Lovely Bones* (2002) and Gayle Forman's *If I Stay* (2007) are narrated from the perspective of a teenage girl that is either already dead or in the process of dying. Susie Salmon, the dead narrator of *The Lovely Bones*, is brutally raped and murdered on her way home from school. She moves on to her 'heaven', from where she continues to watch her loved ones for the next eight years. Mia, the dying narrator in *If I Stay*, has an out-of-body experience while being in a coma after a car crash killed her family and left her severely injured. She narrates from a liminal place between life and death that serves as the background for the principal question that drives the narrative: Mia's decision to live or die. Both narratives portray a form of empowerment in death and dying. The

---

6 | For a longer discussion of the psychology of sex and its psychoanalytical history, see Stephen Diamond, "The Psychology of Sexuality. Why Sex is Still Such a Concern in Psychotherapy."

teenage narrators are, each in their way, endowed with or gain control over their death and (after-)life. Their bodies become crucial in the narratives and for their agency: Susie yearns for a human body, and the growth and experiences it represents, while Mia has to decide to (re-)claim her injured body, the memories and future it holds. The relationship between embodiment and disembodiment, however, is fluid in both narratives.

The Lovely Bones, as argued by Brian Norman, combines a murder plot with elements of a detective and ghost story and very strong influences of a coming-of-age narrative (20). Susie starts her narration with her own demise: "My name is Salmon, like the fish; first name, Susie. I was fourteen when I was murdered on December 6, 1973." (Sebold 1) What follows is a very explicit first chapter that foregrounds the experience of bodily pain, in which Susie's feelings and perceptions and the physical act of rape are central. She is lured into an underground cave by her neighbor Mr. Harvey, who starts to kiss her, shoves his hand under her shirt and rips open her pants. Susie's teenage body is used as an object of adult pleasure with brutal force and violence. After the rape, the reader is confronted with Susie's perceptions of her surroundings and her rapist, but also her own and his body. Her last physical moment on earth is not the loving touch of a body, but violent force and fear—emphasized through a comparison between her heartbeat skipping like a rabbit and his thudding like a hammer (Sebold 15). Her rapist kills her and dismembers her body, puts her in a wax-cloth bag, shoves her into an old safe and dumps it in the local sinkhole—her body never to be recovered.

During the experience of rape and death her disembodied existence already begins to form: "I began to leave my body; I began to inhabit the air and the silence. I wept and struggled so I would not feel" (Sebold 15). Leaving her body is a 'survival mechanism' for Susie, allowing her to disconnect from the brutality forced upon her body. After her death Susie moves on to "her heaven" where she becomes what Alice Bennett has termed a "posthumous narrator" of her own story: As such a dead narrator, according to Bennett, she is in the unique position to also be a witness to the crime she experienced, creating a new voice that makes it possible to narrate death both as a witness and the person experiencing it (108). This position, Sara Whitney argues, restores dignity and agency to Susie and thus grants her a form of (literary) survivorship (355–356). She gains the power to create meaning from her ending. Furthermore, this expanded consciousness as a first-person omniscient narrator from heaven gives her certain privileges: She can experience and describe other character's feelings and she can move around on earth without constraints. But this position is also what makes it hard to pinpoint the degree of embodiment that she experiences in her afterlife: Her existence after death seems to be characterized by a certain degree of materiality—she seems to have a bodily presence and experiences sensory feelings in her heaven—but the fact that the living cannot see her and that she cannot interfere with life on earth positions her closer to a 'ghost' or soul.[7] She seems to be an *embodied mind*, not fully possessing a body, not fully a 'ghost'.[8] Even though she is very active in her heaven, death is connected to passivity for Susie: She can watch but not intervene. This watching takes on the trait of what Norman calls "benevolent haunting" (145): Susie hovers over her family—sometimes even appearing as a reflection—investigating the vacuum of her loss and the feelings of people left behind on earth. This "haunting," her constant presence, is not meant to harm or scare but to hold on to the tenuous connections she still has and does not want to let go off.

However, during the narrative she begins to desire more: she wants to be allowed to grow up. This wish cannot be granted in heaven and is thus realized in the narrative by proxy, through the medium of Susie's younger sister Lindsey. Soon after Susie is murdered, Lindsey's living body begins to remind people of Susie's dead body. While Lindsey is haunted by their resemblance, Susie begins to experience growing up through her sister's life. This connection becomes evident when Lindsey loses her virginity

---

7 | This conception of the body in death, of course, buys into and perpetuates old dualisms of body and mind/soul, in which the latter are seen as in authority over the former.

8 | This premise opens up interesting questions about the conception of an afterlife. For centuries, acceptance of death—the death of others and people's own mortality—has been made easier by ideas about an afterlife, often influenced by religious beliefs. However, just as death has become individualized in the past centuries, so have conceptions of an afterlife become subjective with increasing secularization. The conception of an afterlife in this narrative is a case in point: Susie's heaven is a place shaped by her wishes and desires; it changes shape and meaning according to her mood, feelings and (psychological) needs. However, it is also a shared space: Other dead people populate her heaven, but only those that are somehow connected to her. As such her experience of the afterlife is both individual and communal, but always tailored to her recovery from trauma.

and Susie compares the experiences: The brutality and horror that was forced on Susie's body is a stark contrast to Lindsey's loving experience with her first boyfriend. During the years Susie forms a close connection to her sister, conflating Lindsey's embodied experience of life on earth and her own disembodied experience as a watcher in heaven. Susie claims Lindsey's experiences and body as her own.

Even though Susie emotionally matures considerably during the narrative, her body never changes from that of a fourteen-year-old, "the chest still flat and hips undeveloped" (Sebold 279). She begins to long for the body of a grown woman, envying both her mother and her sister. As Norman has noticed, the position of an observer becomes insufficient for her (147); she wants to experience the feeling of a grown body. This problem is solved through what Sara Whitney calls a finale of magical realism: Susie and a former classmate and friend Ruth swap bodies.[9] Susie falls from heaven into Ruth's body, while Ruth leaves her body for heaven. What follows is Susie's final embodied experience on earth. In her second 'proxy body' she can feel the "marvelous weight" (Sebold 342), the "luscious bounce of breasts and thighs" (Sebold 343) and the "perfect living beauty" (Sebold 347) of a grown-up female body. Susie spends the gift of her borrowed material body by consummating a relationship that started before her death: She has intercourse with Ray Singh, her teenage sweetheart.[10] This experience not only makes up for both the loneliness and passivity in heaven, but also counters being "hurt by hands

---

9 | In the narrative, Susie's soul "touches" Ruth on her way to heaven, forming a special connection between them that leads to Ruth's interest in death, and especially female victims of violence. These special interests construct Ruth as a feminist advocate for women, especially murdered women, and thus a human connection between the living and the dead.

10 | This scene has been examined critically foremost because of its rape imagery. Susie could be seen as a violent penetrator, especially because Ruth's consent can only be inferred. The scene ends for Ruth in permanent trauma, as a "woman haunted" (Sebold 365). For this approach cf. Norman (149 f.). The notion of female bodies being used by others can be highly problematic in a novel addressing rape (cf. Tallent). However, some critics argue that it was Ruth's free choice and her agency that instigated the swap in the first place, and thus stress Ruth's willingness and control (cf. v. Czarnowsky par. 14 f.). Also, the boy that Susie has sex with in Ruth's body is no stranger to her. Ruth and Ray have

past all tenderness" (Sebold 344). Susie compares her sexual experiences on earth—her rape and the new experience of 'making love' with Ray. According to Laura-Marie v. Czarnowsky, by contrasting the sexual experiences *The Lovely Bones* highlights Susie's recovery process: She reclaims her sexuality and sexual agency and leaves her rape trauma behind (par. 5). Susie has deliberately decided not to pursue finding her murderer or visiting her family, rather she experiences for one last time what it means to have a body, to be alive and human. Having a body, here, is closely tied to agency: Ultimately it is a bodily experience that frees Susie and enables her to go on to a new heaven, to let go of her loved ones on earth. (Re-)claiming her own sexuality is a rite of passage for her, not just towards adult-like maturity but also towards a broader acceptance of death.

Like the narrator in *The Lovely Bones*, the narrator in *If I Stay*, Mia, is a first-person narrator. However, she is not omniscient and not yet dead. Thus, she can only narrate what happens around her disembodied self and is not endowed with the privilege of moving around freely or relating other character's feelings. Similar to *The Lovely Bones*, Mia's narrative begins with an explicit scene of damage, pain and death. Mia's story begins with a family trip that turns into a nightmare: An accident kills her parents instantly, while Mia and her brother are badly injured. Mia finds herself standing at the scene, observing the aftermath of the crash. She sees her father surrounded by "gray chunks of what looks like cauliflower" on the pavement—pieces of her father's brain on the asphalt—while her mother is not visibly injured but clearly dead (Forman 16). Another injured body turns out to be Mia herself with one of her legs askew, "the skin and muscle peeled away so that [she] can see the white streaks of bone" (Forman 17 f.). The accident is described in terms of injury, blood and trauma; it is a very bodily experience that is promptly followed by a disembodied one. Mia realizes that she is out of her body, existing in a limbo between life and death. Her disembodied self does not feel pain or any bodily reaction, even though she should be in agony. Emotions are accessible to Mia, but their phenomenological counterpart, feelings and sensations, are not. Her embodied corporeal presence is dislocated from her 'soul' or spirit. While this approach to the body-soul divide and the body-in-death is similar to *The Lovely Bones*, the difference here is that

---

been friends ever since Susie's death and have in their youth been experimenting sexually through kissing.

Mia's body is still alive—she has access to her body and thus a higher degree of agency in the world of the living.

While her body is treated, the 'spirit' Mia tries to find out more about her disembodied state. The particulars are not yet clear to her. She figures out that she does not have supernatural abilities, like floating through walls: She can only do things she could also do in real life, except that they are invisible to the living. Like an embodied person Mia can manipulate certain things in her vicinity, at the same time her experience is clearly disembodied—again a premise that reminds of an *embodied mind*. Soon Mia becomes dissatisfied with the state of suspension she is in and the lack of bodily reactions, being aware of what she is feeling without actually feeling it (Forman 161). She cannot express her emotions in corporeal terms. This lack emphasizes the importance of the body for social and emotional interactions and thereby also a person's construction of self.

In this novel, dying is a disembodied experience: it is not decided by her physical condition, the damage to the body, but by her own will and decision to live, embodied in her 'spirit-like' state. As such, Mia also has a certain degree of agency over her body. The 'mind,' once again, following Cartesian dualist thinking, is in control of the body. Mental tumults, emotions that the disembodied Mia experiences, have consequences for her body. When she is furious about her brother's death and contemplates leaving, her bodily state declines, bringing her back into surgery that saves her body. This approach to death as being decidable ties in with popular notions of death as being preventable: Even though no one could prevent the car crash, by making the right choice Mia can stay alive and get healthy again. She can conquer death.[11] One narrative technique used to do so is that the closeness and stark reality of death is contrasted with life-affirming flashbacks, most importantly Mia's romantic and sexual experience with her first boyfriend Adam. Here, again, the narrative takes up the link between growing up and sexuality, but also the link between desire and death. A romantic relationship is one of the main incentives

---

11 | The general attitude towards death in *If I Stay* is populated by common notions of dying and the afterlife such as death as the "sleep of the dead" (Forman 179). Death never played a huge role in Mia's life, except for the funeral of a friend of her parents and a subsequent conversation about their ideal deaths and funerals. For Mia the afterlife means spending eternity with your loved ones, a comforting and desirable happily-ever-after.

to choose life. While sexuality is not as prominent in this narrative, it is positioned as an important component of growing-up.

Mia's narrative ends with her body. While she is almost certain that she cannot face living on without her family, her boyfriend Adam brings her lifelong companion and dream to her: classical music. The sound of the cello—memories of her life as it was—stirs her up and turns her disembodied state into an embodied one:

"There is a blinding flash, a pain that rips through me for one searing instant, a silent scream from my broken body. [...] I'm lying on my back in the hospital bed, one again with my body. [...] somewhere inside of me I am crying, too, because I'm feeling things at last. I'm feeling not just the physical pain, but all that I have lost, and it is profound and catastrophic and will leave a crater in me that nothing will ever fill. But I'm also feeling all that I have in my life, which includes what I have lost, as well as the great unknown of what life might still bring me." (Forman 233)

As soon as her disembodied self made a decision, she is reunited with her body and feels the full emotional and physical extent of her pain and loss. Materiality, in this narration, is forcefully linked to (emotional and physical) pain. However, as is typical for YA fiction, the narrative ends on a hopeful note, with anticipation of what is to come. Death, for Mia, provides an opportunity for emotional growth.

In both narratives, the relationships between the living and the deceased or deceasing are important. According to Bennett, *The Lovely Bones* sets up connections between the living and the dead in multiple ways: dead people are described as more than their dead bodies; they are portrayed as watching the living, talking to them and wanting connections; the dead are spirits among the living, haunting them in the nicest way possible, sometimes even touching them and changing perceptions. In this sense, *The Lovely Bones* evokes a picture of comfort after death through a disembodied existence. In her unique position as witness and experiencer of death, Susie works as a "native informant" about death and the afterlife for the reader.[12] However, following Tallent, the novel also highlights the passivity of death: the action is where the bodies are and bodies are where the action is. Without a living and breathing body, Susie

---

12 | For an overview of the concept of the "native informant" see Spivak. For a discussion of the "native informant" in the context of death, see Offizier (130).

has no agency on earth. While Mia in *If I Stay* occupies a similar passive position, her still living body provides her with more agency and control. Learning about death for Mia means learning about her own mortality and realizing that affirming life means accepting death, not her own, but the pervasiveness of loss and trauma in life. In Susie's hovering and in Mia's liminal existence between life and death, *dying is an intellectual experience*, which could reassure readers in its implication that life will continue after death.[13] Both narratives, therefore, use a comforting approach to death—even though the physical experiences in the novels are often gruesome, painful and violent. An important component, here, is the theme of sexuality, of experiencing the sensuality of a living body. In both narratives, the body is central to both the experience of life and death.

A Treacherous Body?— (Reviving) the Terminally Ill Body

Jenny Downham's *Before I Die* (2007) and John Green's *The Fault in Our Stars* (2012) portray the fundamentally embodied experience of (terminal) illness. As such, the living body with its flaws, pain and mortality is much more important than in the previous narratives—the illnesses of the protagonists are inscribed on their bodies. Both novels focus on teenage girls suffering from cancer—one thyroid and lung cancer, the other leukemia—and follow a very similar basic plot structure and narrative framework: the protagonists and first-person narrators are terminally ill girls trying to experience life despite their diseases. In *Before I Die*, Tessa wants to experience as many things as possible before she dies. While she works her way through her 'bucket list'—that includes things as varied as taking drugs, driving a car, breaking the law and losing her virginity—she meets Adam and begins a relationship. Similarly, *The Fault in Our Stars* focuses on the relationship between Hazel and Augustus, but here both teenagers suffer from (terminal) cancer. These novels stand in the tradition of others that examine the issues and emotions surrounding terminal illness from the perspective of the sick person. According to Sian

---

13 | Aviva Briefel argues that representations of death as "intellectual experiences" in horror films might reassure the viewer or reader in the implication that life continues after death (97).

Cain, such narratives portray the inherent humanity of the terminally ill: how their teenage protagonists interact, prioritize and live like an average young adult in the face of their disease (n. p.). Important themes, thus, are how the body changes with illness, dealing with and accepting death, as well as growing up despite a possibly limited future.

Ever since Arthur Frank's study on the relationship between phenomenology, health and illness, scholarship has become aware of the central role that the body has in experiencing, narrating and coming to terms with illness. In *The Fault in Our Stars* and *Before I Die* illness is visible on the body. Hazel has to carry around an oxygen tank at all times because her "lungs sucked at being lungs" (Green 8). Her disease shows on the outside, which makes her "irreconcilably other" because "[t]he physical evidence of disease separates you from other people" (Green 144). Hazel juxtaposes her cancer self with her healthy self, showing that illness turned her into another person. Her body has changed because of the treatment, giving her "fat chipmunk cheeks" and a "cankle situation" (Green 9). Cancer treatment has marked her body as Other, as deviating from expectations, which makes her feel insufficient compared to peers and pervasive norms and body images. Bodily changes are also important for Tessa in *Before I Die*: her treatments have left their mark on her body, her hair is only recently re-growing, her thinned out body—as she sometimes claims just "skin and bones"—is something that she has trouble accepting. People react differently to this marked difference, or as Hazel has learned: "Illness repulses" (Green 36). People tend to avoid the sick and dying because they remind them of their own vulnerability and mortality.

Bodily pain and suffering, furthermore, are shown as integral parts of illness. During Hazel's long journey of life-prolonging treatments, she is never free of pain: Underoxygenation causes her to feel pain as a "supernova exploding inside [her] brain, an endless chain of intracranial firecrackers" (Green 105). She often does not feel in control of her body because the pain is always there "demanding to be felt" (Green 142). Her body dictates her life, which hints at an inherent distinction between body and self (or mind). But not just physical pain is described in embodied terms, emotional pain is as well: The emotional devastation of Augustus' death is described in similar terms as the constant physical feeling of drowning from underoxygenation and the resulting pain (Green 263). In *Before I Die,* physical pain is often countered by medical intervention and thus not as present. However, this narrative focuses more on the emotional pain of letting go, of dealing with death and the prospect of dying. Tessa often ponders over what death means in general and for her and struggles with coming to terms with the finality of her diagnosis. It is also this emotional journey that furthers her determination to do all the things that she still wants to do and to complete the ever-growing list of things she still wants to experience.

The omnipresence of pain, decline and suffering is a relentless reminder of the bodily state and the closeness of death. Both protagonists seem to accept their own mortality, but the novels nevertheless hint at ways to keep death at bay. Chris Shilling describes strategies to fight against death, two of which are the deconstruction of death, and love and erotic relationships. According to him, death is "deconstructed" by focusing on how specific causes of mortality can be overcome (199). In *The Fault in Our Stars* this deconstruction is evident in the common trope of battle and fight. Cancer victims are expected to fight until their bodies give up: Hazel's cancer support group consists of "talking about fighting and battling and winning and shrinking and scanning" (Green 5). Cancer as a medical cause of mortality is expected to be conquered. However, as Augustus points out: "What am I at war with? My cancer. And what is my cancer? My cancer is me. The tumors are made of me. [...] It is a civil war, Hazel Grace, with a predetermined winner." (Green 216) All the talk of war and fight are pointless for him, because in the end he is fighting against his own body. The emphasis on 'fight and conquer' puts the sick person in the position of blame for their inability to properly fight a sometimes predetermined war. The image of cancer as a body fighting and betraying itself is also tangible in *Before I Die*. Cancer is framed as a "treachery" of the body, because it is doing something without the consent of the mind (Downham 120). The focus, therefore, is on stopping this treachery through medical intervention. However, the narrative sets in at a point where Tessa has already made the decision to stop aggressive treatments, because it is "[her] illness, [her] death, [her] choice" (Downham 265). Agency, in illness, is undermined by the body but can be reclaimed.

The other survival strategy, love and erotic relationships, is described by Shilling as deferring death by investing hope and meaning in a loved one (200)—a common trope in 'Cancer Lit' for a YA audience. In *Before I Die*, Tessa's discovery of sexuality and romance are central to the narrative. Losing her virginity is one of the main priorities on her list and the first one she tackles head on. She goes out and has a one-night-stand with a boy she does not know. While this is not the most pleasant experience for her, this sexual encounter and the night out nevertheless make her feel more alive (Downham 16).[14] Later, after meeting her boyfriend Adam, sexuality is connected to romance and love and becomes a reviving force. Their relationship and their physical contact is shown as beneficial for her, making her persevere and stronger. These new experiences are not just portrayed as an important stepping stone towards adulthood but also as something that makes her feel comfortable with her own body, that brings the "heat"—life, hope, a future—back (Downham 278). Still, what is noteworthy here is that this form of approaching sexuality is also used as a (moral) lesson that sex in a relationship is 'better,' that it needs a strong connection to romantic love. *The Fault in Our Stars* includes this trope in the romantic relationship between Hazel and Augustus. They have sex during which they both lose their virginity and thus experience a rite of passage towards adulthood together. Similar to Tessa, the experience of sexuality enables Hazel to feel more at ease with her sick and dying body. She feels "breathless in a new and fascinating way" and begins to like her "cancer-ruined" body; the years of struggle, the painful treatments, and the "ceaseless bodily betrayal of the tumors" is suddenly worth it (Green 203). Sexuality gives meaning to her body, it validates the fight and suffering, and redeems the bodily betrayal of cancer and dying.

Dying in both narratives is described in terms of physical decline. In *The Fault in Our Stars*, Augustus's last weeks of life are marked by inexorable bodily deterioration, tiredness, puking, infections, fatigue, pain, and narcotics. His death, then, comes "when the cancer, which was made of him, finally stopped his heart, which was also made of him" (Green 261). Death, here, is a body turning on itself, a body ending a life much too soon, the ultimate form of treachery. However, his death is told and thus interpreted not from his perspective but from Hazel's; again it is a witness making sense of an Other's death. *Before I Die* takes a different approach, one that actually brings it closer to *The Lovely Bones*. Tessa is

---

14 | On a side note, this night out ultimately results in her best friend's pregnancy—a narrative tool that brings together the creation of life (birth) and the loss of life (death) towards the end of the novel. Being around to witness the birth is a strong motivator for Tessa.

the narrator of her own death, or at least her dying—also for her a slow process of bodily decline, of drifting away. It is a noteworthy passage in terms of narration: In the final pages of the book, there is less actual narration from the point of view of the narrator. Rather, the narration becomes unstructured, consisting mainly of her thoughts and the conversations around her, which mirrors her drifting in and out of consciousness, losing and regaining her train of thought. She is narrating her own dying, but through other people's conversations and her own thoughts and memories—moments that she revisits. Still, the narrative manages to stay realistic by ending with Tessa's last thoughts, it stops when her life stops. This approach, however, also means that it is not the person dying or a witness-character who makes meaning of her death—this task falls to the reader.

As Patty Campbell argues, in books where a protagonist (and not just a background character) is dying we come closer to the reality of death (39). *The Fault in Our Stars* deals with death in a very straightforward manner. Hazel and Augustus talk about death and dying a lot because it is a reality for them. Hazel lives in the knowledge that death is the only outcome of her illness, even though she does not know when. Death and human oblivion are portrayed as inevitable. Even though it is a serious topic, the young protagonists often approach death casually, taking away some of its seriousness but not of its tragedy. Through symbols death is also in the middle of Hazel's and Augustus' relationship: They often visit a huge skeleton sculpture in a park—a pervasive symbol of death and decline. Symbolic death is here populated by children using it as a playground; laughter and life position it as normal and omnipresent. However, the young protagonists are also angry about death and the "depraved meaninglessness" of suffering (Green 281). Dying of illness is inherently meaningless and without glory.[15] In that the novel sticks to popular conceptions of senseless deaths. Similar feelings of anger and meaninglessness

---

15 | The removal of death from public view, as described above, and the decline of religion as a structuring force—and with it the prospect of an afterlife that provides meaning to death—meant that death during the nineteenth and twentieth centuries became increasingly connected with annihilation and meaninglessness, see also Offizier (122-123). Death from illness, here, is no exception. Rather, the impression of "preventability" and medical control makes it seem even more meaningless.

abound in *Before I Die*. Tessa thinks a lot about death, what it might feel like, how it manifests itself, what happens afterwards. This confrontation with death is often a point of struggle for Tessa who alternates between acceptance of death as inevitable and revolt against it. Fittingly, death is often connected to many dark images of dust, decay, rotting. It is nothing positive, only a struggle—but one that surrounds us all (Downham 182).

The dying (female) protagonists of *The Fault in Our Stars* and *Before I Die* do not need to learn about their own mortality. However, the proximity of death provides them with learning experiences. The death of a loved one enables Hazel to embrace adolescence as a period of experimentation and development. Her relationship with Augustus has shown her that living and loving are worth the hurt. Tessa's journey toward accepting and then experiencing her own death sends her on a similar road to maturation. Death changes their perspective on life and is a catalyst for emotional growth. In both narratives death and dying become more real and complex, interwoven into all aspects of life and not just singled-out occurrences of violence and trauma. Death, here, becomes familiar and part of day-to-day living.

Conclusion: The Body in Young Adult Fiction

As Margaret Gibson argues, the proliferation and accessibility of death images and narratives—on television, cinema, news stories, novels, images—does not mean that the Western world necessarily has moved past "death denial" towards familiarity and existential acceptance of death. Rather, she says, their pervasiveness might widen the gap between represented and mediated death culture and real-life experiences with death and bereavement—while death in fiction is familiar, 'real' death is not. Still, narrative representations of death might facilitate a more conscious engagement with dying and human mortality; it can be a by-proxy learning experience not just for young adults. In such stories about death the body becomes a component of the story with important implications for the characterization and experience of characters. Looking at embodiment in connection to death in YA fiction can give valuable insights into how death and dying are portrayed and how meaning is made of them.

Social theorists position the body as the site were the self is realized. As such the body becomes a project or a process, an act of becoming and growth. In YA fiction about death the pervasive themes of growth and growing up become enmeshed with mortality and pain. A popular site of growing up in those fictions is sexuality, which for one is a common rite of passage towards adulthood but also always entangled through its biology and bodily enactment with death. Sex, then, becomes dually inscribed as dangerous and desired. In *The Lovely Bones,* having sex and losing one's virginity are central parts of Susie's mental maturation and physical familiarity with growing up in death, even though they can only be experienced by proxy. *If I Stay* positions sexual experiences as natural parts of growing up through flashbacks of Adam's and Mia's developing relationship. Adam becomes a representation of romantic and sexual, bodily desire and as such plays a crucial role in Mia's choice to stay alive. In *The Fault in Our Stars* sexuality gives a new meaning to sick bodies, but also figures as a step towards maturation. It is a way to affirm life and keep death and dying at bay through romantic love. In *Before I Die,* sexuality becomes a means to feel alive, a generative, reviving force that makes a faltering body stronger and more persistent. These love stories in narratives concerned with death function to counter the finality of death. At the same time, they work to position sexuality as needing romantic love to be completely fulfilling and thus create educational lessons for teenagers that reinforce dominant conceptions of sexuality.

Overall, the examined narratives tend to counter harsh aspects of death and dying with soothing elements. Rape and murder, as brutal bodily experiences, are opposed by a cheerful and happy, disembodied, narration from heaven and the continuation of life after death. Accident and trauma are countered with choice, the implication of an afterlife and the possibility for a (happy) future. Terminal illness and death are answered by tropes of fight, the possibility of cure through medicine, empowerment in decision making, support of friends and family, and humor in grave situations. It is a balance between embodied and disembodied aspects, between life and death, growth and seeming finality, suffering and happiness, that makes concepts such as death and dying relatable also for younger audiences. It provides readers with means to live through experiences of loss, grief or illness, and thus to gain, through extension from characters, a greater insight into the self, but also into human mortality.

WORKS CITED

Ariés, Philippe. *Western Attitudes Toward Death: From the Middle Ages to the Present*, trans. Patricia M. Ranum. Baltimore: Johns Hopkins UP, 1974. Print.
Bennett, Alice. *Afterlife and Narrative in Contemporary Fiction*. Houndmills et al.: Palgrave Macmillan, 2012. Print.
Briefel, Aviva. "What Some Ghosts Don't Know: Spectral Incognizance and the Horror Film." *Narrative* 17.1 (2009): 95–110.
Cain, Sian. "YA books on death: is young adult fiction becoming too dark?" *The Guardian* 11 May 2014. Web. 12 March 2015. http://www.theguardian.com/childrens-books-site/2014/may/11/ya-books-on-death-is-young-adult-fiction-becoming-too-dark.
Campbell, Patty. "YA Lit and the Deathly Fellows." *Campbell's Scoop: Reflections On Young Adult Literature*. Ed. Patty Campbell. Lanham: Scarecrow P, 2010. 38–42. Print.
Czarnowsky, Laura-Marie v. "The Postmortal Rape Survivor and the Paradox of Female Agency across Different Media: Alice Sebold's Novel *The Lovely Bones* and Its 2009 Film Adaptation." *Gender Forum. an Internet Journal for Gender Studies* 41 (2013). Web. 10 March 2015. http://www.genderforum.org/issues/gender-and-force-in-the-media/the-postmortal-rape-survivor-and-the-paradox-of-female-agency-across-different-media-alice-sebolds-novel-the-lovely-bones-and-its-2009-film-adaptation/.
Davies, Douglas J. *A Brief History of Death*. Malden et al.: Blackwell Publishing, 2005. Print.
Diamond, Stephen A. "The Psychology of Sexuality. Why Sex is Still Such a Concern in Psychotherapy." *Psychology Today*, Web. 10 May 2014. https://www.psychologytoday.com/blog/evil-deeds/201405/the-psychology-sexuality.
Downham, Jenny. *Before I Die*. Oxford: David Fickling Books, 2007. Print.
Foltyn, Jacque Lynn. "Dead Famous and Dead Sexy: Popular Culture, Forensics, and the Rise of the Corpse." *Mortality: Promoting the Interdisciplinary Study of Death and Dying* 13:2 (2008): 153–173.
Forman, Gayle. *If I Stay*. New York: Speak/Penguin, 2009. Print.
Frank, Arthur W. *The Wounded Storyteller. Body, Illness, and Ethics*. Second Edition. Chicago, London: The U of Chicago P, 2013.

Gibson, Margaret. "Death and Mourning in Technologically Mediated Culture." *Health Sociology Review* 16.5. (2007): 415–424.
Green, John. *The Fault in Our Stars*. New York et al.: Penguin Books, 2012. Print.
James, Kathryn. *Death, Gender and Sexuality in Contemporary Adolescent Literature*. New York: Routledge, 2009. Print.
Norman, Brian. *Dead Women Talking: Figures of Injustice in American Literature*. Baltimore: John Hopkins UP, 2013. Print.
Offizier, Friederike. "Death of the Other: Dying, Alterity, and Appropriation." *The Morbidity of Culture: Melancholy, Trauma, Illness and Dying in Literature and Film*. Ed. Stephanie Siewert and Antonia Mehnert. Frankfurt a. M., New York: Peter Lang, 2012. 119–38. Print.
Owen, Mary. "Developing a Love of Reading: Why Young Adult Literature is Important." *Orana* 39.1 (2003): 11–17.
Sebold, Alice. *The Lovely Bones*. New York et al.: Little, Brown and Company, 2002. Print.
Seelinger Trites, Roberta. "The Harry Potter Novel as a Test Case for Adolescent Literature." *Style* 35.3 (2001): 472–85.
Shilling, Chris. *The Body and Social Theory*. Third Edition. London et al.: Sage, 2012. Print.
Spivak, Gayatri Chakravorty. *A Critique of Postcolonial Reason: Toward a History of the Vanishing Present*. Cambridge: Harvard UP, 1999. Print.
Tallent, Elizabeth. "The Trouble with Postmortality." *The Threepenny Review* 101 (2005): 7–9. Web. 10 March 2015. http://www.threepenny review.com/samples/tallent_sp05.html.
Whitney, Sara. "Uneasy Lie the Bones: Alice Sebold's Postfeminist Gothic." *Tulsa Studies in Women's Literature* 29.2 (2009): 351–73.
Wood, W. R. and J. B. Williamson. "Historical Changes of the Meaning of Death in the Western Tradition." *Handbook of Death and Dying*. Ed. Clifton D. Bryant. Thousand Oaks, CA: Sage Publications, 2004. 14–23. Print.

When Mother Is Dying
Miljenko Jergović's *Kin*

Dagmar Gramshammer-Hohl

INTRODUCTION

In 2013, the Bosnian-Croatian writer Miljenko Jergović published his novel *Rod* (Eng. *Kin*)[1]—an autobiographical family saga of a thousand pages, a "monster of a book" (Valentino, "Otata and Omama," n. p.) that he worked on while his mother was fighting a deadly illness: cancer. She died in December 2012, and the author completed the narrative soon after. The novel was inspired by the stories that Jergović heard from his mother about her relatives and their complicated identities. His entangled family story reflects the collective history of a multi-ethnic, multi-denominational, multi-cultural country, in which borders that separate friend and foe have often run right through the middle of families, occasionally even causing their extinction. Death, thus, is the novel's main motif: in the narrative, the dying of the author's mother, the dying of his family (the Stubler clan), the dying of a city (Sarajevo), a country (Yugoslavia), and of what once meant home to the narrator become deeply intertwined.

Miljenko Jergović was born in Sarajevo (Bosnia-Herzegovina) in 1966. He lived through 18 months of the city's siege before escaping, together with a group of journalists, to Zagreb (Croatia) in 1993, where he has lived ever since. His parents, who had long been divorced and with whom the author maintained difficult relationships, stayed behind.

---

[1] | Russell Scott Valentino's English translation of *Rod* is forthcoming with Archipelago Books, yet not available thus far. Therefore, unless otherwise indicated, all translations of quotations from *Rod* are mine [D. G.-H.].

Jergović's great-grandfather, Karlo Stubler, was of German descent: a Banat Swabian who moved to Dubrovnik and later to Ilidža (Bosnia) under Austro-Hungarian rule. During World War II, Karlo Stubler used to hide his Serbian neighbors and protect them from murdering and pillaging members of the Croatian ultranationalist Ustaša movement. His neighbors, in turn, prevented his deportation to Germany after the communists' coming into power. Jergović's grandfather Franjo Rejc, husband of Karlo Stubler's daughter Olga, had Slovenian roots. Their elder son, Mladen, was drafted into the German army because of his German origin, as a "Volksdeutscher"; he was killed in the war in 1943, shortly after his younger sister Javorka—Miljenko Jergović's mother—was born. The trauma of having forbidden Mladen to join the partisans, her feeling of guilt for his death, would haunt Jergović's grandmother Olga, his "Nona," for the rest of her life: she had thought her son was more likely to survive if serving in the German army. Olga's trauma is passed on to little Javorka. Her being alive is somehow connected to Mladen's death, as if he would have survived if only she, the unwanted child, had not been born.

Jergović's father, a physician and renowned hematologist-oncologist, was the son of a devoted follower of the Ustaša: his fanatic mother even denied him the help he needed when suffering from typhus, because he had fought on the partisans' side. The father's recent death is the subject of what the author called a "farewell essay" ("oproštajni esej"), *Otac* (Eng. *Father*), published in 2010 (Jergović, *Otac* 59).[2] Like *Rod*, it is not only an attempt to come to terms with the death of a parent, but also represents a way to explain national history by telling an intricate family story. Yet, *Rod* is different in many respects, one being its length. Whereas *Otac* seeks for rapprochement with the dying father, *Rod* evades the dying mother—a fact already reflected in the novel's title. In a way, the text performs what it describes, revealing Jergović as a true master of digression: it proliferates just like the mother's cancer cells, the narration becomes "metastatic" and spreads ever further away from its center, the mother's illness and imminent death. The narration, thus, "embodies" what it depicts. This is to be demonstrated on the following pages.

---

2 | Unless otherwise indicated, all translations of quotations from *Otac* are mine [D. G.-H.].

ONE THOUSAND AND ONE PAGES

The novel *Rod*'s scope is a clear reference to the tales of *One Thousand and One Nights*: it is not by coincidence that Jergović's text ends on page 1001. The reason might well be the author's attempt to orientalize his subject—Bosnian history—by hinting at Bosnia's Ottoman legacy and ornamentalizing his prose. However, it seems not so much a question of *how* the tale is told as of *why* it is told: Scheherazade tells her tales because she wants to survive. Each night, she begins a new one, but does not end it, in order to force the king who is eager to hear the conclusion to postpone her pending execution. The purpose of Scheherazade's stories is, thus, to prevent death and prolong life, and this is the very function of Jergović's narrative, of his many digressions and arabesque stories-within-the-story: to delay his mother's death as long as possible, as if telling it would make it definite and irrevocable. This is also the reason why his mother herself permanently reminisces about and recounts the life stories of her dead relatives: to forget about her own illness and dying. As long as she tells stories, she feels "outside" of her sick body, disremembers her suffering and pains and "lives" in the narration ("dok bi ih [priče] pričala, osjećala se kao da je izvan vlastitoga tijela, kao da ne boluje, nego živi u priči" [207]; "Dok tako priča, majka nije bolesna. Onoliko dugo koliko priča traje, nju ništa ne boli" [270]). Storytelling opens up a parallel reality ("paralelna stvarnost" [276]) into which the mother can escape from her deadly disease:

"As long as she is telling stories, she does not think about the illness. Or: as long as she is telling stories, she is not ill at all. If she could do nothing but speak, if I was with her or if we could talk on the phone 24 hours a day, mother would be outside her illness for 24 hours a day. She would be healthy. She would defeat her illness by storytelling, or she would leave her body, she would not need it anymore, entirely having morphed into a story."

("Dok priča, ne misli o bolesti. Ili: dok priča, ona uopće i nije bolesna. Kada bi samo mogla govoriti, kada bih ja bio tu, ili kada bismo dvadeset četiri sata dnevno telefonirali, majka bi dvadeset četiri sata dnevno bila izvan svoje bolesti. Bila bi zdrava. Pobijedila bi bolest pripovijedajući, ili bi napustila svoje tijelo, ono joj više ne bi bilo potrebno, pošto bi se sva pretvorila u priču." [957–958])

The voluminous *Rod* does not represent a novel in the strict sense of the word. Its structure is fragmentary and contains many recurrences, but also gaps—just like family recollections that are told and retold and passed on to (or concealed from) the next generation.

The text consists of seven parts: 1) a short introductory "presentation" ("predavanje"), "Where Other People Live" ("Tamo gdje žive drugi ljudi")[3]; 2) "The Stublers: A Family Novel" ("Stubleri, *jedan porodični roman*"), comprised of 18 titled chapters; 3) "Miners, Smiths, Drunkards, and their Wives: Quartets" ("Rudari, kovači, pijanci i njihove žene, *kvarteti*"), seven pieces of prose in miniature, each consisting of four very short chapters; 4) "Mama Ionesco: A Reportage" ("Mama Ionesco, *reportaža*"), about, or rather around, the life and illness of his mother Javorka; 5) "Inventory" ("Inventarna knjiga"), consisting of 23 titled chapters; 6) "A Calendar of Daily Events: Fictions" ("Kalendar svakodnevnih događaja, *fikcije*"), in which, in Russell Scott Valentino's words, "the familiar constellation of characters returns, and the events of previous sections are danced around, augmented, commented upon" (Valentino, "On Translating Miljenko Jergović," n. p.); and finally 7) "History, Photographs" ("Povijest, fotografije"), comprised of 21 photographs, mostly family photos accompanied by short commentaries.

Obviously, the fourth part, explicitly dedicated to the dying mother, lies precisely at the center of the novel's seven sections. It represents the primary site where the narrative arises, develops, grows, and from where it goes on to "metastasize," to spread to other parts of the narrative body called *Rod*.

As Ingeborg Jandl has observed, the novel's last, photographic section also places the mother's death at its center: the first and last photograph of the gallery are, unlike the rest, colored; the first one shows the family bed where mother Javorka died, and the concluding one the house where she spent her childhood. Jergović took this last photograph shortly before he visited her deathbed. In Ingeborg Jandl's interpretation, this photographic composition, in a way, disassociates the mother's death from the book: the first picture defers her death to an as yet unknown future, whereas the last one eludes her death, leading back to her childhood (Jandl, n. p.).

---

3 | This chapter was published in German translation already in 2007 in the anthology *Der andere nebenan: Eine Anthologie aus dem Südosten Europas*. The U. S. edition appeared in 2013 under the title *The Stranger Next Door: An Anthology from the Other Europe*, edited by Richard Swartz.

Another striking feature of the text is the frequent occurrence of repetitions. So, for instance, the story of Jergović's great-grandfather, Otata Karlo, being taken away by partisans to a holding camp in 1945, prodded in the back with the barrel of a rifle, is told in the very first, introductory chapter "Where Other People Live," and then repeated time and again throughout the book. Grandmother "Nona" Olga's wrong decision of making her son Mladen report for duty instead of letting him join the partisans is another case in point, and so is Otata Karlo's renouncement, repeatedly reported, to take revenge on a certain Boras. One could cite numerous other examples of recurrences. At first glance, these repetitions seem to disturb, to interrupt the narrative flow. However, they clearly illustrate the functioning of communicative memory that subsists in everyday interaction, binding together generations:

"In the Stublers' house all sorts of things were talked about, one and the same story was repeated countless times, built on and invented on [...], and old Karlo engaged in it often and heartily. If his move to Bosnia earned him—or any of us—anything, it was this daily, passionate tale-telling. In other respects, Karlo maybe remained a German, but in tale-telling and the need to constantly replicate stories, Karlo Stubler was indeed a Bosnian."

("O svemu se razgovaralo u kući Stublerovih, ista se priča bezbroj puta ponavljala, nadograđivala i nadomišljala [...], a stari je Karlo u tome rado i često sudjelovao. Ako je od svoga doseljenja u Bosnu išta dobio, ako smo svi mi dobili, dobio je to strasno, svakodnevno pripovijedanje. U drugome je, možda, ostao Švabo, ali u priči, i u potrebi da se priča neprestano ponavlja, Karlo Stubler je bio Bosanac." [73-74])

Repetitive tale-telling is also used to characterize the author's mother and her struggle against her illness. It is interpreted as an attempt to save herself by blaming her doctor, again and again, for not having discovered the tumor earlier and her only son for not assisting her as much as is needed:

"The next day, everything starts all over again [...], I listen and say 'You've already told me that!' but she does not hear me or says: 'And so what if I've told you, do you realize what that man has done to me? It's my neck on the line, not yours!'

And she begins the story all over again, exactly as it happened, not skipping a single detail, as if it is this repetition that is all the sense and cure."

("Sutradan sve kreće ispočetka [...], ja to slušam, kažem – rekla si mi već to!, ali ona me ne čuje, ili govori:
– Pa šta ako sam ti rekla, znaš li ti šta mi je taj čovjek napravio? O mojoj se glavi radi, a ne o tvojoj!
I započinje priču ispočetka, onako kako se dogodila, ne propuštajući nijedan detalj, kao da je u tom ponavljanju sav smisao i izlečenje." [190])

Repetition also has a healing (or "palliative," cf. Lešić-Thomas 11) effect on the narrator of *Rod* himself. He states that one has to reiterate stories until they stop frightening you. Storytelling, thus, is a form of freeing oneself from recollections that prove to be a burden:

"I have already told this but repeat it in a somewhat different manner, as everything has to be repeated here a few more times, and just like in horror stories, where the most dreadful details are repeated so that in the end they scare us a little less."

("Rekao sam već to, ali ponavljam na malo drukčiji način, kao što sve ovo treba još nekoliko puta ponoviti i kao što se u strašnim pričama ponavljaju najstrašniji detalji, da bi na kraju postali manje strašni." [278])

The narrator describes his narrative as proceeding in "concentric circles" ("u koncentričnim krugovima" [91]) from a center that is Karlo Stubler. He constantly thinks of stories that could potentially be incorporated into his text, about novels he could compose; while still pretending to postpone or give them up, he has already written them. At one point, he states that the stories "outpaced" him ("Ubrzo su me priče počele prestizati" [276]). The narrator stops being the master of his tale, as the stories overrun him, they augment and increase and make the reader—as well as the narrator—forget where they started, just as the king in *One Thousand and One Nights* forgets that he wanted to kill his wife at the break of dawn.

The stories told in *Rod* proliferate for one more reason: the narrator does not stick to sheer facts but elaborates on them, adding some detail here, some minor character there, further complicating the already intricate plot. The author-narrator Jergović states that in his 2005 novel *Glorija in excelsis* (Eng. *Gloria in excelsis*), he made up nearly everything, in order to portray his second cousin Željko as truthfully as possible ("U toj je priči skoro sve bilo izmišljeno, da bi Željko mogao biti što stvarniji" [34]). Invention, thus, may lend a story even more authenticity than a supposedly reliable report. On the other hand, writing down the experience of watching his mother die transforms it into fiction, even if every single word is true: "Each written down story stops being veracious, relocates to the realm of fairy tales and fiction, even if it was entirely transcribed from reality." ("Svaka napisana priča prestaje biti zbilja, seli se u bajku i u fikciju, čak i ako je sva prepisana iz stvarnosti." [264])

Fiction slips into the allegedly documentary narrative over and over again, occasionally, maybe, passing unnoticed by the reader who is not familiar with Bosnian history and Sarajevo realities. The Stubler story is sometimes so unbelievable that the fictitious twists and turns that the narrator inserts into the tale do not particularly stand out. A case in point is the story about the construction of the Sarajevo opera, integrated into the chapter "Sarajevski psi" ("The Dogs of Sarajevo," 749–959) about the author-narrator's return to his native city to see his dying mother one last time. It is a weird tale about the opera's architect, Ganimed Troyanovsky, who, just like the Ganymede of ancient Greek mythology, was, in a way, abducted – though not by Zeus to Olympus, but to Sarajevo, by henchmen of the Ottoman serasker (commander-in-chief and minister of war) Omer paša Latas. The fact that the whole tale is italicized insinuates that something is wrong with it (878–924). Still, one has to be aware that there is no opera house in Sarajevo in order to recognize the delusion; apart from the orientalized ornamentation, the story seems to be quite verisimilar. The dying mother, finally, unravels the mystery when her son puts her to the test:

"'Today, early in the morning, I went to Bistrik[4] to see the opera house,' I am telling her, checking if she remembers.
'Where did you go?' she frowns.
'To see the opera house, in Bistrik, where I used to go with Nona.'
She is looking at me and does not know what to say. 'Which opera, there is no opera house in Sarajevo!' She is sad, fighting back tears, because she under-

---

4 | An agglomeration that is part of the municipality of Stari Grad (Old Town) of Sarajevo.

stands I am checking if she remembers. I am checking how clear her mind is. And she understands I am checking how near her death is."

("Bio sam jutros, ranom zorom, na Bistriku, ispred Opere – kažem joj, provjeravam sjeća li se.
Gdje si bio? – mršti se.
Pa ispred Sarajevske opere, na Bistriku, tamo gdje sam išao s Nonom.
Gleda me, ne zna što bi rekla. Kakva Opera, nema u Sarajevu nikakve Opere! Tužna je, zaplakala bi, jer zna da ja to provjeravam sjeća li se. Provjeravam koliko je prisebna. I zna da provjeravam koliko joj je blizu smrt." [954])

By telling the tale of Omer paša Latas planning to build an opera house in Sarajevo, Miljenko Jergović continues the unfinished novel *Omerpaša Latas* by Nobel laureate Ivo Andrić, published posthumously in 1977. The narrative of *Rod*, thus, spreads even beyond its own textual borders. This "proliferating" kind of narration will be at the center of attention in the following section.

PROLIFERATING NARRATION

The scope of Jergović's novel *Rod* results not only from the widely ramified Stubler family tree, but is linked to its primary focus, the mother's illness and dying. The proliferating narration that characterizes the text represents, as I argue, a narrative device whose aim is to reproduce the overwhelming growth and metastasizing of a deadly tumor.

One could quote numerous examples of how the narration veers ever further away from its initial point. For instance, the chapter "Žongler palidrvcima, Furtwängler" ("Juggler of Matches, Furtwängler") from the section "A Calendar of Daily Events" starts from an official train journey of Jergović's great-uncle Rudi, Rudolf Stubler, to Germany. On the train, Rudi becomes acquainted with a strange fellow traveler, Joška Hercl, who begins to tell him his extraordinary life story. Thus, from the train compartment where the two passengers meet, the tale goes back to Joška's childhood in Zagreb, when he was still Josip Stinčić, son of two famous musicians. When the parents realize that little Josip has no musical talent at all, they decide to hide him at aunt Rozalija's place in Graz and proclaim his death, while burying an empty coffin. Rozalija and her mentally disabled daughter Doroteja are Jews, and so Josip converts to Judaism too, and becomes Jošua (Joshua)—Joška. This storyline, which has nothing to do with the Stubler family, and even less with Jergović's mother Javorka, paints the atrocities of anti-Semitism and the Holocaust with Rozalija and Doroteja being deported. Joška survives, because he has taught himself something impossible: juggling burning matches with the fingers of his hand. Therefore, nobody dares to touch him.

Joška's story represents no more than an excursus, though a very long one with many detours, in the account of Rudi's journey to Berlin, where he has business and wants to take advantage of the situation and see the famous conductor Wilhelm Furtwängler, whom he admires so much. In what follows, the narrative further develops the life stories of Jewish musicians whom the German conductor managed to save, and of another one who perished. In the end, even Rudi does not know which parts of the tales he was told are true and which are pure fiction.

The fact that the story-within-the-story-within-the-story contains many digressions is addressed several times in the text itself. So, for instance, after a long diversion concerning a "Concert for Rain and Piano" that Joška's father gives to commemorate his allegedly dead son, the narrator states:

"Now let us slowly return to the compartment where Joška is still telling Rudi the story of his life. But before, to make the tale complete, we will take a look at what was going on in Zagreb, at the Mirogoj Cemetery, on Friday, September 1, 1939, while the whole of Europe was shaking under the boots of German soldiers marching across Poland."

("Sad krenimo polako nazad, u kupe u kojemu još uvijek Joška prepričava Rudiju svoj život. Ali prije toga ćemo, da bi priča bila cijela, pogledati što se u Zagrebu, na Mirogoju, događalo u petak, 1. rujna 1939, dok se cijela Europa tresla pod čizmama njemačkih vojnika koji su marširali kroz Poljsku." [515])

Commenting on another digression concerning the music student Josip Mrak, who has to guard Maksimilijan Stinčić's grand piano at the cemetery, the narrator likewise observes:

"Josip Mrak's serene disposition and airiness would be a good topic for a Croatian social novel, which, alas, will never be written, as will not so many other novels either that we occasionally mention, but enough of that, we have already veered too far away from the story of Rudolf Stubler's journey to Berlin and his encounter with the juggler of matches Joška Hercl while the train was at a still at the Zagreb main station in the late summer of 1954."

("Vedra narav i lakoća Josipa Mraka dobra su tema hrvatskoga društvenog romana, koji će, na žalost, kao i toliki drugi romani koje prigodno spominjemo, ostati nenapisan, ali nećemo o tome, ionako smo predaleko otišli od priče o putovanju Rudolfa Stublera u Berlin i o njegovome susretu sa žonglerom palidrvcima Joškom Herclom, dok je vlak stajao na zagrebačkome glavnom kolodvoru, kasnoga ljeta 1954." [514])

Another example of proliferating narration is the chapter "Dnevnik pčela" ("Diary of the Bees") about a notebook that the author-narrator finds and that, obviously, belonged to his grandfather Franjo Rejc. Just like other members of the Stubler clan, Franjo was passionate about beekeeping. The bee diary includes observations and notices on the condition of his beehives and the measures he used to take. In this chapter again, the notebook only serves as a point of departure for a number of nesting stories. The most disturbing digression contained in this chapter is the tale beginning with Karlo Stubler's acquaintance from Dubrovnik, Gertrude Seghers-Stein, his children's first music teacher. When her youngest son Adrian contracts diphtheria and falls seriously ill, Gertrude commissions prayers with the Jesuits. The friar who takes the task upon himself is Don Emanuel Prpić, referred to as Pop Manojlo. The reader then learns not only the story of Adrian's tragic death but also the unbelievable tale about the Jesuit. The narrator comments on this insertion as follows:

"One cannot stop a tale, following it through to the end, without saying everything about everyone. Hence a little on Don Emanuel, called Pop Manojlo, from Dubrovnik. In this way, we will delay and dilute the account of the fates of Maximilian Seghers-Stein and Mrs. Gertrude, and make it more bearable to those who hear about it for the first time."

("Nemoguće je zaustaviti priču, voditi je kraju, a ne reći sve o svima. Zato još o don Emanuelu Prpiću, dubrovačkom popu Manojlu. Tako ćemo odgoditi i razvodniti sudbine Maximiliana Seghers-Steina i gospođe Gertrude, učiniti ih podnošljivijim onome tko ih prvi put sluša." [677])

One might add that this digression also fulfills the function of "delaying and diluting" the account of mother Javorka's dying.

Don Emanuel's story is related on the basis of the different names he has borne throughout his life. A child of poor parents, little Marko Prpić has to stay home alone while his mother and father go to work. One day, he knocks at the door of the monastery across the street and from then on spends his days with the clergymen and -women. After his studies in Rome where Marko becomes Don Emanuel, he is moved to Dubrovnik and named Pop Manojlo. There he is made the victim of an intrigue: his fellow clergymen accuse him of having abused a choirboy, they cut off his ear, and chase him away. He turns into Ostoja Jednouhi (Ostoja One-Ear), a lunatic hermit, wandering through Herzegovina and living in caverns. In 1939, Orthodox monks accommodate the sick and moribund man; he recovers, and they admit him to the monastery, naming him Ignjatije, after Ignatius Theophorus, the God-Bearer. Next, members of the Ustaša come to the monastery, trying to silence him as the last witness of the Dubrovnik child abuse intrigue. When Ignjatije learns from his fellow friars what the Ustaša threatened to do to him in the name of the Catholic Church, he transforms into an avenger, joins a group of Serbian Chetniks but leaves them soon too, straying through destroyed villages, finally renamed, again, as Pop Avet (Spook). Picked up by a group of partisans, he transforms once more, this time into Pop Španac (The Spanish) because of his good relationship with the partisans' commander who fought in the Spanish Civil War. One day, lying in ambush, he kills a member of a German patrol. The circumstances of this incident are told in a way that makes clear who the killed young soldier must have been: Jergović's uncle Mladen. After the war, the reader finds Pop Prpić in Innsbruck, helping people, be they war criminals or not, move overseas with falsified documents. He is finally killed in Chicago by the UDBA, Tito's secret police.

The proliferating kind of narration so typical of *Rod* in general, and of the previously mentioned story-within-the-story-within-the-story in particular, is best summarized in the following quotation:

"What followed is described most accurately in the *Memories of a Hermit*.[5] Whoever is interested in it may go and find the book, for we don't have time for this part of the tale, nor would it help us with our inquiry or with Ignatije Prpić's

---

5 | A fictitious work left behind by the obviously no less fictitious character Prpić.

story, which is embedded in the story of the Seghers-Stein family, which, in turn, is embedded in the story of the summer of 1943 that will end with Mladen's death in Slavonia."

("Sljedeća etapa opisana je vrlo pomno u *Upamćenjima jednog pustinjaka*. Koga zanima, neka potraži knjigu, jer mi za taj dio priče nemamo vremena, niti bi nam pomogao u našem istraživanju, kao ni u priči o Ignatiju Prpiću, koja se nalazi u priči o porodici Seghers-Stein, a ona u priči o ljetu 1943, koje će završiti Mladenovim stradanjem u Slavoniji." [692-693])

An illustrative example of how the narrative "metastasizes" in *Rod* is the following passage from the tale about Ganimed, the fictitious architect of the fictitious Sarajevo opera mentioned above. In this paragraph, Ganimed is conversing with Omer paša Latas's henchman Sarchione, condensing the narrative device used throughout the novel:

"Ganimed was in an unexpectedly good mood. He walked arm in arm with Sarchione and started to babble incessantly, jumping from one topic to another, about the violin makers of Cremona and the difference between maple and walnut wood, he babbled about Goethe, Dante, and Shakespeare, [...], about the healing effects of melancholy [...]. Then he went on about the daguerreotype, [...], and about the Russians being a bloodthirsty and sentimental folk, [...], and then he related the story of a certain Jean Marais[6] who murdered twenty-seven young women in Lyon before being arrested and taken to Paris, where they would cut his head off by guillotine, and who then said he was content with this, that he had killed all those miserable women to finally see Paris and die ..."

("Ganimed je bio neočekivano dobro raspoložen. Držao je Sarchionea pod ruku, i bez prestanka brbljao, skačući s teme na temu, o kremonskim graditeljima violina i o razlici između javorova i orahova drveta, o Goetheu, Danteu i Shakespeareu, [...], o ljekovitim karakteristikama melankolije [...]. Zatim je brbljao o dagerotipiji, [...], pa o tome da su Rusi krvoločan i sentimentalan svijet, [...], pa je, zatim, pričao o nekom Jeanu Maraisu, koji je u Lionu ubio dvadeset sedam mladih žena, prije nego što su ga uhvatili, a poslije su ga vodili u Pariz, da mu na pariškoj giljotini sijeku glavu, i tad je Jean Marais rekao da je time zadovoljan, zato je ubijao sve te nesretnice, da napokon vidi Pariz i umre ..." [895])

---

6 | In fact, Jean Marais was a French actor and sculptor (1913-1998).

Interestingly, the story that Ganimed relates, which is as far as can be from the subject of mother Javorka's dying,[7] culminates in the death of the narrated character. Just like the author-narrator Miljenko Jergović, who in the chapter "Sarajevski psi" after many narrative detours finally ends up in Sarajevo, coming to see his gravely ill mother for the last time,— and on the occasion imagining his own death—Ganimed's many digressions ultimately lead toward the point from which he himself started his journey, Paris, and toward death.

The close link between the narrator's return to the mother, to the motherland, and death is not incidental. It will be discussed in the following section.

SICK MOTHER, SICK MOTHERLAND

In Miljenko Jergović's work, the motherland is repeatedly linked to the image of cancer. For instance, in his novel *Dvori od oraha* (Eng. *The Walnut Mansion*), the émigré Moritz Ferrara feels his lost homeland growing inside him like a "tumor of the soul":

"Moritz Ferrara would die from an illness that had no name but could be most accurately described as a tumor of the soul. His homeland would grow inside of him, until it sucked in all his vital fluids, softened his bones, and killed him in the end, either in Milan or in some other city." (*Walnut Mansion* 146)[8]

("Moritz Ferrara umrijet će od bolesti koja nema imena, a najbliže bi se mogla opisati kao tumor na duši. U njemu će rasti njegov zavičaj, sve dok mu ne posiše sve životne sokove, razmekša mu kosti i na koncu ga ubije; u Milanu ili u nekom drugom gradu." [*Dvori od oraha* 232])

---

7 | Though rather not by incident, Ganimed's explanations start from a comparison of maple and walnut wood, whereby in Croatian, the first name Javorka—the name of the author's mother—is derived from "javor" ("maple"), whereas the walnut plays a significant role in Jergović's 2003 novel *Dvori od oraha* (Eng. *The Walnut Mansion*).

8 | The English translation of *Dvori od oraha* is by Stephen M. Dickey and Janja Pavetić-Dickey (Jergović, *Walnut Mansion*).

The protagonist's, Regina Delavale's, brother Luka Sikirić who is also forced to live in exile, likewise learns that he suffers from cancer. His illness parallels Moritz Ferrara's: Luka's tumor also seems to be provoked by homesickness, and so he returns to his native Dubrovnik because he wishes to die at home.

Tumors and metastases are metaphorically linked to the homeland yet in another way: in the essay that the author wrote on the occasion of his father's death, *Otac*, he states that his homeland's "shared and separate national histories" are "interspersed with wars" like his father's old body is interspersed with metastases ("nekoliko zajedničkih i odvojenih nacionalnih historija prorešetanih ratovima, kao njegovo [očevo] staračko tijelo metastazama" [7]). He speaks of the danger of "even more monstrous metastases" growing ("još nakaznije metastaze") because of a falsification of the past, when there seem to be only heroes and victims on one side and only perpetrators on the other (155). The motherland, thus, is as sick as is the mother (or, the fatherland as sick as was the father).

In the novel *Rod*, the author-narrator's native city is repeatedly equated with the figure of the mother. Post-war Sarajevo is described as "her [the mother's] city throughout, as cracked up, destroyed, and cordial as she was herself" ("Sarajevo je tih nekih poslijeratnih doba sasvim bivalo njezinim gradom, pomalo ludim, u sebe urušenim i prisnim, kakva je bila i ona, luda, urušena, i srdačna" [360]). The narrator speaks of "the womb of Sarajevo" ("utroba Sarajeva" [860]), and he yearns to forget Sarajevo and his mother alike: "I strove to forget [...] Sarajevo, the name and place are but sheer torment to me now, and mother who, I believe, is already waking, waking from the pain, and her dying body that has begun rotting alive [...]." ("Trudio sam se zaboraviti [...] Sarajevo, jer mi je od tog imena i mjesta ostala još samo muka, i mati koja se, vjerujem, sada već budi, bude je bolovi, njezino odumiruće tijelo, koje je živo počelo trunuti [...]." [929])

He is alienated from his native city like he has been estranged from his mother throughout his life: as he states, his grandmother Olga was a substitute mother to him. Nevertheless, he does not succeed in feeling like a stranger in Sarajevo ("ja, na svoju žalost, nikada u ovom gradu neću biti stranac" [869]), even if he would wish so, nor does he manage to deny his sympathy with his mother. The narrator-author is forced to carry Sarajevo on his back like a heavy burden that he cannot get rid of ("[...] ga vučem, taj moj grad, na plećima gdje god se pokrenem. Pognuo sam se i zgrbio od Sarajeva i njegove težine" [941]), and the mother weighs equally heavy on him, her unrealizable wishes and expectations weigh heavy on his conscience: she wants him to make her healthy again, to procure pharmaceuticals and therapies that work wonders. He craves freeing himself from having to think about and to go back to Sarajevo, since he desires to avoid any confrontation with the motherland that he has lost as well as with the mother that he lost already as a child and that he will definitively lose in the near future. Thus, the encounters with the dying old mother and with the native place are reflected in one another; they disclose what the narrator feels dying within himself and what he will have to bury: everything that he once thought was his.

Conclusion

In the novel *Rod*, the lethal disease of metastatic cancer and the painful process of dying that it involves are more than the narrative's subject. As has been demonstrated in this article, the proliferation of metastases also serves as a metaphor to describe the author's war-torn, "dying" country where conflicts are not solved, but grow and generate ever new conflicts. Last but not least, "metastasizing" also represents a narrative device that textually performs what it depicts.

At one point in the novel, the narrator claims that dying cannot be described, since it entails thoughts and feelings that have no name ("Postoji umiranje, koje se u priči ne može opisati, jer su to misli i osjećaji koji nemaju svoga imena" [*Rod*, 263]). I dare to disagree with him about this: through the device of what may be called "proliferating narration," the text movingly displays how a woman or a man suffering from cancer is overpowered by the disease, as are close relatives who must recognize that they are helpless in the face of this illness. With *Rod*, Miljenko Jergović gives the reader an idea of what cannot be told because it belongs to the realm of the body; yet of how narration is able to *embody* what seems to be beyond words: "Literature serves the purpose, among other things, of expressing over and over again, throughout life, that which resists being put into words, and which the writer always has the impression is on the tip of his tongue." ("Književnost, između ostaloga, i služi tome da se cijeloga života iznova pokušava reći ponešto od onoga što se ne da utjerati u riječi, a piscu se uvijek čini da mu je na vrh jezika." [*Otac*, 117–118])

WORKS CITED

Jandl, Ingeborg. "Fotografie, Erinnerung und Fantasie in Miljenko Jergovićs Familientexten *(Mama Leone, Otac, Rod)*." *Österreichische Beiträge zum Internationalen Slawistenkongress 2018* (=Wiener Slawistischer Almanach: Sonderband). Ed. Peter Deutschmann, Imke Mendoza and Alois Woldan, Frankfurt/Main et al.: Lang [in print].
Jergović, Miljenko. *Dvori od oraha*. Zagreb: Durieux, 2003. Print.
Jergović, Miljenko. *Otac*. Beograd: Rende, 2010. Print.
Jergović, Miljenko. *Rod*. Zagreb: Fraktura, 2013. Print.
Jergović, Miljenko. *The Walnut Mansion*. New Haven, London: Yale UP, 2015. Web. 17 January 2017. http://www.mylibrary.com?ID-834628.
Jergović, Miljenko. "Where Other People Live." *The Stranger Next Door: An Anthology from the Other Europe*. Ed. Richard Swartz, Evanston: Northwestern UP, 2013. 99–112. Print.
Lešić-Thomas, Andrea. "Memory, Narratology and the Problem of Authenticity: A Story of Pain." *Interpretations, European Research Project for Poetics and Hermeneutics*, vol. 2: *Memory and Art*. Ed. Kata Kulavkova, Skopje: Macedonian Academy of Sciences and Arts, 2008. 101–118. Web. 4 March 2018. www.academia.edu/11350641/Memory_Narratology_and_the_Problem_of_Authenticity.
Valentino, Russell Scott. "On Translating Miljenko Jergović." 2016. Web. 13 February 2018. pen.org/on-translating-miljenko-jergovic/.
Valentino, Russell Scott. "Otata and Omama." 2016. Web. 13 February 2018. russellv.com/tag/miljenko-jergovic/.

Storytelling in the Age of AIDS
Narrative Possibilities and the Exigencies of Loss
in Dale Peck's *Martin and John. A Novel*

Ariane Schröder

> "We tend to narrate the history of the feminist and lesbian/gay movement [...] in such a way that ecstasy figured prominently in the sixties and seventies and midway through the eighties. But maybe ecstasy is more persistent than that; maybe it is with us all along. To be ecstatic means, literally, to be outside oneself, and thus can have several meanings: to be transported beyond oneself by a passion, but also to be beside oneself with rage and grief."
> JUDITH BUTLER, *PRECARIOUS LIFE*, 24

In its November 24, 1986 issue *The New Yorker* printed a short story by Susan Sontag called "The Way We Live Now." Five years into the epidemic, it was the first piece of fiction published in the magazine that directly addressed AIDS and its socio-cultural repercussions in the United States. Written entirely as a concatenation of conversational fragments, the narrative opens as follows:

At first he was just losing weight, he felt only a little ill, Max said to Ellen, and he didn't call for an appointment with his doctor, according to Greg, because he was managing to keep on working at more or less the same rhythm, but he did stop smoking, Tanya pointed out, which suggests he was frightened, but also that he wanted, even more than he knew, to be healthy, or healthier, or maybe just to gain back a few pounds, said Orson, [...]. But did he have a good doctor, Stephen wanted to know, [...] it was only in the last six months that he had the metallic

taste of panic in his mouth, because becoming seriously ill was something that
happened to other people, a normal delusion, he observed to Paolo, if one was
thirty-eight and had never had a serious illness [...]. (Sontag n. p.)

The reader encounters a multitude of voices that variously express concern, empathy, curiosity, presumptuousness or sadness about the story's central character, a man in his thirties stricken with AIDS. Although he is the only subject of discussion, the main hero remains without name or voice in the text. He is never speaking, he is only talked about. Through this simple literary technique, Sontag is able to offer a pointed critique of the socio-cultural response to this health crisis in the United States: that those actually suffering in this epidemic were almost always excluded from the discourse about AIDS. U.S. mainstream media representations of people with AIDS (PWAs) generally reduced them to the state of victimhood or identified them exclusively with their illness. What is more, the AIDS crisis was not perceived as a political challenge for the nation as a whole but as an isolated phenomenon that only affected certain minority groups.

The dominant images propagated of PWAs in the U.S. media were those of gay men and of intravenous drug users. As Jan Zita Grover has argued, their supposed lifestyle exclusively focused on "pleasure seeking," so when AIDS hit anyone not directly associated with drug or gay culture, media outlets and politicians interpreted it "as an assault from diseased hedonists upon hard-working innocents" (Grover 23). Consequently, U.S. media acted as a cultural echo chamber for what I would call a "hierarchy of culpability," in which gay men and drug users were seen as responsible for their infection with HIV, while hemophiliacs, blood or organ donation recipients and—most of all—children were seen as the "innocent victims" of this epidemic. Biomedical, political and media narratives frequently put in place a rhetorical *cordon sanitaire* between those associated with HIV and a "general population," or what Richard Goldstein has called "the implicated and the immune" (17).

Simon Watney has argued that AIDS did not only cause "a medical crisis on an unparalleled scale, it involves a crisis of representation itself, a crisis over the entire framing of knowledge about the human body" (*Policing* 9). So how did authors—specifically gay authors directly affected by the epidemic within their community—respond to this crisis of representation in their literature? How did they counter the American mainstream's "'the way we live now' syndrome," as David Román has called it, which is defined by the fact that "the representation of gay men with AIDS only solidifies dominant cultural images of gay men" (64)? In the following I will argue that anyone addressing AIDS as a literary subject invariably encounters very specific biomedical, political, ethical and aesthetic quandaries that need to be acknowledged, or ignored at the risk of just reiterating gay stereotypes.

While the first years of the epidemic saw literary production that mostly aimed at educating and informing the public about AIDS-related issues, the late 80s and early 90s saw an ever widening field of so-called "AIDS literature."[1] Michiko Kakutani has described the evolution of this genre as beginning with "memoirs and journals [...] followed by a growing number of documentary-like novels and short stories, and in recent years by increasingly metaphorical and idiosyncratic works of fiction" (quoted in Pearl 24). In the following I will analyze what could be considered one of the most experimental literary artworks of this latter period, Dale Peck's novel *Martin and John*. My aim is to illustrate how the author is able to liberate his narrative—in form and content—from the discursive limits of AIDS and the conventional tropes commonly associated with the representation of this disease and its principal sufferers. In doing so, the novel manages to simultaneously convey the subjective specificity of individual loss and the collective trauma of a community at the height of this singular epidemic crisis.

How to Have Literature in an Epidemic

Before addressing Peck's novel in detail, it is necessary to provide a short overview of the discursive force-field surrounding AIDS, the biomedical, political, ethical and aesthetic impediments that delimit artistic expression. The discourse on HIV/AIDS is structured within a clearly hierarchical framework with biomedicine as the ultimate arbiter of the disease's "truth." Cindy Patton has argued that "science serves as the master discourse that administers all other discourses about AIDS" (53) because

---

[1] | The literary critic Michael Bronski has even deemed the rubric of "AIDS literature" as in itself an expression of homophobia, because he claims that without denial, oppression, and indifference, these works would be called "American literature" (quoted in Schulman 50).

"AIDS" emerged as an unstable and constantly developing medical concept before it entered public consciousness. Since science exerts such great control over the semantics of the epidemic, we are unable to articulate anything about AIDS without a prior critical engagement with its biomedical knowledge culture.

Because this strange new disease occurred first in previously healthy young gay men in urban centers of the U. S. east and west coast in 1981, biomedical discourse soon began to redress this *correlation* between illness and sexual identity as *causality*. This was enabled by a medical establishment that to a large extent still saw homosexuality as inherently pathological, which further facilitated "the forward slippage from corruption theories of homosexuality to contagion theories of AIDS" (Watney, "Spectacle" 77).[2] Thus, early on in the epidemic crisis, as Cindy Patton claims, "homosexual AIDS" became a stabilized medical entity, it represented the "real" or "original" AIDS against which other demographic groups had to articulate their difference (66). While biomedical research made significant inroads in HIV/AIDS research throughout the first decade of the crisis, the way medical discourse represented gay men as culpable in their own infection with the virus, deeply affected the political response to AIDS—both in the conservative climate of the Reagan administration and within the gay community itself.

In his essay "Esthetics and Loss" the writer Edmund White poignantly addressed the impact of HIV/AIDS on gay men in the United States: "To have been oppressed in the 1950s, freed in the 1960s, exalted in the 1970s, and wiped out in the 1980s is a quick itinerary for a whole culture to follow" (215). He addresses the cultural impact the epidemic has had in the United States as vital subject for art, specifically literature. His remarks moreover illustrate two important points: on the one hand, the enormous speed with which the lesbian and gay movement had staked

---

2 | Homosexuality was not only interpreted by many at the time as "abnormal" due to socially conservative convention but also had a long and problematic history within U. S. medical sciences, especially in psychology and psychiatry. It was only since 1973 that the American Psychiatric Association had actually removed homosexuality from the *Diagnostic and Statistical Manual of Mental Disorders* (DSM). And the DSM would retain the pathological condition "ego-dystonic homosexuality" (EDH), defined as "being in conflict with one's sexual orientation" until 1987.

out civil rights and living spaces in a country that had until Stonewall[3] not only discriminated against but legally prosecuted them. On the other hand, it showed that AIDS did not only present an existential threat to gay individuals but to the community as a whole. Because open gay life took only place in a few urban clusters in the U. S., the Castro district in San Francisco or New York City's Greenwich Village seemingly turned from vibrant and lively quarters into "gay cemeteries" in just a few years. One can only imagine what it must have been like for so many young independent men (who oftentimes had left a homophobic family environment behind) to suddenly have to rely on others for help; for them to accept the fact that life would be over before it had even really begun. Many would soon come to realize that there was no governmental support system for them: no legal aides, no psychiatrists, no social workers—only overcrowded hospitals that oftentimes provided nothing more than palliative care, if they decided to admit PWAs at all. Moreover, growing media awareness of the epidemic did not improve matters, it just aggravated the stigmatization, fear and discrimination of people with AIDS.

Thus, when the author and activist Larry Kramer began calling the AIDS epidemic a "gay holocaust" many within the community did not see this as an exaggeration.[4] His comments not only evoked a collective fear of universal gay death but also addressed the fact that many felt purposefully neglected by the U. S. government. But while the geographical clustering of gay men in just a few cities might have initially exacerbated the spread of HIV amongst them, this concentration also would become their lifeline. As Cindy Patton has pointed out by contrasting the two groups most visibly affected at the beginning of the epidemic—gay men and intravenous drug users—the former had an "autonomous and

---

3 | A raid on the Stonewall Inn (a gay bar) in New York City's Greenwich Village on June 28, 1969 sparked violent clashes between law enforcement and LGBT demonstrators who were protesting police violence and discrimination. It is widely believed to be a watershed event of the gay and lesbian liberation movement in the United States. Gay Pride parades across the globe, often called "Christopher Street Day," reference Stonewall as this was the street where the bar was located.
4 | To claim that there was a genocide or holocaust, thus a deliberate killing of any of the epidemic's victims, is of course not only an indefensible claim but an outrageous exaggeration. But provoking and inflaming others with his rhetoric has always been an essential part of Kramer's writing and public persona.

highly articulate infrastructure for mobilizing politically around AIDS" and existing community newsletters, magazines and newspapers would become essential in disseminating information as well as rallying for political action (17).

Because the gay community felt physically threatened by the inaction of the U.S. government and the misrepresentation of the disease in the mainstream media, AIDS literature produced in the early period of the epidemic was almost exclusively activist and political in nature. Michael Denneny characterized it as "writing in response to a present threat; it is in it, of it, and aims to affect it. [...] this AIDS writing is not only being produced in the trenches, as it were, but is being published, read by its public and evaluated by the critics in the midst of the crisis" (46). In his argument Denneny evokes the "Lost Generation" of World War I whose devastation similarly brought about a canon of exceptional texts written by young raw talents under deadly and traumatic circumstances.[5]

Most early works about HIV/AIDS were aesthetically unsophisticated texts that served two main purposes: dealing with the immediate personal trauma inflicted by illness and death, as well as educating the readership about AIDS and its consequences. Therefore, the early to mid-eighties saw a dominance of both drama and short fiction, two genres that promised easier access either through direct engagement or brevity. Novels that dealt with the crisis were scarce. From the mid-eighties onwards AIDS literature began to become more stylistically experimental and more complex in its content. However, the syndrome's imposition of methodic constraints oftentimes led to formulaic, repetitive texts. In his extensive study on AIDS novels, Steven Kruger claims that there were fundamentally only two major cultural narratives available to talk about AIDS that he calls "the narrative of irreversible decline" and "the narrative of uncontrollable spread" (75–6). The first one charts the course of an individual's illness, very often from the onset of symptoms to the diagnosis, the character's ongoing suffering and eventual death. The second one offers a collective perspective on the "historical trajectory of

---

5 | "Lost Generation" refers to the American generation born between 1883 and 1900, those that came of age during World War I. Ernest Hemingway popularized the term in *The Sun Also Rises* (1926) by using it as an epigraph credited to Gertrude Stein ("You are all a lost generation"). Other notable writers include F. Scott Fitzgerald, T. S. Eliot, Sylvia Beach and Ezra Pound.

the epidemic" (Kruger 76) and addresses questions of origin and method of spread.[6]

Moreover, what all AIDS literature needed to somehow confront was the problem of the ending to their narratives. At the height of the epidemic, before any successful therapeutic measures were found, death from AIDS was a foregone conclusion. Yet, no matter if a text chose to portray the death from AIDS or leave it out, stories about people with AIDS were—if depicted in a realist tradition—always representations about the progressive decline of health, of debilitating illness and mental anguish. This inherent hopelessness hampered readers to derive aesthetic gratification from these narratives, as Andrew Holleran has stated: "As admirable as the writing or publishing of books about AIDS may be, I really don't know who reads them with pleasure—because I suspect there is one thing and one thing only everyone wants to read, and that is the headline CURE FOUND" (12).

Furthermore, the portrayal of people with AIDS—especially in life narratives—carries grave ethical implications that should not go unmentioned here. Michael Denneny has pointed out that epidemics turn the privacy of death into a social event. In these instances, he claims, "the individual death is both robbed of its utter privacy and uniquely individual meaning and simultaneously amplified with the resonance of social significance and historical consequence" (Denneny 37). Thus, any representation of PWAs that turns their illness into a symbol for something else or uses their suffering as a cheap plot point to generate drama, is essentially exploiting the suffering of real-life individuals. Hence this kind of writing is always a tight-rope act of speaking to the gay community as a collective without diminishing a person's singular trauma. In this context, the most essential task of AIDS literature, or what Denneny calls "its innermost principle" is simply "the act of bearing witness" to both individual suffering and the potential demise of a whole subculture of American life (48).

---

6 | Paul Monette's memoir *Borrowed Time* (1988) is probably one of the most commercially successful of such "irreversible decline" narratives, as it charts the course of his lover's illness from diagnosis to death. The most famous example of the "uncontrollable spread" version is likely Randy Shilts's *And the Band Played On* (1987), a broad portrayal of important political, medical and cultural actors during the first six years of the epidemic.

NARRATING AIDS IN *MARTIN AND JOHN*

At the time when *Martin and John* was published in 1993, Dale Peck was twenty-six years old. His young age is significant here, because Peck would thus become one of the main literary voices of a generation of gay artists who had neither a first-hand experience of gay liberation in the 1970s nor an idea of gay sexuality outside the shadow of HIV/AIDS. John Clum has in this context distinguished between the "'Stonewall generation,' who once thought it had found paradise and lost it through AIDS" and authors like Peck, who "experienc[ed] pain and loss without saving memories, present love, or dreams of a future" (Clum 667). Yet although Peck's writing does not participate in a nostalgic longing for a time before the epidemic, it is nevertheless similarly occupied with the question how such traumatic loss—both personal and collective—affects memory and our ability to tell stories. It attempts to translate the experience of individual bodily disintegration and the vanishing of a whole culture into an artwork that still resonates with a cultural market oversaturated with more orthodox and formulaic narratives about AIDS.

The novel was also published during "one of the bleakest stretches of the AIDS pandemic" (LaPointe n.p.) when the death rate in the United States was highest and the supposed miracle drug azidothymidine (AZT) had proven to be ineffectual. Successful treatment with antiretroviral therapy (HAART) that significantly extended the life of HIV-positive people was still another three years away. Thus, Peck's narrative inserts itself into a decade-old literary debate about the meaning of AIDS, just before therapeutic advancements would significantly shift the image of the disease from inevitably fatal to possibly manageable.

From the outset of *Martin and John* it becomes clear that for Dale Peck telling the story of AIDS necessitates a refusal to respect genre distinctions between fiction, autobiography and history and a break from literary realism in favor of postmodernist techniques. The author's claim in the title of his book that his text represents "a novel" feels almost like a provocation as the author's repeated narrative distortion of time, space and characterization belie conventional expectations of this form of literature. Aine McGlynn has therefore categorized the work as a "high postmodern novel" that is characterized by "its playful and shifting narrative style, self-consciousness about the creative process, unstable characterization, challenge to authorial convention, comfort with profanity, and unashamed treatment of taboo" (262). As I will show in the following analysis, by choosing fragmentation over cohesion in his storytelling, Peck is not only able to distance himself from any moral commentary about the epidemic and the potential culpability of gay men in their own infection, he also is able to evade the seemingly inevitable narrative of "irreversible decline" so common in most AIDS fiction.

Peck's "novel" at first glance looks more like a short-story collection as it consists of an assortment of small stream-of-consciousness vignettes intercut by lengthier narratives. The italicized vignettes offer snippets from the life narrative of a young man named John as told from his own perspective. They trace his development from infancy to adulthood, how he experiences the loss of his mother and physical violence at the hands of his father, how he leaves rural Kansas behind for New York City where he meets Martin, falls in love with him and loses him to AIDS. This linear and elliptical narrative ends with John back in Kansas, in the process of grieving and writing, while a bottle of AZT on the shelf signals his own infection with HIV and uncertain future. The vignettes are complemented with eight short stories that provide alternative versions to the "reality" produced in the italicized texts. In these stories the characters have the same or similar names but shifting affiliations, motives and identities. As the narrative progresses, the distinctions between what is supposed to be John's "real" autobiography and his "invented" fiction begin to blur as fantasies, memories and traumatic experiences converge. Monica Pearl has pointed out that in both a biomedical as well as in a cultural context "[t]he narrative of AIDS itself is unreliable" (30). *Martin and John* not only imposes this uncertainty on the reader, it also actively undercuts any attempt to get at some essential "truth" of the story. What is more, the collapsing polyphonic structure of the text also offers an adequate formal expression of what AIDS can do to the human body and mind: its fragmentation, disintegration and eventual dissolution. "The reality of AIDS," David Kaufman has claimed, "may be too virulent, in a sense, to be captured through customary fictional devices" (347) and I will in the following look at some of the book's chapters in more detail in order to illustrate how Peck finds alternative modes of representation for the gay male experience at the height of the epidemic.

The first chapter, an italicized vignette called "Here Is This Baby," not only marks the beginning of John's existence and establishes a circular narrative of life, it is also already fraught with themes that remain central throughout the whole book: despair, family violence, problematic relationships, complicity and guilt. John's mother Bea is presented as an inexperienced young housewife, distraught that her baby simply won't stop crying. In her distress she calls up her husband Henry at work who reacts annoyed and quickly becomes aggressive. When he returns home early, his violent anger made manifest by the fierceness with which he closes the car door, the baby suddenly and inexplicably stops crying and Bea complains *"I'll be damned if he's not shutting up at just the right time, lying in my arms with his eyes wide open and innocent like he hasn't done a thing, and don't he just know who's going to get it now?"* (M & J 4, emphasis original)[7] At this point the narrative stops and the reader anticipates that Henry will physically abuse his wife, and that somehow—however unwillingly—John is complicit in this act of violence. The guilt of the passive observer who is unable or unwilling to offer protection from harm becomes a recurring motif throughout the text.

The next chapter, "Blue Wet-Paint Columns," is set a few years later in Long Island, when Henry forces Bea to have another child although pregnancy poses a significant health risk to her. Little John watches in horror as his mother's miscarriage leaves her severely debilitated. Unable to look after her, Henry moves his wife to a care facility and takes John with him to Kansas, separating mother and son forever (M & J 14). Here, the heterosexual encounter is marked as dangerous, reproductive sexuality as deadly. Through this depiction, Peck destabilizes the commonly assumed link between homosexuality and death in the age of AIDS. By framing sexuality as inherently unsafe, he foregoes any debate about personal culpability about HIV infection that is so often part of AIDS narratives. At some point or other most of these texts invariably discuss the potential moment of infection, which is oftentimes depicted as a transgressive act.[8]

---

7 | All references to this edition of Dale Peck's novel *Martin and John* will be quoted forthwith as "M & J".

8 | In his famous AIDS memoir, *Borrowed Time*, for example, Paul Monette confesses his guilt over the infection of his lover Roger. His own lack of monogamous commitment is made responsible for Roger's infection: "The through line of my guilt, as an overdetermined actor would have it, went back to Joel and the unhappy months of 1981. If I hadn't had the deadborn affair with Joel I wouldn't have collapsed the way I did. If I hadn't been so full of havoc, Roger would never have gone east alone in October, never gone home with the freshman lawyer he

In *Martin and John*, the author resists the urge to fit his narrative about the affliction into a moral belief system. I would therefore argue that AIDS is never treated accusatorily here, it does not mean anything beyond devastating illness and death, it is but one more fact of life.

Throughout the following vignettes and stories the reader for the first time notices problems with the consistency of both narrative and characters. John's parents in "Driftwood" live in Kansas on a farm and the family is traumatized by the previous death of John's older brother. In the next story, "Transformations," Henry is dead and Bea drowns her sorrows in alcohol. "The Search for Water" brings John back to his hometown on a visit to his stepmother Bea, who recently divorced her husband Henry. More and more, one realizes that these stories provide alternative realities to the plot that slowly progresses in the vignettes. It is of course not coincidence that these stories, which detail John's adolescence and sexual awakening, are also the moment when Martin appears in the narrative. He is a young runaway in "Driftwood" with whom John shares a first romantic encounter, the lover of both Bea and John in "Transformations," and John's boyfriend in "The Search for Water."

This narrative structure is evocative of the literary games of Donald Barthelme or John Barth which have often been criticized for being an end in themselves. However, Peck's text is able to rise above mere experimentation and novelty because it is anchored in the author's emotional investment in his characters. At the core of each of these stories there is an emotional consistency, a bond between one John and one Martin that provides narrative continuity and stability. As Kaufman has argued, "all the Martins and all the Johns are somehow different yet at once the same, connected by emotional truths that betray their alikeness" (347). The reader's simultaneous disorientation and recognition is further enabled by the repeated recurrence of seemingly insignificant details: a circle-like scar around the eye, a silver ring as treasured family heirloom, a disfigured hand, an unexpected gesture (legs lifted in the air, shaped like a V) all appear in more than one story. Like musical fugues, these elements establish significant connections between the narratives or question their meaning. Also, by constantly rearranging the different Martins and Johns

---

met in Cahoots after seeing Nicholas Nickleby. He'd come back from that trip to the run of ambiguous viral misery that ended up misdiagnosed as amoebas. We both agreed it must have been that contact." (Monette 88-9).

in urban or rural spaces, with a working or middle class background, as young or old, Peck manages to transcend the singular trauma of AIDS and makes visible its ramification for the gay community as such. Accordingly, Catherine Texier has argued that "[b]y breaking the story line and blurring the identity of his characters and the hard boundaries between the stories, Dale Peck succeeds in exploring the experience of being gay with a remarkable complexity and depth of feeling" (n. p.).

Although *Martin and John* is a narrative about the trauma and loss instigated by AIDS, the disease is only addressed specifically in the last quarter of the novel. While the earlier sections are mostly concerned with John's coming-of-age, sexual experimentation and the trials and errors of emotional relationships with the ever-changing Martins, the novel provides no extended portrayal of physical decline that is so common for most AIDS narratives. Also, the text evades the typical biomedicalization of AIDS, the authoritative power of health care professionals or therapy regimes remains absent from the text. Instead, the vignette plot jumps from Martin and John finding their most deeply affectionate and intimate bond yet in "The End of the Ocean" to Martin's gruesome death in "Circumnavigation." Both men are in the bathroom, John watches Martin through the mirror while the other is taking a bath:

"Behind me, water slapped the tub's sides, and when I turned, Martin was looking at it slosh between his legs. He didn't see my face, and I made an effort to pull it together. Martin's back was bowed, the notches of his vertebrae stood out like walnuts, his legs splayed like those of a baby who's just fallen, and the weight of his chin pressed on the catheter that poked from his chest. He was looking at a thick red and brown stream that leaked from his anus and ran between his legs down the center of the tub to the drain." (M & J 164, emphasis original)

Peck provides a visceral look at a man in the last stages of this dehumanizing disease: emaciated to his bare bones, helpless and immobile like a small child, suffering from debilitating opportunistic infections and constant diarrhea.[9] That the stream running out of him is not only

---

9 | The narrative, for instance, mentions that Martin suffers from cryptococcosis, a fungal infection that can lead to fatal forms of meningitis or pneumonia. Moreover, the reference to the breast catheter indicates a then common treatment for cytomegalovirus, a dangerous herpes infection.

brown but red indicates that Martin has an intestinal hemorrhage and both men realize without many words that it is too late for John to get help as "Martin's life slipped out the drain" (M & J 165). John stays with him, passively observing him:

"After a while the stream coming from Martin's body was just red, and then it was clear, and for a moment I thought the water draining from the tub came from his body, and then I realized, Of course, he's stopped hemorrhaging, and then, when I touched him with my left hand—my right hand can't really feel temperature—I noticed that his skin was no warmer than the water coming from the shower and that the water had gone cold long ago." (M & J 166, emphasis original)

This scene is brutal in its unflinching look at the devastation of this illness, which is often cloaked in melodrama[10]—there is no tearful goodbye, no palliative care, no alleviation of Martin's suffering, only the bleak and degrading death of *"a six-foot-two-inch man who weighed eighty pounds and who'd had all the shit and blood and water and air sucked out of him"* (M & J 166, emphasis original), literally drained of life.

After this fraught chapter, the rest of the novel further dismantles the already tenuous narrative pact with the reader. In the short story "The Gilded Theater," Martin is suddenly alive and well, he is an older man engrossing the younger John in his affluent Manhattan lifestyle. At one point in the narrative Martin exclaims confidently: "I will certainly not die of something as ordinary as AIDS, John. How—he paused, searching for a word—how *mundane!*" (M & J 181, emphasis original). In this context, the novel's narrative strategy to abandon character consistency in favor of variation and fragmentation has the additional advantage that it disposes of the problem of the ending that all authors who address AIDS face. As Reed Woodhouse has stated: "In one sense no one dies, in another, everyone does" (205). In a gesture reminiscent of Scheherazade, Peck is able to make use of what Wendy Farris has called "an intriguing aspect of all literary discourse," namely "its capacity to simulate the postponement of human death through the prolongation of fictional life" (811). Yet, the repeated reinvention of Martin and John never functions as utopian wish

---

10 | Probably best exemplified by Andrew Beckett's (Tom Hanks's) death scene in the blockbuster movie *Philadelphia* (dir. Jonathan Demme) that also premiered in 1993.

fulfillment because the alternatives that follow are just as bleak, fraught with disillusionment, physical violence and sexual exploitation. John's loss of Martin, his father or his mother is always the outcome in these narratives, only the way this loss manifests itself changes. The effect is to integrate AIDS as an inevitable part of life—albeit a catastrophic event—but not more devastating than all the other forms that loss can take.

Adding to the disorientation that Martin is alive again, the next chapter named "Lee" abandons the clear formal distinction between supposedly autobiographical and fictional content, between italicized and non-italicized passages. Scenes of emotional conflict between Martin and John blend with violent sex between John and an anonymous partner.[11] The narrative constantly shifts between these two story lines, now without the italics signaling a change in perspective. In what reads like a flashback to an earlier point in the narrative before his death from AIDS, Martin expresses his extreme resentment about John's apparent health. He claims that John only remains at his side out of pity, while the latter can only voice meek opposition. As John tries to embrace him, Peck creates a meaningful and compelling tableau of the two bodies:

"Then he bend his head to the side and I saw my head in the mirror perched above his body and I knew what he was doing, but I stood there and let him do it. Look carefully, he said, and I looked at his drooping nipples and the lines of his ribs and his ashen skin and my face. This is going to be you one day, he said. And I hope it's soon" (M & J 194).

With Martin's body superimposed on John's head the scene establishes a devastating simultaneity of Martin's deadly present and John's potentially lethal future. It is indicative of Martin's rage about his illness just as much as it addresses the survivor's guilt of the still-healthy John.

The intercut sex scenes in which his unnamed partner repeatedly hits John—as the latter demands—can be read as both John seeking atonement for his guilt and his attempt to find a physical expression for the grief that Martin's death has caused him. This sexual encounter, which is entirely void of actual intimacy, culminates in John being anally penetrated by a gun, but when he begs the other man to pull the trigger, he

---

11 | If he is the eponymous "Lee" of the chapter's title—or whom else this name refers to—is never explicitly stated.

becomes so disturbed that he flees from the room. In this moment, alone, humiliated and almost suicidal with anguish, John regains some sense of self again, as the narrative settles back into a more formally stable italicized vignette:

"In the sudden quiet I hear myself sob aloud and I think that at last I've succeeded, for I cry only for myself, and if any thought of Martin remains, or of my mother, or of my father, they founder in a sea of other names, and nameless faces, and in the faces of hundreds of men whom I remember by a common name, a name that remains unconnected to any identity no matter how many times it is assumed. And that name, I must remind myself, is my own: John." (M & J 196-7, emphasis original)

Here, Peck makes clear that "John" functions as a stand-in for a whole community suffering from the physical and psychological repercussions of the AIDS epidemic; all of those people who fall ill and die and all of those who bear witness to their dying. Yet this universalizing gesture does not trivialize or dilute the raw emotions surrounding Martin's illness and death, as the reader has already become emotionally invested in the bond between the two men, even if the parameters or conditions of their relationship change from narrative to narrative.

While in "Lee" John tries to overcome his grief through anonymous and violent gay sex, in the next story, "Fucking Martin" he seeks fulfillment in heterosexual practice: he sleeps with his friend Susan in order for her to become pregnant. John's thoughts however, constantly circle around Martin whose dying wish it was that he should help their friend conceive a child (M & J 217). Accordingly, with this reproductive purpose in mind, sex with Susan is void of actual physical desire, because for him, John states, "she made sex seem unerotic, less like fantasy, more like life" (M & J 203). He realizes that this affirmative, potentially life-giving act is only symbolic and cannot bring his lost lover back from death. Realizing this, John begins to cry as Susan looks at him: "'Dale?' she whispers" (M & J 219). This moment of autoreferentiality acknowledges the presence of the author and the fundamental importance of his own personal experiences for the text. Yet, it still enforces its prerogative to be understood as fiction, not as an autobiography. As Peck tears down the presumed "fourth wall" between him and the reader for one instant, he then immediately reinstates "John" as the principal agent of the story. However, the narrative focus shifts from John's perspective to an omniscient narrator who comments on the impossibility to fully grasp "the sum of life" in narrative: "Inevitably, things have been left out. Perhaps they appear in others' stories. Perhaps they were here once and John's forgotten them. Perhaps some things he remembers didn't really occur. But none of that matters now" (M&J 220). By consciously inserting himself into his novel, Peck manages to reflect on his personal grief without becoming lost in its particulars.

Andrew Holleran, speaking about the first years of the AIDS crisis, had claimed that "[n]ovels weren't needed; [...] The truth was quite enough; there was no need to make it up. The attempt to imagine such scenes seemed impertinence of the worst kind" (13). *Martin and John*, I would argue, manages to stake out a space between fact and fiction that acknowledges the very real horrors of the epidemic while simultaneously making room for different voices, offering more than just a personal testimonial. In this way, the novel offers, as John Champagne has claimed, "an extended deconstruction of the binary 'remembering/forgetting'" (185), which becomes even more pronounced in the ultimate chapter of the book.

The last vignette, "I Divide My Life in Two," sees John's return as the narrator of his and Martin's story. He lives in a small place in Kansas with an AZT bottle nearby, waiting to become necessary when he himself betrays the first symptoms of AIDS. While it has been futile to replace the void left by Martin with anonymous sex or procreation, he finally finds a way to express his loss and reclaim his memories through the act of writing, of storytelling. Reiterating the circular life narrative, the novel ends with the story of its own initiation. Martin had encouraged John to write (M&J 224) and as he sits in his room, the first pages of *Martin and John* begin to take shape: "*I wrote: this is not the worst thing I remember, and then, I don't know why, but I wrote something that hadn't happened. Everything's been a little confused since then, what's real and what's invented, but it all seems to make more sense too*" (M&J 225, emphasis original). The narrative self-consciously makes transparent the complex process of writing about memories and their rearrangement in fiction. John confesses that this act of self-expression allows him to gain control over his life narrative and his complex emotions of grief, guilt and anxiety at the same time.

Moreover, John realizes that he has used storytelling in order to cope with traumatic experiences all his life:

"I remember making up my first stories at night, kept awake by the sound of my parents fighting in the other room. Every fiction is always opposed to some truth, and the opposition in these stories was easy to spot, for they were about a happy mother, happy father, happy John. But this changed. Soon the stories I imagined were as horrible as the one I lived. I found a power in it, and that power increased as the imagined horror became more and more like the events of my life. You can search for a meaning in that. I tell myself that by reinventing my life, my imagination imposes an order on things and makes them make sense." (M & J 224, emphasis original)

While in childhood storytelling provided a mental escape route from domestic violence, as an adult it allows him to reclaim power from AIDS and the way it seems to dictate the life narratives of so many gay men during the epidemic crisis. What he argues for here, is that he has learned that in order to overcome fear or grief, it does not help to simply displace or repress these emotions. Instead, he feels empowered by his ability to look his own nightmares in the eye unflinchingly and let his imagination dictate their shape. Formally, storytelling also becomes the only consistent structuring principle of Peck's novel, which according to Richard Canning allows the "fiction to reveal and to question how the ordering of our experiences, thoughts, and memories conditions what they mean to us" (Canning xl). Whatever Martin *meant* to John in all his various incarnations, what all these different narrative strands point to is the inescapability of losing him. Thus, the novel as a whole represents an elaborate elegy on loss, grief and the potential for self-healing that can be found in narratives. Judith Butler has stated that "loss must be marked and it cannot be represented; loss fractures representation itself and loss precipitates its own modes of expression" (Butler, "Loss" 467). In this sense I would argue that *Martin and John* provides a persuasive strategy to represent what is seemingly unrepresentable through fragmentation, rearrangement and reiteration. Especially the impermanence of authorial identity and the shifting of names, places, relationships emphasize the unprecedented scale of epidemic suffering and death at hand: that there are thousands of "Johns" and "Martins" who experienced similar catastrophes in the age of AIDS. Thus, this novel becomes both testament of and emblem for the loss of individual lives and the loss of a culture.

WORKS CITED

Butler, Judith. "After Loss, What Then?" *Loss. The Politics of Mourning.* Ed. David L. Eng and David Kazanjian. Berkeley: U of California P, 2003. 467–473. Print.

———. *Precarious Life. The Powers of Mourning and Violence.* London and New York: Verso, 2004. Print.

Champagne, John. "Nietzsche, Autobiography, History." *Journal of Homosexuality,* 34:3–4 (2008): 177–204. Web. 28 December 2107. DOI:10.1300/J082v34n03_10. 17.

Canning, Richard. "Introduction." *Vital Signs. Essential AIDS Fiction.* New York: Carroll & Graff, 2007. xi–xlvii. Print.

Clum, John M. "'The Time Before the War.': AIDS: Memory, and Desire." *American Literature,* 62.4 (1990): 648–667.

Denneny, Michael. "AIDS Writing and the Creation of a Gay Culture." *Confronting AIDS Through Literature. The Responsibilities of Representation.* Ed. Judith Laurence Pastore. Urbana & Chicago: U of Illinois P, 1993. 36–54. Print.

Farris, Wendy B. "1001 Words: Fiction Against Death." *The Georgia Review.* 36.4 (1992): 811–830.

Goldstein, Richard. "The Implicated and the Immune. Responses to AIDS in the Arts and Popular Culture." *A Disease of Society. Cultural and Institutional Responses to AIDS.* Ed. Dorothy Nelkin et. al. Cambridge: Cambridge UP, 1991. 17–42. Print.

Grover, Jan Zita. "AIDS: Keywords." *October.* 43 (1987): 17–30.

Holleran, Andrew. *Ground Zero.* New York: William Morrow, 1988. Print.

Kaufman, David. "Heroes with a Thousand Faces." *The Nation,* March 15, 1993. 347–349.

Kramer, Larry. *Reports from the Holocaust: The Making of an AIDS Activist.* New York: St. Martin's, 1989. Print.

Kruger, Steven F. *AIDS Narratives. Gender and Sexuality, Fiction and Science.* New York & London: Garland, 1996. Print.

LaPointe, Michael. "A Vibrant, Elegiac Novel of the AIDS Pandemic That Shouldn't be Forgotten." *The New Yorker,* January 30, 2018. Web. 30 January 2018. http://www.newyorker.com.

McGlynn, Aine. "Martin and John." *Encyclopedia of Contemporary Writers and Their Works.* Ed. Geoff Hamilton and Brian Jones. New York: Infobase Publishing, 2010. 262–263. Print.

Monette, Paul. *Borrowed Time. An AIDS Memoir.* Orlando: Harcourt, 1988. Print.
Patton, Cindy. *Inventing AIDS.* New York and London: Routledge, 1990. Print.
Pearl, Monica B. *AIDS Literature and Gay Identity. The Literature of Loss.* New York and London: Routledge, 2013. Print.
Peck, Dale. *Martin and John. A Novel.* New York: Farrar, Straus and Giroux, 1993. Print.
Román, David. *Acts of Intervention. Performance, Gay Culture, and AIDS.* Bloomington and Indianapolis: Indiana UP, 1998. Print.
Schulman, Sarah. *The Gentrification of the Mind. Witness to a Lost Imagination.* Berkeley: U of California P, 2012. Print.
Shilts, Randy. *And the Band Played On. Politics, People, and the AIDS Epidemic.* New York: St. Martin's Griffin, 1987. Print.
Sontag, Susan. "The Way We Live Now." *The New Yorker,* Nov. 24, 1986. Web. 4 December 2017. https://www.newyorker.com.
Texier, Catherine. "Loves of a Young Hustler." *New York Times,* February 28, 1993. Web. 7 January 2018. http://www.nytimes.com.
Watney, Simon. *Policing Desire. Pornography, AIDS and the Media.* Minneapolis: U of Minnesota P, 1996. Print.
——. "The Spectacle of AIDS." *October.* 43 (1987): 71–86.
White, Edmund. "Esthetics and Loss." *The Burning Library. Essays.* New York: Knopf, 1994. 211–217. Print.
Woodhouse, Reed. *Unlimited Embrace. A Canon of Gay Fiction, 1945–1995.* Amherst: U of Massachusetts P, 1998. Print.

Realism and the Soul
The Philosophy of Virginia Woolf's Illness

Vira Sachenko

WOOLF AND COMMON LIFE: A REALIST APPROACH

Biographers and critics diverge greatly in narrating Virginia Woolf's illness[1], while psychiatry struggles to define mental illness itself, as well

---

1 | What we know of Woolf's mental history (besides the generous volume of her literary achievements) is shaped into categories brought to our attention not only by psychiatry, but by psychoanalysis, medicine, literature, and Woolf herself. Virginia Woolf has been sexually abused by her half-brother(s) throughout her childhood and youth—events which appear highly traumatic in her recollections. She was said to be genetically predisposed to manic depression (Caramagno 12), although the impact of 'biology' in the psychopathology of this disorder is highly debated. What is fairly consistent, is that she suffered periods of "mania" and "depression" her whole life, meaning at times she was extremely elated, confident, active, prolific to the point of delirium, and, at other times, she felt depleted, was apathetic or sad, and disempowered. These states made her find herself unable to perform daily tasks, confusing things, hallucinating, talking to herself on the street or becoming violent towards people around her. She had a complicated relationship with food (called by many an eating disorder), and complained repeatedly of influenza, fever, sleeplessness, "fidgets", headaches, and muscle pains. Almost all of these symptoms can be and have been explained as appropriate responses to life events, or to socio-political dominance of patriarchy, as well as rebellion against war and imperialism. There have also been sustained efforts to pathologize or simply somatize Woolf's madness and to fit it neatly into a diagnosis. Some, like Perry Meisel, have interpreted some of Woolf's symptoms as "the kind of derealization most familiar clinically, not as psychological, but as partial epilepsy" and suggested that hers was a "strictly somatic disorder" ("Woolf and Freud" 339).

as procedures of diagnosis and treatment (Bolton; Rose)[2]. The disagreements are as diverse as biographers' political beliefs and professional contexts, but the famous Hermione Lee quote, which begins her chapter on madness, informs much of the work published in the last decade, "Virginia Woolf was a sane woman who had an illness" (Lee 171). The difference in calling Woolf's condition an *illness* rather than *madness* or *insanity* is tremendous. Rendered through the prism of early-twentieth century patriarchy, Virginia was seen as a *capricious woman* plagued by *bouts* of *madness*: unusual, threatening behavior, as well as passive phases of sulking in bed, refusing to eat, in other words, a *hysteric*. From the humanist perspective (backed by earlier feminist critiques of psychiatry), Woolf's creative ways were complex: she was in a codependent relationship with her husband, but also a genius—she had a "method to her madness" and thus was not seen as ill (Kenney 184). Since the 1970s, readers informed by psychoanalysis, among others, have offered a legion of explanations that helped to liberate Woolf not just from the sombre labels of *ill* or *mad*, but from the notion that she was somehow *generally* off the course of the *common* reality (Naremore; Meisel; Whiteley; Abel; Zwerdling). A number of authors began to claim that Virginia Woolf was a realist, that there was ground to her inconsistency in her own attempts to describe herself at different times as ill, mad, depressed, melancholic, angry, etc, and that this inconsistency reflected real conflicts not just in Virginia's character, but in society as a whole. All this variety suggests that, in thinking about Woolf's illness, and our own, "[we] do not stand at a unique moment in the unfolding of a single history, but in the midst of multiple histories" (Rose 252).

---

2 | A contemporary psychiatrist following a recent manual, such as *Diagnostic and Statistical Manual of Mental Disorders*, 5th Edition (DSM-5), would invariably diagnose Woolf with a subtype of depression or bipolar disorder. And that, as Derek Bolton rightly points out in his outstanding study, can be both interpreted as "madness"—i. e. a form of deviation from the norm that makes people uncomfortable, and as "illness"—a pathological abnormality that can be physiologically studied and cured (if not at this point in history, then—eventually). In the words of another doctor and researcher, "In psychiatry, diagnostic boundaries are mapped by consensus and fenced off by the criteria published in DSM. Arguing about them is as pointless as arguing about the rules of tennis—one might dispute a particular call, but the rules of the game are there in plain black and white." (Mackinnon)

Faced with the sheer volume and prominence of *symptoms* over time, Woolf has certainly recognized her own states as *common* phenomena, which at times confused and terrified her, and over which, at times, she gained a sense of control, which gave her the confidence to share the insight with her readers. Woolf, being the subject of the contradictory claims of medicine and literature, psychiatry and politics, was profoundly aware of her own and others' capacity to render her condition in any number of ways, including ways that would deny her basic freedoms by depriving her of her already scarce rights as woman and putting her in an asylum, which her husband wisely decided against. She was also aware of the limits her illness presented internally, in practicing these basic freedoms: there wasn't much she could do when she was sick with fever or extremely depressed, and especially not when she was explicitly ordered by doctors to refrain from all her favorite activities. Woolf was highly anxious about the need to make decisions day in and day out, based on ever proliferating opinions on mental illness, her own credibility and capacity to analyze, and what she and those around her called *symptoms*. On the day of her death that decision was suicide; but for the majority of Woolf's life it was struggling on, working through it in writing, trying various *treatment methods* offered by doctors and devising her own[3].

---

3 | There is by now a tradition of interpreting Woolf's writing as therapy, which Hermione Lee warns us not to take too literally, for this would presumably reduce the value of Woolf's writing. Maxwell Bennett suggests that in the last years of her life Woolf has devised a practice of autoanalysis, not too much unlike psychoanalysis. Perry Meisel ("Woolf and Freud") goes even further in suggesting that evidence about Woolf's social circle suggests that she read not just Freud, but was in contact with, and heavily influenced by, Melanie Klein—an issue addressed at length by Elizabeth Abel, who claimed that Woolf was familiar with both Freud and Klein and developed criticisms of both methods. Woolf's diary entries from the 1920s (especially from 1926) show her recording her "states of mind" regularly, trying to trace step-by-step the changes in her moods and the various actions that change them. (*Diary* 3, 112) These are especially prolific in resembling contemporary psychotherapeutic techniques for managing mental illness, such as Dialectical Behavioral Therapy (DBT) which is based on the practice of mindfulness derived from Buddhist thought, but the crux of which is not much unlike Marxist practice, with the key difference in that it is performed by individuals and usually in solitude.

In her 2017 monograph, Pam Morris sets out to demonstrate that Virginia Woolf was a *worldly realist*. Wordly realism[4] "conveys a materialist, non-hierarchical and encompassing perception of existence, a horizontal continuity of self, social world and physical universe" (Morris 5). Morris makes a strong case for reading Woolf as a realist, showing how she drew from both sides of the debate on materialism and idealism contemporary to her. Morris also points to the very important fact that the rigid distinction between realism and modernism has to a great degree been sustained by the "Stalinist era" ideological oppositions in politics, albeit she discounts Georg Lukács' approach as "over-partisan" and his oppositions as unproductive (Morris 9). For Morris, Woolf's realism must be studied not just for the sake of understanding her writing properly, but in order to train our ability to analyze and critique the modern world, in which idealism of the disembodied mind (classically attributed to Woolf also) is still regularly charged with being a condition of possibility for Western imperialism[5], as well as the cause of the climate disaster that is upon us (Moore et al.)

I argue, with Morris, that this intersection of realism and idealism, as well as body and mind, is where we should place Woolf's *soul*, and more specifically her *realist* position. However, rather than downplaying the historical and conceptual complexity of the ideological opposition in politics which Morris attributes to the era of Stalin, I look at the particular approaches to *materialism* of Lukács and Woolf to see if they have retained any of their contemporary urgency. I begin with the very collision which is taken as the nominal source of the problem of Woolf's categorization as a *realist* or a *modernist* writer: of Woolf's notorious mention as a bourgeois thinker by Lukács. Having clarified Lukács's concerns with Woolf and with the approaches he associates with her, I look at Woolf's *treatment of illness* by re-reading her early essays, primarily "Modern Fiction" (1921) and "On Being Ill" (1926). These essays provide some overview of the sophistication of Woolf's writing style—her discourse on *form*—and her

---

4 | To elucidate this term, Morris draws on Roy Bashkar's *critical realism*, as well as Jacques Rancière's *dissensual regime*.

5 | This point, however, is not new. It has been made convincingly (and in direct relation to Virginia Woolf's work) by Meisel *(Absent Father)*. For a different take, see the analysis of imperial ego in *Mrs Dalloway* (181-3), and Weinmann. Even Lukács alludes to this proposition in *The Meaning of Contemporary Realism*.

struggle with mental illness—her ideas about *soul*. I hope to demonstrate, that, in spite of the stark political boundary that is still consistently drawn between the demands of a radical version of the political Left (which is not simply "Stalinist") and liberal democracy (Douroux), Lukács and Woolf had more in common than meets the eye.

What they had in common was a broad philosophical approach to all questions of life, Platonic in its origins, and palpably marked by an interest in the question of the relation between individual and common, singular and typical, particular and universal—a formalism which grew for Lukács into a partisan position, and which brought Woolf to a more aporetic approach to the common life of all. In the language of *revitalizing sociology*, the discord between Woolf's and Lukács' views of mental life have to do with *older* sociology and "can be our guide in helping to identify intersections between sociological and biological attention" (Fitzgerald, Rose and Singh 138). Such attention it afforded here through the concept of *materialism*, which has been associated, at the dawn of the twentieth century, both with biology and sociology, nature and nurture. As Nikolas Rose repeatedly claims in *The Politics of Life Itself* (2007), contemporary psychological materialism has been unjustifiably tied to the organ of the *brain*, and away from the social notions of *environment*. In proposing to look at the challenges of applying Lukács' critique to Woolf's understanding of illness I intend to foreground precisely this essential connection between biology and sociology, psychology and politics, particular soul and collective form.

The Soul as Realist Domain: Lukács' Trajectory

In this late work, *The Meaning of Contemporary Realism*, published in English in 1963, Lukács contradicted the claim that modernist literature is *by definition* anti-realist. For Lukács, all modernist literature was not uniformly flawed, as contemporary renditions of his thought often suggest. Lukács read and borrowed unapologetically from many modernist writers, but he deemed the fragmentation expressed in their persons (souls) and works (forms) to be dangerous. The contradictions of capitalism which expressed themselves in the biological material of human life and sociological material of literary worldviews were to Lukács *real* and *common* to all, and his critique of modernism (as his critique of social realism) had to do with exposing the false premises, pretense of knowledge, and lack of formal understanding that led writers to propose models of human life which were [unnecessarily] limited by experience of the necessarily classed life under capitalism. Lukács deemed the problem of psychopathology to be central to modern literature, inasmuch as he saw literature to be a reflection of human behaviors and ideological attitudes, as well as a guide for future human actions—individual and collective. ("Franz Kafka or Thomas Mann?" 81) He proposed a distinction between realism and modernism which framed the concept of *realism* as a reaction to *angst* (fear or anxiety as a basic condition of modernity, invoked by capitalism, fascism, war, imperialism, etc.). Lukács saw *angst* as a state produced almost universally by alienation from our practical nature as humans, and condemned the modernist response to *angst* as unnecessary amplification, hopelessness, and nihilism. Most importantly, the modernist response to *angst* was unsatisfactory, because it placed ideological limits on the exploration of reality and its properly social dimensions, which Lukács saw to be the only way to truly overcome *angst*.

One such harmful limit was what he called the literary myth of solitude *as eternal condition of man*, which led to the collective normative stance that society was made out of individuals who could never truly understand or support one another. Literature written on the assumption that humans were solitary beings was a problem because it was "complicit with the forces of alienation" (*Soul and Form* 3) [6] Lukács insisted that solitude was (and should be represented in literature as) "a specific social fate, not a universal *condition humaine*" ("Ideology" 20).

Solitude and atomization of individuals (social isolation from each other) were the primary factors of why people found themselves overwhelmed by *angst*, perceiving the world as a chaotic and an essentially hostile place. Lukács was worried that abundant portrayal of hopeless solitary trajectories in literature meant that these portrayals were inevitably being read as conceptions of reality, thus depriving the readers of harboring their social potential: "[...] the modernist writer identifies what is necessarily a subjective experience with reality as such, thus giving

---

6 | Alienation in the most basic Marxist sense: being unable to manage and enjoy life collectively due to the inherent flaws of the property system, which created class divisions that guaranteed the alienation of people from their work, as well as from opportunities for *real* freedom.

a distorted picture of reality as a whole (Virginia Woolf is an extreme example of this)." ("Franz Kafka or Thomas Mann?" 51)

In his analysis, Lukács employed the philosophical distinction between abstract and real potentiality, where potentiality was defined as the spectrum of possibilities—of movements of the *soul*—that was richer than actual life. He also relied on the *developmental model* of character formation in both life and art: "innumerable possibilities for man's development are imaginable, only a small percentage of which will be realized" ("Ideology" 21–2). Both abstract and real potentialities pertained to human existence (and that of literary characters). What distinguished them was whether they actually took place: abstract potentialities were states, experiences and actions we *imagined to be possible*; real potentialities were those that ended up taking place—and thus showed themselves to be *real*.[7] Realist literature, then, needed to "demonstrate both the concrete [i.e. real] and abstract potentialities of human beings. [...] A character's concrete potentiality once revealed, his abstract potentialities [would] appear inauthentic."[8] ("Ideology" 23)

Real humans could not demonstrate a *final* set of real potentialities, for what would seem "authentic" to them at any given moment was bound up completely with the time of their life, stage of their (and collective) development, socioeconomic conditions they were in, i.e. the *environment*. This is why the purported modernist claim that we are, by nature, solitary, to Lukács was not just ideological (an imagined "realism") but unnecessarily limiting: both in reference to our souls—because it prevented us from uniting with others politically and "breaking the chains of capital", and in the context of literature, which was to be a guide of potentialities beyond

---

7 | "Situations arise in which a man is confronted with a choice; and in the act of choice a man's character may reveal itself in a light that surprises even himself" ("Ideology" 22) and "concrete potentiality is concerned with the dialectic between the individual's subjectivity and objective reality" ("Ideology" 24).

8 | This Lukács illustrates with an example from *The Indifferent Ones* by Alberto Moravia, in which the character of Michel makes up his mind to kill his sister's seducer. At this point the potentialities of what is going to happen are abstract—he may kill him, or not, or change his mind. But once Michel proceeds with the murder, the real potentialities are revealed in that "Michel's character emerges as what it is—representative of that kind of background from which, in subjective fantasy, he had imagined he could escape" ("Ideology" 23).

the scope of those imagined by us in the course of our personal experience. This is why bourgeois literature was riddled by false understanding, at the root of which was the belief (the non-truth) that the social whole was composed of 'atoms' of individuals. In spite of possibly having a *tendency* toward egalitarianism or solidarity between those individuals (and, especially, cross-class identification), it would have always to preclude the postulation of the abstract potentiality of the common, and with it also its practical implementation. In Butler's words, Lukács was trying to show (from his earliest work and onwards) that "the soul [was] not a purely interior truth, but comes into its own in the act of expression itself" (4), and that this expression developed in relation and in relationships with other people.

Lukács' critique of modernists like Freud and Woolf was that they subscribed to the faulty version of reality, in which an individual life was not in every way typical of all other life, and in which the principle of realism inherent in dialectical materialism was denied in favor of "naturalism", tendencies, and allegories—reified fragments of reality, all essentially nihilistic and void of [political] truth. This problem was due to the modernist's reliance on the wrong approach to psychopathology (psychology and psychoanalysis), which, in turn, was given credence by the conventions of the European novel: Clearly, this[9] is not strictly a scientific or literary-critical problem. It is an ideological problem, deriving from the ontological dogma of the solitariness of man. ("Ideology" 30)

Lukács drew a stark line between the approaches of Pavlov and Freud. For Lukács, as for Soviet psychiatry, Pavlov's science was characterized by the view that "mental abnormality is a deviation from a norm", while Freud was seen as relying "on understanding of the normal personality in the psychology of the abnormal" ("Ideology" 30). The importance of this difference relied on Lukács' commitment to the Aristotelian concept of man as social animal, which Lukács saw to signify constant dynamic development which transformed "normality" by changing reality. Man was like

---

9 | "This" refers to the difference between the approaches of Freud and Pavlov, a subject that deserves its study. The recent 900-page biography of Pavlov (2014) continues to inspire evocative reviews of the relevant questions (Rossiianov, eng. transl. Seay). For a discussion of the relevant themes of ideology and optimism in the aborted adoption of Freudian psychoanalysis into Soviet psychiatry, see Proctor.

other animals insofar that man learnt and was shaped by the environment; but man was also rational and could use this reason to transform his own reality. Nevertheless, man was a universal category—a type—particular only by way of the context he was shaped by.

According to his rendition of Pavlov's experimental model for human psychology, Lukács saw "mental abnormality" under capitalism as a sign of *protest*. Because he saw their means of protesting as extremely ineffective and hypocritical, he charged the modernists with escapism through their "attenuation of reality" (focus on overwhelming emotions, "ghostly aspects of reality", fragmentation of personality), and thus with failure to provide adequate solutions to the challenges presented by the particular conditions of capitalism ("Ideology" 25–29). Unable to protest meaningfully, modernist writers created characters who were paralyzed by the psychological labels they received or invented for their characters (as well as stuck in experiences which might have given birth to these labels), thus denying the inherently social nature of all human experiences—in their lives *and* in their works.

Pointing out what he considered a blind spot in modernist experiments, he claimed that "with Joyce the stream-of-consciousness technique [was] no mere stylistic device; it [was] itself a formative principle governing the narrative pattern and the presentation of character" ("Ideology" 18). Against Joyce, and Woolf (who was considered to be in the same category), he claimed that the governing principle in place in much modern literature [was] *not* dynamism of the mind—as the stream-of-consciousness form would lead us to believe. Instead, it [was] a *Weltanschauung*, an ideology, or, simply, a worldview, which was static. In other words, while modern literature *seemed* to be dynamic in displaying the various "states" which came one after another in the stream-of-consciousness, as well as in using this device in combination with others, this "worldview" behind it did not change substantially based on these states (*angst* was not overcome by changing the *environment* that created it). This charge was a more totalizing rendition of his 1930's thesis about *Tendenz* literature, in which Lukács accused bourgeois writers of inability to display any kind of true *partisanship* with the proletariat, only, at best, a vague *tendency (Tendenz)*, or aspiration for a more equal existence.[10] Without partisanship, there

---

10 | The problem with *tendency*, according to Lukács, was that it was not based in practice or "real, objective or material production", but in a "morality", an "ought",

would be no transformation (namely, no transformation of underlying property relations), as the initial *Weltanschauung* would be carried over between mind and form, and, most importantly, allow no transformation of each through praxis. Lukács' critique of the modernist *Weltanschauung*, then, was so "over-partisan" because he believed that partisanship with the proletariat was the only way to overcome the *necessary classed* existence of what the modernists saw as *reality*.[11]

EMBODIED SOUL: WOOLF'S REALISM

The contradictions of life which emerged in every field of human activity were well familiar to Woolf, as they are to anybody who tried writing about her, especially on the issues of mental abnormality and madness. However, the way Woolf's name entered the canon of English literature was less ambiguous. Each decade seems to bring a rendition of criticism of Quentin Bell's 1972 biography of Woolf—one of the most influential texts, often cited as a major benchmark in the history of creating the *insane* Virginia. Some credit is due to Bell's initial ambivalence on the subject: he positively announced that he didn't know enough about Woolf's mental illness and garnished the term breakdown with quotation marks, hesitant that this was the right word to describe what happened after her mother's death (Bell 44). However, in a gesture rightly depreciated by nearly all feminist critics, he then proceeded to write perhaps the most famous lines of this biography, "[f]rom now on she knew that she

---

which was an ahistorical distortion, an ideology. ("'Tendency' or Partisanship?" 37) In other words, Lukács was concerned that bourgeois literature was not based in truth (that our lives are socially conditioned), including the social truth of human existence, the horizon of which *could be* something like communism.

11 | The Left's insistence on forging immediate partisanship with the proletariat was a suggestion Woolf vehemently disputed in 1931, in her "Introductory Letter" to a book by Co-Operative Working Women published by the Hogarth Press: "They want baths and money. To expect us, whose minds, such as they are, fly free at the end of a short length of capital to tie ourselves down again to that narrow plot of acquisitiveness and desire is impossible. We have baths and we have money. Therefore, however much we had sympathised our sympathy was largely fictitious." ("Introductory Letter" xxv-xxvi)

had been mad and might be mad again," and rushed to call her illness "cancer[12] of the mind" (Bell 44). Despite intended narrative simplicity, Bell's account of Virginia's last full day alive is an evocative demonstration of the *many* forces and perspectives on her madness that confused Woolf, and found no resolution in biographical writings. Bell attempted to undo these contradictions from the beginning, and proclaimed that "it was a symptom of Virginia's madness that she could not admit that she was mentally ill" (Bell 224). However, instead of producing a basis for this claim, Bell described Woolf's final consultation with a physician, Octavia Wilberforce, as a *demonstration* of Woolf's own identification of her *disorder*. In this encounter, Woolf first said that there was nothing the matter with her but, upon closer inspection, admitted that she was afraid of going mad—and being unable to write *again*—which was usually one of her biggest complaints about feeling unwell. According to Bell, Virginia begged Wilberforce not to prescribe her the hated rest cure[13] and was told that depression was like an appendix: once removed, a scar was all that

---

12 | And what a tremendous insight that could have been! For narrative medicine practitioners and phenomenologists, Woolf's illness may well be compared to cancer, inasmuch as the pain and confusion brought about in the sick body makes equal demands on the receiver of these complaints: to believe the patient (or oneself), to feel solidarity with them before the shared sense of danger that is recognition of mortality (Avrahami 8). For an analysis of the demands cancer makes on the body see Barbara Rosenblum's *Cancer in Two Voices* (1991), quoted in Avrahami (58-69)—the aporias Woolf reached in the descriptions of her states of mind she noted in her diaries are strikingly similar to those of Rosenblum.

13 | Rest cure was a treatment method devised by the American neurologist Dr. S. Weir Mitchell in the 1900s. It was most commonly prescribed to women with severe nervous symptoms, such as hypochondriacs, hysterics, and neurasthenics. Although commonly seen as highly oppressive to women, the rest cure is described as effective for some patients and as one of the "less barbaric" treatment methods used on women at the time. One of the main objectives of the rest cure was to limit the patient's interaction with family members, relationships with which were seen as having a major effect on the development of nervous illness (Bassuk). "Resting," however, also meant being ordered to stay in bed for weeks, avoid all activity, being fed excessively (especially dairy). For Woolf, this meant a ban of all of her favorite activities—walking, reading, writing, and corresponding with friends—which is why she despised such therapy. Perhaps even more importantly, it meant re-establishment of the kind of control over her life from the side of

would remain, unless inflamed by dwelling upon it. Bell does not specify what reaction Virginia had to this statement. The next day, however, Woolf walked into a river with stones in her pockets; her body was found three weeks later.

Bell's effort to narrate the encounter—between Woolf and herself, Woolf and Wilberforce, Woolf and Bell—demonstrates that there was no consensus about Virginia's *madness* (not in the early 1900s, nor posthumously). There was, of course, and still is, some local consensus *within* the specific discourses that have taken up Woolf's life for examination. Psychiatrists have worked with her as a neurasthenic, then a manic depressive, then a bipolar "case". Woolf's own pursuit of making sense of the pain she suffered is documented in her diaries and her literary writing, of which an important devaluation was made for decades, privileging "Woolf's *Diary* (or her manuscripts, for that matter) as the 'authentic' place where the 'real' Woolf can be found, while her other texts [were] seen as the crippled result of compromise and self-betrayal" (Nikolchina 34). But there is no place where the subjects of illness and death are taken up more explicitly and then in one essay. "On Being Ill" is a published attempt to outline the ways in which the affairs of the body and the mind have an immediate and defining impact on us. However, this form is not a mere rendering of Woolf's ideological prejudices; it's an attempt to work through the profoundly social problems which Woolf is concerned with five years prior, in "Modern Fiction".

At the end of *Virginia Woolf and Neuropsychiatry* (2013)—a work that literally reduced Woolf to a *neurochemical self* by claiming to analyze how her brain chemistry defined her life—Maxwell Bennett considers Woolf's use of the word *soul*. He proposes that sometimes Woolf uses it as a pseudo-religious term to refer to an ancient view of the soul as a thing devoid of subjective features which goes underground whilst the body is sleeping or dead (194–5). The second use of the word, for Bennett, is strictly synonymous with the *mind*, which he takes to be an individualizing force forming our inner life, emotions, senses. This allows Bennett to assert later that, "[t]o 'lose one's mind' is usually reserved for those occasions when one's rational abilities are not correctly used, as in the severe depression suffered by Virginia Woolf" (199). Bennett thus credits Woolf,

---

the doctor she would no longer allow at the end of her life, and which she criticized heavily in *Mrs Dalloway*.

"together with Joyce, as pioneering the literary technique of 'stream of consciousness'. It is characterized by a flow of thoughts and images, which may not always appear to have a coherent structure or cohesion. Writers who create stream-of-consciousness works of literature focus on the emotional and psychological thoughts of their characters." (199-200)

Bennett then draws on the history of consciousness in the West to historicize Woolf's "mind" as a "Cartesian product" and as such one that vaguely has to do with the *body* insofar as the body is a vessel through which the impressions reach the *mind*. Bennett's story reflects a common reduction of Descartes and is in fact a characterization of that which in Anglophone literatures is called "Cartesian", but his analysis of Woolf and her mind-body concept is misleading[14]. By identifying the soul with the mind he negates the distinction that Woolf makes over and over again, and one that is crucial to her philosophy. Bennett cites passages from "Modern Fiction" as proof that Woolf was a dualist who believed in the primacy of mind over body. He further implies that Woolf's concept of the mind is reflected in her legacy as a stream-of-consciousness writer. Bennett's citations reflect a popular misconception about Woolf[15], so it is not surprising that he too fails to notice the difference that Woolf draws between herself and Joyce—both in "Modern Fiction", and, more fundamentally, in her reworking of these ideas in "On Being Ill". In talking about Joyce's method of recording the workings of the mind, Woolf *concludes* that,

"[i]t fails because of the comparative poverty of the writer's mind, we might say simply and have done with it. But it is possible to press a little further and wonder whether we may not refer our sense of being in a bright yet narrow room, confined and shut in, rather than enlarged and set free, to some limitation imposed by the method as well as by the mind. Is it the method that inhibits the creative power? Is it due to the method that we feel neither jovial nor magnanimous, but centred in a self which, in spite of its tremor of susceptibility, never embraces or creates what is outside itself and beyond?" ("Modern Fiction" 161-2)

---

14 | For an elaborate analysis of how Woolf's realism is a *critique* of Cartesian philosophy, see Whiteley. Whiteley's claim is that Woolf's improvement on Cartesian philosophy was her outlining of the limits of knowledge. However, "Woolf celebrate[d] triumph of mind over matter" (24).
15 | This was noticed by Naremore already in 1972. (122)

Woolf here is not attacking Joyce personally, the "poverty of the writer's mind" pertains to everyone, including herself. To her, not only is the form of the stream-of-consciousness novel limited (as Bennett understood it, and as Woolf described *Ulysses*, and what she means by "the method"), the mind itself is. Moreover, as James Harker demonstrates, the mind is not only limited, it is very often, in Woolf's work, wrong in its judgments. The mind becomes "centered in a self" and produces little beyond itself (or what it *already* knows as real). Naremore thus describes the technique as claustrophobic and connects it thematically with Woolf's preoccupation with being "egotistical"—a complaint she often had for herself and others. (123)

This oscillation—between this selfishness, or privacy, and unity, or communion with others who always already surround one, egotistical or not—is rendered by Naremore as the key tension in Woolf's life and work. This tension is manifest in the "'screen-making' habit of human personality" which, according to Woolf, "probably" preserves our sanity (Naremore 134). Although this "screen-making" is contradictory to seeing "the thing itself", it is "a device of shutting people off" and a way to not "dissolve utterly" (Diary 3: 104). Perry Meisel contributes to this study by analyzing the Woolfian "self" as the process of *ascesis*, a complex procedure of temporarily capturing certain "territories" of the world as pertaining to that "self" which nevertheless always remains tentative, virtual, without thick boundaries (*Absent Father* 112–3, 121). When this self is forced into the condition of permanence by total identification with it, it becomes a condition of ownership, property, or capture of capital (173). Such identification is intoxicating (204), because it provides a sense of wholeness within a reality that is fractured, contradictory, and in which many versions of it collide (211). According to Meisel, Woolf learns this theory from reading Walter Pater (her second "father" whose work she studied a great deal and whose name barely figures as a reference in her records). She then falls into its very traps:

"For Woolf [...] literature is common ground because it allows her to trespass and expropriate without paying the price in unacknowledged influence [of her real father, Leslie Stephen, and her symbolic father, Walter Pater, as well as of everything and everyone else of which her experience was composed]. It allows her to seize and colonize a territory not properly her own and so build on it a 'new house' [...]. In Woolf's hands, the tools of [world']s power are also the tools of its disassemblage, even though they are, paradoxically, the tools of her new and greater power [as a literary and a feminist authority]." (*Absent Father* 242)

Clearly ambivalent about the harshness of his own conclusions, Meisel asserts that the lack of agreement between Woolf's late works, after all, "forbid[s] us to believe any moment in Woolf's career to be more conclusive than another." (*Absent Father* 243) Incidentally, this is precisely Woolf's critique of the mind and the literary technique associated with capturing it.

To return to Lukács' terminology, the mind produces a *Weltanschauung* when its position is not in common relation with—the "body", and the minds and bodies of others (or of other times), to the flux of the world in common. Although *spiritual* is the word Woolf uses to speak of Joyce, it seems to have not been picked up by the canon of literary theory on Woolf. Pam Morris points this out, as she explains that Woolf took

"the oppositional terms 'materialists' and 'spiritualists' from her father's usage. Leslie Stephen refers to materialists as those subscribing to the doctrine that matter is the ultimate reality, while spiritualists, he defines as those that believe the mind is the only reality. In other words, spiritualists subscribe to idealism, a mode of thought to which Woolf is largely hostile." (57-8)

Woolf knew, just like Lukács (especially the young Lukács of *Soul and Form*), that life happened beyond the mind, and beyond form. However, she criticized both the *idealism* and the *materialism* of her time for their ideological prejudice. Like idealism, materialism was an overly neat approach. Materialism failed to let life "live" in it with all its inconsistencies. Woolf wrote, of Arnold Bennett's fiction: "There is not so much as a draught between the frames of the windows, or a crack in the boards" (MF 158). Life's variety and inconsistency could not be fully contained in materialist approaches to realism, because "materialists [...] spend immense skill and immense industry making the trivial and the transitory appear the true and the enduring" (MF 159). In other words, materialism failed to accommodate the knowledge of change and difference—the *realities* of *other* times and places, and lacked universality. Of H. G. Wells, Woolf wrote:

"He is a materialist from sheer goodness of heart, taking upon his shoulders the work that ought to have been discharged by Government officials, and in the plethora of his ideas and facts scarcely having leisure to realise, or forgetting to think important, the crudity and coarseness of his human beings." (MF 159)

Here, again, materialism was inadequate because it was (at least in the work of H. G. Wells) utopian, and did not account for the existing procedures at work in society (like governments to whom the power to make political decisions was allocated), as well as the limitations of existing human beings which were vivid and obvious to Woolf (their "crudity and coarseness"). This reformist perspective certainly undermined the property claims of revolutionary hypotheses (such as Lukács') but it also underscored the effects Lukács too saw and attributed to primitive accumulation: that reality of the class and labor divisions shaped minds in ways that were *crude* and *coarse*. What distinguishes Woolf was *how* she thought about these psychopathological distinctions and *why* she found them crucial in the development of a *common* reality (if such was to be possible).[16]

In the end, Woolf asserted, there was no one method of capturing life. A writer must "have the courage to say that what interests him is no longer 'this' but 'that': out of 'that' alone must he construct his work. For the moderns 'that', the point of interest, lies very likely in the dark places of psychology." (MF 162) What is crucial to see is that Woolf doesn't identify with *these* moderns. For her, English fiction had much to learn from Russian: "If we are sick of our own materialism the least considerable of their novelists has by right of birth a natural reverence for the human spirit" (MF 163). Surely idealizing Russian literature, Woolf, however, admired "the inconclusiveness of the Russian mind" (which was unlike the "English mind") and suggested that "unquestionably they see further than we do and without our gross impediments of vision" (MF 163). She concluded with a proposal to draw from both traditions (and their comparison). But she insisted on the necessity to focus not on devising methods, or even experiments, but on writing about *everything* that exists: "everything is the proper stuff of fiction, every feeling, every thought; every quality of brain and spirit is drawn upon; no perception comes amiss." (MF 164)

---

16 | "In Woolf's fiction, moments of shared being lead to dissolution of the competitive and individualistic self." (Morris 200) However, it is not clear, whether this communion can go on beyond 'moments'.

Learn she did, from Russian writers in general, and specifically from "Gusev," the 1890 short story by Anton Chekhov, which Woolf cited in "Modern Fiction" in her critique of the modernists' obsession with the mind. Reading Chekhov helped Woolf to think about the *common* mortality of all, regardless of class, rank, political or religious persuasion, or form of political activism. Above all, "Gusev" was for Woolf a meditation on the non-human qualities of nature and on the fraudulence of the very distinction between *man* and *nature*. Chekhov's realism accounted not only for human life and conquest, but for illness, misery, and death, after which human bodies were dumped overboard "like a carrot or a radish" without this being comic or tragic, only "vague and inconclusive" (MF 163). Chekhov's realism was refreshingly unheroic, and presented "the horizon much wider from his point of view" (Woolf qtd. in Rubenstein 62).

Smuggling Chekhovian narrative devices into English literature, Woolf made them the property of the mind in the form of "On Being Ill". She translated Chekhov's formally transgressive (MF) short story into the already canonically inconclusive essay form. Instead of multiple identifiable characters and omniscient narration, she focused on rendering singular trajectories against the backdrop of group phenomena, specifically the trajectories of bodies that become "ill" against the military conformity which was most relevant to her time. This allowed her to think not only about the sociological issues like the First World War and the epidemic of the Spanish Flu that followed it (as well as wiped out at least one fifth of the world's population) (Hindrichs), but about the less obvious relationships between the singular perspectives inherent in illness and the demands of society. Accordingly, Woolf also worked through her own contradictory responses to Chekhov's fiction, which she admired equally in its seemingly opposing tendencies. On the one hand, Woolf was keenly interested in Chekhov's exploration of the solitary journeys of individuals suffering from ensuing mental and physical distress resulting from their social isolation and emotional deprivation, which served to "reinforce Woolf's conviction that it is impossible to truly know another person" (Rubenstein 67–8). On the other hand, Woolf considered Russian literature (and specifically Chekhov) to have an expansive effect on the English heart, such that dissolves boundaries (between individuals) and helps [us] become democratic, "if to love the poor and hate the rich is democratic" (Rubenstein 178).

ILLNESS, MATERIALISM AND COMMON LIFE IN "ON BEING ILL"

Faithfully reforming English literature in the image of Chekhov, Woolf attempted to show that (modern) literature's concern was not solely with the mind, and that the body was not "a sheet of plain glass through which the soul look[ed] straight and clear, and save for the two passions such as desire and greed, [was] null, and negligible and non-existent" (*On Being Ill* 4). The soul, an entity composed of body and mind, was alive and incapable of being captured fully by any form. Nevertheless, form could conceivably capture a rendition of this problem. Woolf laid out just this in "On Being Ill": when mental or bodily capacities were inhibited, the soul's movements would be defined by this limitation also, sometimes privileging imaginative faculties of the mind over the experiences of the body, and vice-a-versa. Thus, the mind could become "a slave" to the wars of the body, its possibilities rendered through the difference experienced by the body, making the sufferer unable to think about things in ways they did when they were well. At the same time, when the body is restrained in movement (due to illness or some other limit or vulnerability), the mind could roam freely and explore the possibilities of the soul which frequently go unnoticed in the body's usual rhythm. Woolf's insistence on the psychically disabling experiences of illness makes it extremely easy to read this essay as one equating *mind* (which is 'spirit', moment, a state) with *soul* (which is personality, the composite of body and mind), thus falling into the same "Cartesian" trap Bennett describes. But the journeys the mind makes, exploring its "virgin forests" and "snowfields", are still embodied ("[a]ll day, all night the body intervenes"), even if its journey lacks the usual "pretence" of life in health. (*OBI* 4; 11–2)

In "On Being Ill", fever and melancholia have equal corporeal effect. Woolf uses the two interchangeably[17] as signifiers of illness. *Mental* illness is equated with the *physical*. Although one appears to one in the *mind* and the other is felt strongly in the *body*, they both disrupt the body's movement in a certain direction. The metaphors Woolf uses in this essay reflect this dynamic. Those unbothered by illness are "the upright", an "army" "marching" to "battle". Illness, however, prompts a spatial shift,

---

17 | See, for instance, "[t]hose great wars which the body wages with the mind a slave to it, in the solitude of the bedroom against the assault of fever or the oncome of melancholia, are neglected" (5).

a turning away from, "deserting", "raising [their] feet", "floating on the stream", "looking around", "looking up", "lying recumbent" (*OBI* 12–13). This is how Woolf understood the embodied mind, not a mind that ruled a body which "is a sheet of plain glass through which the soul looks straight and clear" and was negligible (*OBI* 4), but a mind that was extended into its hands and feet, and a subject to the challenges that came upon them: "the unending procession of changes, heat and cold, comfort and discomfort, hunger and satisfaction, health and illness, until [...] the inevitable catastrophe; the body smashes itself to smithereens, and the soul (it is said) escapes." (*OBI* 5) Here, as elsewhere, the soul is nothing more than a placeholder for this relationship between the *body* and the *mind* (the idealist/spiritualist insights into reality and the materialist ones), another word to mean identity, character, spirit, subjectivity.[18]

For Woolf, the soul's full potential was always to remain unknown, the mind was only able to imagine some of it and the body could test the reality of this imagination. However, against Bennett, this potential was not the religious hope of the afterlife or some idea that the soul goes under ground at night, but precisely the opposite: a unity of everything and everyone in life, boundaryless, and "democratic". Further, this democratic potential, as well as its solitary recognition, are written in physical metaphors, suggesting a profoundly material dimension of both social isolation and the idea which Pam Morris terms *wordly realism*—that horizontal unity of all in which each may become vulnerable and isolated (199).

"On Being Ill" begins by implicating the reader in the shared experience of being ill in Woolf's use of "we" as the main pronoun on the first pages, as in "we are so frequently forced to think of [illness]" (*OBI* 3). The use of the "we" demands identification from all, but this is hardly an ideological generalization, as both the category of illness and the experience itself is undoubtedly universal. However, soon after these initial pages, the pronouns change, with the focus shifted onto the "body", singular, or "it", signaling that each instance of illness is a potential for a *particular development*. She also utilizes the singular "body" to speak of human experience in general: being embodied, being ill, wanting connection, etc, but each narration of the experience of embodiment is written from the point of

---

18 | Or, as Woolf attempts to designate the same thing in a character elsewhere, "quiver, life, soul, spirit, whatever you are of Minnie Marsh" ("An Unwritten Novel" 58) and "the creature *within*" (*OBI* 4; emphasis mine)

view of a singular body. In Lukács' terms, Woolf generally refers to illness as a real possibility for everyone—we all can and will get sick at one point or another, because we already know ourselves to have been sick as we know the general human vulnerability to illness. Becoming ill is both an abstract and a real possibility for everybody.

The particular experience of *a* soul (namely exclusion, othering, desertion, exile—whatever words we use to narrate this difference) is seen as a real possibility because Woolf herself has learned it through experience (praxis): by becoming ill herself as well as by being referred to as mad. But these experiences are also seen as abstract possibilities for souls in general, because Woolf has undergone them herself. It was real for Woolf that her undeniably classed experience of illness prompted her (and allowed her the time) to pick up on this particular form of *memento mori*—the contemplation of non-human things. It was also a feature of this particular reality that allowed Woolf to read Chekhov and to reflect on the matters of nature and human democracy, and to come to the understanding that to describe everything that is, including the moral indifference of nature was a way to contextualize human action within that indifference.[19] In this way, Woolf postulated a reality that was not only intersubjective, but undeniably not known as common—not just in the sense of property relations that defined it, but in terms of lack of common grounds on which all experiences would be verifiable directly (Whiteley 148), or on which a common language of illness could be devised *(OBI)*. Skeptical not only of Cartesian assumptions about the power of introspection (Whiteley 155), Woolf was strongly aware of the limitations of the narratives of progress inherent in Lukács' model of human development (and of the proposal to understand illness as a beginning of a revolutionary sequence[20]). For Woolf, our mor-

---

19 | We can read "On Being Ill," via "Modern Fiction" and Chekhov, as an attempt to think about the indifferent reality of nature, of plants and rocks and the sky, within which human passions and desires find a place and allow us to get caught up in our plans and projections. In foregrounding the ambivalence of the ill body toward the affairs of civilization, Woolf also develops her view of reality as such in which Anthropocentric ambition will always be conquered. (*OBI* 16)

20 | Meisel goes as far as to suggest that the composition of the self (specifically, of Mrs Dalloway) "is the result, not of a sure and natural process of development, but a discipline and curtailment that makes the 'parts' given to Clarissa in time past cohere and harmonize" with the help of a mirror. (*Absent Father* 171)

tality and vulnerability were also our individualizing features, such that they could disable, disincline, dissuade from common life for reasons that were deeply material and environmental, but which made identification with someone different from oneself entirely imaginary. In her "Introductory Letter" to the collection by co-operative working women she grapples precisely with this problem of understanding: "[...] we tried in the Guild Office that afternoon to explain the nature of fictitious sympathy and how it differs from real sympathy and how defective it is because it is not based upon sharing the same important emotions unconsciously" ("Introductory Letter" xxix).

Like Lukács, Woolf believed that consciousness (and reality) were class-specific. Unlike him, she considered this "barrier [...] impassable" in her lifetime (even though the democratic unity was ultimately desirable), precisely because such redistribution was precluded by the difference that shaped the souls of the rich and the poor. (Introductory Letter xxviii–xxix). With Lukács, we can read the realism of "On Being Ill" as an expression of Woolf's *subjective* experience, i.e. the sense that she herself did not find the conditions under which to create meaningful collectivity or, as she puts it, to receive true sympathy from other human beings. However, instead of postulating her subjective experience as *reality* (as Lukács suggested she did) Woolf was aporetic precisely about the individual boundaries that precluded the co-creation of a common reality:

"That illusion of a world so shaped that it echoes every groan, of human beings so tied together by common needs and fears that a twitch at one wrist jerks another, where however strange your experience other people have had it too, where however far you travel in your own mind someone has been there before you—is all an illusion. We do not know our souls, let alone the souls of others. Human beings do not go hand in hand the whole stretch of the way." (*OBI* 11-2)

For Woolf, illness was the experience that revealed her *embodied* difference from all other beings, and afforded her solitude in this difference, her "desertion" of common desires and goals.[21] Illness was transformational.

---

21 | As well as those structures of being that otherwise oppress us. For example, Jane Salisbury suggests that, for Victorian women, for whom illness was often one of the rare opportunities for solitude, privacy, and freedom, it was also a *perverse chance to develop oneself*: "The ill female body, neutered by the sickroom, is

It brought "spiritual change" (*OBI* 3) and made "the world change [...] its shape" (*OBI* 8). However, this uprooting[22] wasn't necessarily initially willed or even intended (as is the case with Lukács' proposal that the modernists *protest*), nor did it happen through knowledge or certainty about the world. In the privacy and solitude of her bedroom and her soul, she had enough *rashness* to become an *outlaw* (*OBI* 22), targeting one screen (boundary, separation of the common) at a time.

Works Cited

Abel, Elizabeth. *Virginia Woolf and the Fictions of Psychoanalysis*. Chicago, The U of Chicago P, 1989. Print.
American Psychiatric Association. "Bipolar and Related Disorders." *Diagnostic and Statistical Manual of Mental Disorders: DSM-5*. 5th ed., Washington DC: 2013. 123–54.
Avrahami, Einat. *The Invading Body: Reading Illness Autobiographies*. Charlottesville: U of Virginia P, 2007. Print.
Bassuk, Ellen L. "The Rest Cure: Repetition or Resolution of Victorian Women's Conflicts?" *Poetics Today*, vol. 6, no. 1/2, 1985, pp. 245–257. www.jstor.org/stable/1772132.
Bell, Quentin. *Virginia Woolf: a Biography*. London: The Hogarth Press, 1990. Print.
Bennett, Maxwell. *Virginia Woolf and Neuropsychiatry*. Berlin: Springer, 2013. Print.
Bolton, Derek. *What is Mental Disorder? An Essay in Philosophy, Science, and Values*. New York: Oxford UP, 2008. Print.
Butler, Judith. "Introduction." *Soul and Form*. Ed. John T. Sanders and Katie Terezakis. New York, Columbia UP, 2010. Print.
Caramagno, Thomas C. "Manic-Depressive Psychosis and Critical Approaches to Virginia Woolf's Life and Work." *PMLA* 103.1 (1988): 10–23.

---

liberated from the aggressive desires of men, the clinging demands of motherhood, and the oppressive conventions of Victorian and Edwardian mores." (61)
22 | The "ancient oaks" (*OBI* 3) are an abstract enough metaphor that they don't have to signify anything in particular, except *some* kind of rooted materiality which becomes uprooted in illness—be it neural connections, class relations, or the patriarchy.

Chekhov, Anton. "Гусев" ["Gusev"]. *Полное Собрание Сочинений и Писем*. [*The Complete Edition of Works and Letters*], vol. 7, Ed. Vadim Ershov, 2006. Web. 6 January 2018. http://az.lib.ru/c/chehow_a_p/text_0070.shtml.

Douroux, Philippe "Alain Badiou: 'I hold firm to the communist hypothesis'...Laurent Joffrin: 'Which no one wants anymore.'" *Verso Blog*, Web. 20 December 2017. https://www.versobooks.com/blogs/3544-alain-badiou-i-hold-firm-to-the-communist-hypothesis-laurent-joffrin-which-no-one-wants-anymore.

Fitzgerald, Des, Nikolas Rose, and Ilina Singh. "Revitalizing Sociology: Urban Life and Mental Illness Between History and the Present." *The British Journal of Sociology* 67.1 (March 2016). Web. 6 January 2018. doi:10.1111/1468-4446.12188.

Harker, James. "Misperceiving Virginia Woolf." *Journal of Modern Literature* 34,2 (2011): 1–21. Web. 8 January 2018. www.jstor.org/stable/10.2979/jmodelite.34.2.1.

Hindrichs, Cheryl. "Virginia Woolf and Illness." *Virginia Woolf Miscellany* 90.1 (Fall 2016): 44–48.

Kenney, Susan M., Edwin J. Kenney, and Jr. "Virginia Woolf and the Art of Madness." *The Massachusetts Review* 23.1 (1982): 161–85.

Lee, Hermione. *Virginia Woolf*. New York: Knopf, 1997. Print.

Lukács, György. "Ideology of Modernism." *The Meaning of Contemporary Realism*. London: Merlin P, 1979. Print.

——. "Franz Kafka or Thomas Mann?" *The Meaning of Contemporary Realism*. London: Merlin P, 1979. Print.

——. "'Tendency' or Partisanship?" *Essays on Realism*. Ed. Rodney Livingstone. Cambridge, Mass.: MIT P, 1980. Print.

Mackinnon, Dean F. "The 'Hard' and 'Soft' Phenotypic Boundaries of Bipolar Disorder." *Psychiatric Times* (2016). Web. 17 September 2016. http://www.psychiatrictimes.com/special-reports/hard-and-soft-phenotypic-boundaries-bipolar-disorder/page/0/1.

Meisel, Perry. *The Absent Father: Virginia Woolf and Walter Pater*. New Haven, Yale UP, 1980. Print.

——. "Woolf and Freud: the Kleinian Turn." *Virginia Woolf in Context*. Eds. Bryony Randall and Jane Goldman, Cambridge: Cambridge UP, 2012, 332–341. Print.

Morris, Pam. *Jane Austen, Virginia Woolf and Worldly Realism*. Edinburgh, Edinburgh UP, 2017. Print.

Moore, Jason W. Ed. *Anthropocene or Capitalocene? Nature, History, and the Crisis of Capitalism*. Oakland, PM Press, 2016. Print.

Naremore, James. "A World without a Self: The Novels of Virginia Woolf." *NOVEL: A Forum on Fiction* 5.2 (1972): 122–134.

Nikolchina, Miglena. "Born from the Head: Reading Woolf via Kristeva." *Diacritics* 21. 2/3 (1991): 30–42. Web. 7 January, 2018. www.jstor.org/stable/465189.

Proctor, Hannah. "'A Country Beyond the Pleasure Principle': Alexander Luria, Death Drive and Dialectic in Soviet Russia, 1917–1930." *Psychoanalysis and History* 18. 2 (June 2016): 155–82. Web. 7 January, 2018. doi:https://doi.org/10.3366/pah.2016.0187.

Rose, Nikolas. *The Politics of Life Itself: Biomedicine, Power, and Subjectivity in the Twenty-First Century*. Oxford, Princeton UP, 2006. Print.

Rosenblum, Barbara. *Cancer in Two Voices*. Spinsters Book Company. 1991. Print.

Rossiianov, K. "Ivan Pavlov and the Moral Physiology of Self." Trans. N. Seay. *Kritika: Explorations in Russian and Eurasian History*. 18.1 (2017): 203–209.

Rubenstein, Roberta. *Virginia Woolf and the Russian Point of View*. New York: Palgrave Macmillan, 2009. Print.

Salisbury, Jane. "'The Borderland between Life and Death': The Spatial Politics of Illness in *The Years*." *Virginia Woolf Miscellany* 90 (Fall 2016): 61–63.

Weinmann, Michael. *Language, Time, and Identity in Woolf's The Waves: The Subject in Empire's Shadow*. Lanham, MD: Lexington Books, 2012. Print.

Whiteley, Patrick J. *Knowledge and Experimental Realism in Conrad, Lawrence, and Woolf*. Baton Rouge, Louisiana State UP, 1987. Print.

Woolf, Virginia. "An Unwritten Novel." *Monday or Tuesday*, New York: Harcourt, Brace and Company, 1921, 45–70. *HathiTrust*. Web. 10 February 2018. https://hdl.handle.net/2027/mdp.39015001800351.

——. *Introductory Letter. Life as We Have Known It*. Ed. Margaret L. Davies, New York, W. W. Norton & Company, 1975. Print.

——. *The Letters of Virginia Woolf*. Ed. Nigel Nicolson and Joanne Trautmann. London: The Hogarth Press, 1978. 6 vols. Print.

——. *Moments of Being*. Ed. Jeanne Schulkind. St. Albans: Triad/Panther Books, 1978. Print.

——. *The Diary of Virginia Woolf.* Ed Anne Bell. New York/London: Hogarth Press, 1980. 5 vols. Print.
——. "Modern Fiction." *The Essays of Virginia Woolf,* edited by Andrew McNeillie, vol. IV, London: The Hogarth Press, 1994, 157–65.
——. *On Being Ill by Virginia Woolf with Notes from Sick Rooms by Julia Stephen.* Ashfield, Massachusetts: Paris P, 2012. Print.
Zwerdling, Alex. *Virginia Woolf and the Real World.* Berkeley, U of California P, 1986. Print.

The Illness Is You
Figurative Language in David Foster Wallace's Short Story "The Planet Trillaphon"

Anita Wohlmann

In David Foster Wallace's first-person short story "The Planet Trillaphon As It Stands in Relation to the Bad Thing" (1984), an unnamed, twenty-one-year-old, highly eloquent, Brown University student tries to convey what "severe clinical depression"—the "Bad Thing"—is really like (28–29). He reports several anecdotes, which illustrate the gravity of his condition, before he stops his account and delves into an elaborate description of what it means to suffer from depression. In this descriptive section, he first refers to established similes, such as the sensation of drowning, suffocation under a glass jar, or falling into a black hole that has no ground. Then, he suggests his own set of comparisons that feel more apt to him. "To me it's like being completely, totally, utterly sick" (29), he maintains. He locates the feeling of sickness in the stomach as a sense of nausea and then spreads this comparison across the entire body: "your feet, the big muscles in your legs, your collarbone, your head, your hair, everything, all just as sick as a fluey stomach" (29). He continues: "Imagine that every cell in your body, every single cell in your body is as sick as that nauseated stomach. Not just your own cells, even, but the e.coli and lactobacilli in you, too, the mitochondria, basal bodies, all sick and boiling and hot like maggots in your neck, your brain, all over, everywhere, in everything. All just sick as hell." (29) The narrator pushes the microscopic view further and invites his readers to join him on the imaginative ride through the "funhouse orbitals" of the human body (29). In a next step, he elaborates on how "the Bad Thing" attacks the body's defense mechanisms by sabotaging the sick person's voice and legs, making it impossible to call for help or run away. The disease is "open-ended" (29). Eventually, the narrator ends his imaginative journey through the human body when he reaches the culmination of his comparisons in the equation of self and sickness: "you're the Bad Thing yourself! The Bad Thing is you. Nothing else: no bacteriological infection or having gotten conked on the head with a board or a mallet when you were a little kid, or any other excuse; you are the sickness yourself. It is what 'defines' you." (29) Similar to a dramatic denouement, the narrator comes full circle at the end of the segment when he returns to the three initial similes: "there is no surface to the water [...] you bonk your nose on the jar's glass and realize you're trapped [...] you look at the black hole and it's wearing your face" (29–30). Eventually, the narrator closes the descriptive excursion, acknowledging that his explanations do not protect him from feeling that the Bad Thing is reaching out for him. He then returns to his account of the events that have sent him to the Planet Trillaphon—the metaphor he chooses to describe the effects of the anti-depressant he takes after a failed suicide attempt.

A number of figurative devices operate in "The Planet Trillaphon." Similes and synecdoches are used when the illness is described via source domains such as the glass jar or the hole or the human body. In moving from body part to body part, the narrator uses synecdoches when he asks a fictive 'you' to imagine that every single nauseated bodypart stands in for the whole body that is afflicted by illness. Moreover, established metaphors, such as 'illness is war', are the basis for the narrator's self-description as a "troubled little soldier" (27). He also uses metaphors when he likens his experience of being on an anti-depressant with being away from "good old Earth" and living on a different planet (26). The spatial distance between the planet Trillaphon and earth describes the emotional detachment the narrator experiences when he is on drugs. Personification, one might argue, is used when the illness is called the "Bad Thing." The capitalization turns the simple words into a proper name, and together with the repeated use of the Bad Thing as a noun, it is suggested that the illness is a living being that acts, to some extent, on its own. Similarly, when the black hole is imagined having "vague teeth in it" or "wearing your face" (28, 30), the hole, i.e. the illness, is personified. The face is also a pars pro toto of the entire person. Thus, when the hole is imagined to wear the person's face, the hole and the person are one. Personification and synecdoche, in a way, prepare the full equation of the illness with the person. Such identifications of illness and patient have been problematized, among others, by Susan Sontag (1978) and Paula Treichler (1999), who have highlighted the dangers that are involved when the socio-cultural features associated with an illness (such as HIV/AIDS, cancer or tuberculosis) are mapped onto and equated with a patient's personality. Siri Hustvedt has argued that the full identification between illness and self is particularly prominent with neurological and psychiatric illnesses (7). Whereas people *have* cancer, they *are* schizophrenic or bipolar (7). Drawing on the work of Katherine Staiano, linguist Suzanne Fleischman argues that the possessive "I have"-construction posits illness as an external object, thus creating distance between patient and pathology (8–9). The "I am"-construction, however, is an existential statement in which a pathology is incorporated as part of a suffering individual (8). Such an identification with an illness is often felt to be very real. Problematically, it may increase patients' isolation, sense of otherness and failure, as well as their likelihood for self-blame.

In this essay, I want to explore the use of figurative speech, more particularly the move from comparison (as in simile and metaphor) to equation or identification (as in synecdoche) by focusing on the relational nature between the two things that are brought together: target domain and source domain.[1] Relationality is crucial, on the one hand, on the level of figurative speech itself: Consisting of source and target domain, metaphor, simile, and synecdoche draw on notions of sameness, similarity, contiguity, difference and gaps. The relational nature between source and target is thus a crucial criterion in understanding the potentials and dangers of using figurative speech in describing and explaining illness. On the other hand, relationality is also significant on the level of the specific situation or context in which a figure of speech is embedded: Who speaks to whom? Which intentions are involved? And what is the relationship between speaker and listener, narrator and reader? In "The Planet Trillaphon," the figures of speech are used by a narrator, who addresses a fictive reader; and they are interpreted by real readers. This relation between figurative speech and narrative context suggests narrative theory as a crucial tool in analyzing figurative speech. However,

---

1 | Source and target are the prevailing terms in cognitive metaphor theory (Kövecses; Lakoff/Johnson). Other terms for the domains are vehicle and tenor (coined by I. A. Richards), primum comparandum and secundum comparatum (used in rhetoric), or donor domain and recipient domain (translated from Harald Weinrich's notion of "Bildspender" and "Bildempfänger").

such an approach is often met with hesitations in narrative theory where researchers have been reluctant to incorporate figurative devices, such as metaphors, because they are difficult to place within narrative paradigms (Fludernik "The Cage Metaphor"). At the same time, there is a tradition of research that considers the boundaries between metaphor and narrative to be more porous than the disciplinary separation of metaphor theory and narrative theory suggests.² After all, it seems quite obvious that metaphors are often embedded in narratives and that some metaphors—such as life is a journey—may even project mini-narratives of their own.³ (As my wording signals, metaphor is often used as an umbrella term that encompasses simile, metonymy, synecdoche and personification.)

It thus seems appropriate to take into account both the relational nature that is constitutive of figurative speech as well as the relation to the narrative, in which figures of speech are embedded. In doing so, my argument on the relational quality of metaphors follows Martha Stoddard Holmes, to whom metaphors and similes (and by extension metonymies or synecdoches) are neither inherently good nor bad. Metaphors and the relationships they create

"have the potential to become relationships of hierarchy or exploitation: perhaps the tenor drives the vehicle (imagine Pavarotti in a Maserati); he is simply using it.

---

2 | Paul Ricoeur, for example, published *The Rule of Metaphor* (1975) and the three volumes of *Time and Narrative* (1983, 1984, 1985) as separate research projects, but he claims in the first volume of *Time and Narrative* that they actually form a pair and were conceived together (ix). Also, see the work of Hanne; Biebuyck/Martens; Fludernik ("The Cage Metaphor", *Beyond Cognitive Metaphor Theory);* Ritchie.
3 | A variety of terms are presently circulating, which conceptualize this link between metaphor and narrative. Eubanks speaks of mini-narrations which metaphors can unfold (the relationship between metaphor and narrative is mainly one of licensing); Ritchie analyzes metaphorical stories, in which several metaphors are linked via a story, which then functions as a vehicle that is mapped on a target, the speaker's story; Musolff explores how metaphors in politics are developed into scenarios; and to Biebuyck and Martens metaphors can unfold as paranarratives parallel to an underlying epinarrative. Musolff's notion of metaphor scenarios probably comes closest to what Wallace is doing, but Musolff's "scenario analysis" is based in critical discourse analysis and is directed towards cognitive metaphor studies.

But not always: at the same time, the vehicle may carry the tenor where it wants. There is the potential for mutuality, as well, and the potential for ethical consequences." (Holmes 270)

To better understand the power and limits of figurative speech, an approach that combines metaphor theory with narrative theory offers a rich, critical vocabulary, as I aim to demonstrate in the following analysis.

My approach in this essay is based on a larger research project on narrative-based metaphor analysis. Elsewhere, I explore how narrative criteria, such as characterization, space, and tone can inform metaphor analysis. Here, I will focus on irony, focalization, you-narration and narrative structure to suggest that, alongside metaphor theory, narrative theory may enhance our understanding of the role of figurative speech in relation to the body and illness. In this essay, I will first explore the narrator's use of figurative speech from the perspective of metaphor theory before I will expand this scope and analyze how particular narrative devices complicate the meanings and functions of the figures of speech. In this sense, this paper and my larger project are a response to the call for "metaphoric literacy" (Holmes 272) and "metaphor competence" (Hanne 227) in the field of Health Humanities.

Before I start, I want to provide some context to David Foster Wallace's short story and clarify my approach. "The Planet Trillaphon" was Wallace's debut as a writer. He wrote the story as a student at Amherst College, studying philosophy and avidly reading postmodern writers, such as Thomas Pynchon and Donald Barthelme. The story was published in the Amherst Review, a year after Wallace had withdrawn from school for the second time to get treatment for his depression. The autobiographical background of "The Planet Trillaphon" and the many similarities between the narrator and Wallace's life suggest a reading of the story as an illness narrative or "autopathography" (Hawkins). Wallace's biographer D.T. Max fuels such a conflation of author and narrator when he finds that "the authorial 'I' and the 'I' of the narrator parallel each other in the story in a way they would never again in Wallace's fiction" (*Every Love Story* 34). However, it is difficult to determine Wallace's relation to his first launch into (creative) writing. Max suggests that Wallace may not have been very proud of this early story or may have found it "too revealing" (*Every Love Story* 310 n9), given that Wallace never republished "The Planet Trillaphon," as he did with his other stories. Max adds that, in the early 1980s, Wallace had not yet decided which career he wanted to pursue, whether he wanted to dedicate his full attention to philosophy or to literature. The story may have been a trial balloon. Given this uncertain context of the story, I use a close reading approach to focus on the formal qualities of the narrative. While I do think that the story can also be productively read as an insightful illness narrative that offers us access to the experience of severe clinical depression and other psychiatric symptoms and diseases (such as hallucination, bipolar disorder and depersonalization),[4] my focus in this essay is the role of figurative speech in relation to illness, hoping that an emphasis on the formal qualities of the text and the combination of metaphor theory and narrative theory will make a theoretical contribution to the field of Health Humanities, where the focus on narratives has been strong and metaphors have enjoyed an ambivalent reputation, ranging from critical rejection and skepticism to the embracement of metaphor's ambiguity in caring for the sick (e.g. Sontag; Hutchings).

FROM SIMILARITY TO SAMENESS:
SIMILE, SYNECDOCHE AND FULL IDENTIFICATION

For my analysis, I will focus on a segment of six paragraphs in the middle of "The Planet Trillaphon" (pages 28 to 30), in which the narrator tries to explain the Bad Thing. The section is remarkable for several reasons: it is replete with different forms of figurative speech, it introduces a second-person narration (which is practically absent from the rest of the story), it seems to pause the sequence of events conveyed in the preceding and following paragraphs and, in this freezing of narrative time, the section resembles a description, an introspection or commentary. Despite the lack of narrative events, the segment unfolds a form of narrative drive given the way in which the narrator imaginatively moves through several source domains as if he progressed from one micro setting or space to the next. The segment also illustrates a progression from simile to synecdoche to full identification. In this sense, the segment seems to have a culminating point, namely the moment when the illness is fully equated with the sick

---

4 | In fact, I have used the story repeatedly in narrative medicine courses with medical students and professionals as well as with students of literature studies.

person, which is the ultimate impasse or trap in the narrator's explanation of what it means to suffer from depression.

Let me first clarify the terminology. Metaphor, simile, metonymy, and synecdoche share an important characteristic: they refer to one thing by way of another. Similes and metaphors draw on likeness and transfer characteristics from one domain (the source) to another (the target). Crucially for metaphor and simile, source and target may share similarities, but they are fundamentally distinct. In other words, a source domain (such as war) may have features that are comparable with the target (illness), but the relationship is one of similarity only, not of sameness. Metaphor and simile are different in one significant aspect: similes use linguistic indicators, such as "like" or "as," when they explain one thing by way of another. For example, while "illness is war" is a metaphor, "illness is like war" is a simile. In a metonymy, the relationship between the two domains is one of contiguity and association: When we speak of the White House (source) instead of the American government or the people who work in the White House, we refer to the White House as a thing that is closely associated with the American government or the president. The source can be used as a stand-in for the target. In a synecdoche, the source can also be a stand-in, but the relationship between source and target is different: the source is part of the target domain. For example, a wheel is part of the whole car, and the expression "she is just a pretty face" (Whitsitt 73) uses the face as a pars pro toto for the entire person. A synecdoche can also make the reverse movement and use the whole for a part, for example when we refer to America but only mean the United States. Metaphor theory has become the field with the most comprehensive research on figures of speech, which is why I will sometimes refer to metaphors as a kind of umbrella term that encompasses simile, synecdoche and metonymy. In metaphor theory, synecdoches are often treated as a subcategory or special case of metonymy, but this approach has been challenged. For example, Samuel Porter Whitsitt argues that a lumping together of synecdoche and metonymy erases the important feature of difference and contiguity in metonymy (74)—a criterion that seems of particular relevance for illness experiences.[5]

---

5 | Fleischman, for example, mentions the common parlance in health care when a patient is referred to as "the gall bladder in room 312," which problematically reduces the patient to a body part and directs the treatment toward the "synecdochic sign" (21-22). Similarly problematic are, according to Fleischman, the uses

This distinction of the terminology is crucial for the way in which the troubled little soldier in the short story deals with his predicament. When the narrator presents and elaborates three well-known metaphors (water, jar, hole), he starts out with similes, as for example when he quotes

"some people [who] say it's like having always before you and under you a huge black hole without a bottom, a black, black hole, maybe with vague teeth in it, and then your being part of the hole, so that you fall even when you stay where you are (...maybe when you realize you're the hole, nothing else ...)." (28-29)

In this simile, the illness is defined by way of selected features that are transferred from the source, the hole, which is dark, bottomless and undetermined (and potentially unlimited) in its spatial dimensions. Hole and illness, at this stage, are entirely different entities. But the hole is also ascribed human features, such as teeth, and, at the end of the segment, the hole is "wearing your face" (30). With this personification, target and source domains are modified: it is no longer the illness that is described, but the person who is ill. The inanimate hole morphs into a hole with human features. Thus, the personification is interwoven with a synecdoche, namely the suggestion that the person—the narrator or the 'you'—is "part of the hole" (28). The dissimilarity between source and target—the hole and the illness/person—has disappeared; target and source have become one entity and "the Bad Thing just absolutely eats you up" (30). Hole, illness and person have become identical.

A similar move from difference to sameness, from comparison to identification, occurs when the narrator suggests a source domain of his own choice, namely single body parts that are nauseated. "[A]ll just as sick as a fluey stomach" is clearly a simile, but as the description progresses, it is less and less clear if the references to sick body parts still fulfill the central criterion of a simile, namely the transfer of features from a source domain that is different from the target. In fact, the singular body parts are not different from the target, i.e. the person. Thus, when the narrator goes through each body part—"your feet, the big muscles in your legs, your collarbone, your head, your hair" (29), and then moves

---

of metonymy. She speaks, for example, of "metonymic contamination" or "guilt by association" when "characteristics of a disease or affected body part transfer to the patient as an individual" (e. g. a "lazy muscle"; 20).

beyond the skin into the body's interior, the microscopic elements of cells, molecules and atoms—all of these sick singular parts of the body belong to a human being. Together, the single sick parts form a human being, and the sickness of each part seems to add to and exacerbate the sickness of the whole. Again, the move from simile to synecdoche prepares the final movement, which is the equation of sickness with self: "you are the sickness yourself. It is what 'defines' you" (29). In this final movement, source and target become interchangeable because they are considered the same: "you're the Bad Thing yourself! The Bad Thing is you" (29). The identification is complete.

One might argue that this conflation is less a matter of full identification than a form of literalization: What was originally meant to be figurative assumes a literal, material quality. For example, to some patients, it may feel utterly real and consistent with their experience that HIV/AIDS is a punishment from God (Sontag; Treichler). Following this line of thinking, what has been a metaphor originally, namely a way to explain something unknown and abstract by referring to something entirely different which seems more graspable, has lost its figurative function. The source has become structured by the target, which is a process that has occurred in conventionalized metaphors, such as when we speak of the legs of a table. The figurative nature of the comparison is no longer transparent, and the fundamental difference between source and target seems to have disappeared. Whereas this process is relatively unproblematic for the legs of a table, there are more serious implications with regard to illness. The physician Abraham Verghese (2004), for example, who worked with HIV patients in the 1980s, is convinced that metaphor can kill: "I lost two of my patients to suicide at a time when the virus was doing very little harm to them. I have always thought of them as having been killed by a metaphor, by the burden of secrecy and shame associated with the disease." (n. p.)

As Verghese's example illustrates, the full identification with illness can imply that the social and cultural ascriptions, values and norms that are associated with a figure of speech take on a material reality. Holmes defines the potential danger in terms of appropriation and colonization which occur when source and target do not remain visible and transparent through a lexical indicator. In her distinction of metaphor and simile, Holmes quotes Julie Carlson who maintains that "simile teaches us 'to perceive in relation not to is, which conflates identities, but likeness'"

(271). Adapting Holmes' phrasing, a person with an illness thus may be like a black hole or like a drowning swimmer or like a Bad Thing—but is still him- or herself (271). However, "you're the Bad Thing yourself" and the subsequent "The Bad Thing is you" (29) erases all difference and postulates sameness instead of inviting us to consider a similarity. The individual becomes appropriated by and subjugated to the illness. Therefore, as Holmes argues, "metaphors, in equating two things, have the potential for colonization through conceptualization" (271). In fact, as I have demonstrated above, "the illness is you" is not a metaphor, but the point Holmes makes about the erasure of difference and the danger of appropriation and colonization seems applicable nonetheless. The consequences of moving from simile to full identification thus have an ethical dimension, involving questions of power, hierarchy and the restriction of options and alternatives. What Doty defines as the tentative quality of figurative speech, namely its nature as an "act of inquiry (not an expression of what we already know)" suggests that metaphor proposes to see something in a different or new way (79–81), is replaced by a prescriptive or normative statement about what is or what is supposed to be. Whitsitt raises a similar point when he speaks of "the violence of synecdoche" in comparison to metonymy (74). Synecdoches illustrate a "desire to make Two things, One," a "desire to reduce Two to One" (74). While Whitsitt ascribes the notion of desire to researchers who treat synecdoche as a special case of metonymy, I find the wording suggestive because it draws attention to the relational dimension of figurative speech (and, as a matter of fact, all language). Thus, following Holmes and Whitsitt distinctions, some types of figurative speech, such as metaphor or synecdoche, may be more problematic than others. However, as I see it, each type of figurative speech can be put to different uses, which may be invitational or prescriptive, tentative or commanding, expanding or limiting options.[6] What is crucial is the context and how the relational nature of metaphor is understood.

---

6 | For a number of neurological diseases, the inability to identify the source as distinct from the target can also be symptomatic of cognitive diseases and can thus serve as a diagnostic tool (Reuber et al.). Similarly, in Elizabeth Outka's analysis of actualized metaphors in literary texts (where ghosts are not understood as metaphors of past traumas but appear as literal and real), such literalized metaphors are a symptom of psychological trauma (255). Healing then lies in restoring the ability to recognize the figurative dimension of the comparison (267).

Full identification with an illness therefore need not be problematic. It may be the result of having integrated an illness into the story of one's life. For Siri Hustvedt, who suffers from migraine and a mysterious shaking disorder, full identification with her illness implies that she has become "curiously attached" to her migraines (189): "I cannot really see where the illness ends and I begin; or, rather, the headaches are me, and rejecting them would mean expelling myself from myself" (189). For Hustvedt, her illness is thus not (or no longer) a mysterious Other or a hostile invasion from outside. "The shaking woman," as she has labelled her affliction, moves from the third person into the first person and becomes a part of the self. Full identification is thus not necessarily a symptom or a problem to be overcome, but the potential result of an attempt to live with a chronic disease. From this perspective, full identification may foreground a collaborative relationship between self and illness, and need not imply erasure or closure.

And yet, in "The Planet Trillaphon," full identification with the illness indicates the destructive nature and terrible consequences of depression. The narrator struggles to integrate the illness into his life, to understand it and communicate about it. His narrative illustrates the devastating and harmful nature of his disease, in which full identification and the erasure of difference between self and illness is a symptom of the disease. This point is further emphasized when the narrator, in the section following his attempt to describe the Bad Thing, relates the events that led to his suicide attempt. When the narrator travels home to his parents for the holiday season, an accident occurs during the bus ride for which the bus driver is fully responsible. Injured and afraid of losing his job, he starts crying, and the narrator cannot help but relate to the bus driver's predicament.

"I felt unbelievably sorry for him, and of course the Bad Thing very kindly filtered this sadness for me and made it a lot worse. It was weird and irrational but all of a sudden I felt really strongly as though the bus driver were really me. I really felt that way. So I felt just like he must have felt, and it was awful. I wasn't just sorry for him, I was sorry as him, or something like that. All courtesy of the Bad Thing." (30)

This collapsing of boundaries between the narrator and the bus driver, the full identification between two separate entities, is, from a medical perspective, a warning sign of the narrator's alarming condition. Dr. Kablumbus, the narrator's doctor, says afterwards "that's when the Bad Thing really got [the narrator] by the balls" (31). The narrator can no longer distinguish between himself and the other, and this hyper-empathy, the fact that he truly seems to feel the other's pain, misleads him to make a terrible mistake: When he tries to help the bus driver, the narrator secretly places money and marijuana in the bus driver's pockets. Later, he realizes that this clumsy effort will very likely exacerbate the bus driver's desperate situation. But there is no going back. The damage is done. At home, the narrator pulls "about three thousand electrical appliances" into his bath tub. He survives and is sent to "the Troubled Little Soldier Floor" (31).

Aside from reading this scene as a symptom of the narrator's illness, as Dr. Kablumbus does, or as a dramatic moment in the downward spiral of narrative events, we can also understand it as a comment on the dangers of over-identification, of ignoring difference and assuming sameness in the (mis)use of figurative speech. As the anecdote suggests, identification and empathy can lead to false projections and a problematic appropriation of the Other's experience (Whitehead 5). It can also be based in "a narcissistic or even imperialistic assumption of identity between the self and the storytelling Other" (Fitzpatrick 198). If we lose our distance, if we feel as someone else, our tunnel vision makes us believe to know what is best for the Other. Thus, the story expands the problem of full identification from the level of figurative speech (i.e. between source and target, self and illness) to the relationship between self and other. We may wonder about our relationship with the narrator and his plight. How are we to position ourselves towards the narrator? And how does the narrative shape our involvement as readers?[7] What is at stake when we identify with the narrator?

Narrative Contexts

"The Planet Trillaphon" embeds the narrator's numerous figures of speech within a narrative that is full of irony and a type of language that produces ambivalent effects. The narrator describes himself as "not incredibly glib"

---

7 | For the sake of simplicity, I will not distinguish here between real readers and fictive readers, even though this is another, possibly productive dimension to consider in combining metaphor theory and narrative analysis.

compared to the "very glib guy on the television" who used the underwater metaphor to describe depression. However, the narrator's impressive articulateness and eloquence, which he likes to showcase throughout the story, proves the opposite (28–29). The narrator's ironic, sarcastic tone also seems to ridicule the actual severity of his situation and produces an odd notion of detachment and incongruity. When he speaks of his suicide attempt, for example, he belittles the gravity of the situation and speaks of a "very silly incident" or a "really highly ridiculous incident" (26). He summarizes his distressing experiences of crying, nausea and hallucination as "all this extremely delightful stuff" (28), and when he talks about the horrifying experiences of hallucination, he comments "Weird, weird, weird" (26) or wonders "Boy oh boy, how the heck is the Bad Thing able to do this?" (29). In speaking ironically about deeply unsettling experiences, he seems to hold them at a distance, trying to not let them overwhelm him emotionally. Irony appears as a means of self-protection. The difficulty to position ourselves in our relation to the narrator is amplified by the narrator's linguistic register, which sways between an impressive eloquence that reflects his intellectual capacities and an extensive use of colloquial language, juvenile expressions ("Holy cow!") and pop-cultural references. The narrator's use of language[8] may increase identification and attachment or may result in estrangement and detachment, depending on the readers' age, cultural context and personal tastes. This double nature of the narrator's diction thus produces a paradoxical effect. On the one hand, the narrator's use of colloquial language makes him more approachable; he appears at eye level. On the other hand, we may wonder if we ever really come close to him. After all, instead of giving us his name, he describes himself as a "troubled little soldier" (27), a metaphor that is touching but also belittling and mocking, refusing to unveil his identity and acknowledge the severity of his situation. Thus, we encounter a narrator who appears as a clever, self-reflexive person, who does not settle for simple answers; but we may also wonder about how much we can and should trust him.

---

8 | According to D.T. Max, this use of language in "The Planet Trillaphon" is typical of Wallace's style, which he would develop throughout his career. Wallace "conjured the world in two-hundred-word sentences that mixed formal diction and street slang, technicalese and plain speech; his prose slid forward with a controlled lack of control that mimed thought itself" ("The Unfinished" n. p.).

In other words, the narrative situation raises doubts about the narrator's reliability. This sense of skepticism or suspicion is increased by the use of internal focalization. The story's "psychological centre" is a first-person narrator (Nünning and Nünning 118), who has confessed to us in the beginning of the story that he suffers from hallucination. It is through the focalizer's particular filter of perception and consciousness that we experience and learn about the events and reflections (Nünning and Nünning 118). Focalization foregrounds a particular way of seeing the world and thus echoes the function of metaphor which Mark Doty describes as "a form of self-portraiture" and as a "perceptual signature, a record of an individual way of seeing" (79–80). Focalization, similar to metaphor and simile, thus constructs an alignment between the reader and the narrator's perception. One might even argue that in conveying a metaphor through a focalized perception, the "perceptual signature" of both narrative situation and figurative speech are intensified.

The second-person narration that is so prevalent in the segment under discussion produces a crucial double effect: The you can be understood as relating either to the narrator himself or to the reader. For example, when the narrator maintains "I had previously sort of always thought that depression was just sort of really intense sadness, like what you feel when your very good dog dies" (28), he seems to be speaking to himself, thus conjuring up a kind of split or second identity. In this sense, "the *you* covers up for an *I* of the protagonist in the grip of narrative experience" (Fludernik, "Second Person Fiction" 222; original emphasis). Following Ursula Wiest-Kellner, the you narration may emphasize the otherness and isolation of the protagonist (qtd. in Schwibbe 208). But the second-person narration also seems to address the reader, especially when he uses imperative verbs: "Imagine your whole body being sick like that: your feet, the big muscles in your legs, your collarbone, your head, your hair, everything, all just as sick as a fluey stomach. Then, if you can imagine that, please imagine it even more spread out and total" (29). In combining the second-person address with imperative verbs ("Imagine"), the narrator trespasses the boundaries of the text. He establishes a dialogic communication with the (fictive) reader and, simultaneously, makes this addressee into an "actant," who "instantiates an existential bond with his or her former (discourse) self, positing a subjective verisimilar identity between the address-you and the protagonist-you" (Fludernik, "Second Person Fiction" 221–222). The narrator and fictive reader thus blend into a hybrid diegetic creature (Wiest-Kellner qtd. in Schwibbe 208).

Focalization, second-person narration and imperative verbs produce an ambivalent effect on our relationship with the text. On the one hand, we are invited to follow the narrator's imaginative journey through several source domains and pars pro totos. We are asked to imagine, body part after body part, what it would mean if each of them were sick. In doing so, the narrator's invitation to imagine resembles visualization techniques used, for instance, in autogenic training, biofeedback and autosuggestion. Thus, when the narrator zooms from outer space and from his detached position into the molecular sphere of his body to describe the utter sense of sickness and desperation that has befallen every atom of his body and self, this imaginative movement may suggest a similar mental journey performed by the reader, who is pulled deeper and deeper into the chasms of despair, making it difficult to stay distanced and detached. On the other hand, the use of the second-person narration also invokes a meta-discourse and thus the opposite of immersion, namely detachment and critical distance (Wiest-Kellner qtd. in Nünning and Nünning 116). In pulling down the fourth wall (Konstantinou 91), we become aware of our function as readers and we can self-reflexively consider our position towards the claims made in the text. Thus, similar to the use of irony, focalization and second-person narration invoke contradictory effects on the quality of our relation and identification with the narrator.

The structural composition of the segment under discussion is also noteworthy. The imaginative journey through the body is framed by three metaphors the narrator has picked up elsewhere—water, the glass jar, and the black hole. They appear at the beginning of the section and the narrator returns to them at the end of his attempt to define the Bad Thing. The section thus comes full circle and appears complete and whole. The three similes signal that we have come to the end of an epistemological journey that aims at explaining and understanding what the illness is and feels like. And yet the journey is not over for the narrator who "can feel it [the Bad Thing] reaching out for me, trying to mess with my electrons. But I'm not on Earth anymore" (30). On the formal level, we might have reached the end of the journey, but the open-endedness of the illness itself undermines any sense of closure. The struggle to communicate what depression is and feels like will continue. This notion of impossible closure is intensified at the ending of the short story: The narrator tells us about his suicide attempt and his commitment to a mental hospital, where he meets a girl, May, with whom he falls in love. She dies in a car accident soon after, which sends the narrator into yet another crisis. He explains why he changed the name of his antidepressant ("Tofranil") to "Trillaphon" and elaborates on the side effects of the drug.[9] He then maintains: "Being far away sort of helps with respect to the Bad Thing. Except that is just highly silly when you think about what I said before concerning the fact that the Bad Thing is really." (33)

The story ends mid-sentence (and at the bottom of the page). In refusing to provide closure and in withholding a sense of unity or wholeness, we are confronted with a blank space. This gap is crucial in many ways. It suggests that there is no sufficient or satisfying explanation or description of the experience of depression. The ending leaves things open and flexible and holds the reader in suspense. When I read the story for the first time, I remember that I flipped pages, returned to the electronic pdf file and started searching online—convinced that I was missing a page, that there had to be a proper ending. Similarly, when I taught the short story, my students kept asking me if I had mistakenly given them an incomplete document. This moment of uncertainty, the longing for a proper ending, and the gradual realization how accustomed we are to this narrative convention, increases, as I believe, the power of the story as it makes us reflect on our default positions and desires for closure and wholeness. Thus, we can read the ending and the gap it leaves as a meta-textual comment on the problems involved in erasing gaps—an issue that is negotiated on several levels of the story: on the level of the figures of speech, when self and illness have become one; on the level of the characters, when the narrator overidentifies with the bus driver; and on the level of the reader's relationship with the work, when the story's use of irony, focalization, you-narration and closure invite ambivalent relations and involvements with the text, its narrator and overall topic.

---

9 | Tofranil is an existing antidepressant. Trilafon is also an FDA-approved drug (a type of Perphenazine), which is used in the treatment of psychoses, involving symptoms such as hallucinations, nausea, and vomiting (see https://en.wikipedia.org/wiki/Perphenazine).

Conclusion

A key term in my analysis has been the relational nature between source and target, illness and self, between the characters in the text and between narrator and reader. I have suggested that "The Planet Trillaphon" is a rich story that illustrates the ambivalences involved when similarity and difference turn into identification and sameness, when the otherness of a source domain or person is no longer acknowledged or recognizable. The text itself critically reflects on these issues and we are invited to challenge the identifications that occur in the text and between text and reader. Analyzing the story from the double perspective of metaphor theory and narrative theory raises awareness for the multiple possibilities of relating to figurative speech, its meanings, interpretations and uses. Even though "the illness is you" does not seem to leave much space for choice, distance or difference, the narrative in which this equation is embedded emphasizes the relational, collaborative act involved in understanding figurative speech.

Donald Davidson elaborates on this notion of collaboration in metaphor interpretation. He also highlights the imaginative potential of language and figures of speech. To Davidson,

"[m]etaphor is the dreamwork of language and, like all dreamwork, its interpretation reflects as much on the interpreter as on the originator. The interpretation of dreams requires collaboration between a dreamer and a waker, even if they be the same person; and the act of interpretation is itself a work of the imagination. So too understanding a metaphor is as much a creative endeavour as making a metaphor, and as little guided by rules." (qtd. in Garber 240)

While there might be no rules in metaphor interpretation, there are useful concepts and approaches, as I have tried to show, that can guide our understanding and open up alternative interpretations and meanings. They can be helpful to tease out the fundamental wrongness that lies at the heart of comparing two distinct entities. After all, every metaphor or figure of speech is, to some degree, false because metaphor consists in a "calculated absurdity" of the act of comparison (Strub qtd. in Zimmermann 74). It is an inherent contradiction that strikes us in a metaphor and that produces its defamiliarizing effect. Therefore, to the novelist and essayist Walker Percy, metaphor "asserts an identity between two different things. And it is wrongest when it is most beautiful" (Percy 81–82). Metaphors thus rely on disobedience to reason, on mistake and absurdity, and on the inherent instability of language and meaning (Garber 253). Even if difference is eliminated through an equation of source and target, the equation carries "a kind of intentional or motivated solecism: a mistake or a crime elevated to a position of rhetorical power" (Garber 240). I have argued here that, when difference is erased and full identification appears inevitable, one of the options we have is to pay attention to the contexts in which a metaphor or figurative speech is embedded and the ways in which this context may challenge full identification and help reinstate difference. Narrative devices, such as irony, unreliability, focalized perspectives and a narrator's self-reflexivity, can shed a new light on the fundamental absurdity of metaphor and, in doing so, they provide a "distancing aspect" which gives us a choice in our interpretation (Doty 80).

The example that I have analyzed here is a (possibly) fictional or semi-fictional account and therefore, one might argue, the narrative components are more elaborate than they would appear in ordinary speech or in a medical report. Elsewhere, I have used this narrative-based approach to metaphor in my analysis of an illness narrative, namely Arthur Frank's *At the Will of the Body*, in order to show how narrative analysis can be helpful to understand how established yet problematic metaphors, such as the "illness is war" metaphor, are challenged and creatively reimagined (Wohlmann, forthcoming). Margaret Morganroth Gullette's research is dedicated to reveal and resist the absurdities of the identification of age with decline, an equation that leads her to argue that ageism literally kills people. Physician and literary scholar Rita Charon provides an intriguing example of a non-literary account of a doctor-patient encounter, in which both figurative speech and narrative play a central role in understanding the patient's body. Charon summarizes an hour-long consultation with a patient who came to her with inexplicable and incongruous physical symptoms. Charon's summary of the encounter focuses on a number of different source domains—for example, a network of unrelated bodily symptoms, illness as an alien invasion—which Charon and her patient explored and tested as a means to understand the young man's experiences and to find a solution to his pain. The patient's body is compared to a metal tube or a garden or "a *most* mysterious and powerful instrument, rather like a renaissance harpsichord" (39; original emphasis). After having described some of the metaphors, Charon emphasizes the subjective, focalized perspective of her summary, stressing self-reflexively that "it may have been *my* impress" or "it comes to me now as I write" (38–39; original emphasis). Charon thus presents the metaphors as an invitation, an inquiry into what both patient and doctor do not know. She asks her patient to consider different comparisons by proposing to imagine a range of source domains. Given that the metaphors are embedded in a subjective account and based in a relational and collaborative endeavor between patient and doctor, none of these metaphors can be final. And yet and quite understandably so, the underlying desire to channel disparate, incongruous symptoms into One solution or One diagnosis is clearly present in the account, and eventually the illness is described as "some kind of migraine equivalent" (38). Unfortunately, we are not told in this short account if the patient's symptoms ceased or if the migraine medication helped. Closure, in Charon's account, is provided on a different level—the patient feels heard and understood—which is rendered to us through the perspective of a doctor who experiences, in response to the patient's comment, a "combination of exaltation and consummation" and a feeling of "having achieved something" (39). We are told that the patient gave permission to publish the account, but we are given only sparse information on the temporal dimensions that are involved. What happened after six weeks when the patient was supposed to return to the clinic? Which effect did the medication and explanations have? The point of these questions is that, in addition to the narrative devices I have studied in Wallace's short story, the role of time and its potential impact on the use of figurative speech is another, potentially important element to consider in a narrative-based metaphor analysis. We know that some of Charon's metaphors occurred in communicating directly with the patient, others suggested themselves later when she rewrote her notes and tried to understand what had happened. From the suggestion that the patient's body might be a communication device which is "telling him something he otherwise could not know," Charon retrospectively comes to think of the patient's body as a "renaissance harpsichord" when she rewrites the notes for the article (39). This subtle shift in the source domain—from embodied communication instrument to a music instrument from the Renaissance—has distinct temporal dimensions and we may wonder about the additional questions that the source domain raises: Who plays the harpsichord? Which piece is performed? Who is the composer? And, how does the harpsichord sound? Is it tuned?

As I mentioned earlier, researchers in the field of metaphor theory and Health Humanities have called for metaphor literacy and metaphor competence and this appeal seems particularly pertinent when figurative speech is used in relation to illness and the body. In Health Humanities, narrative is a dominant approach even though it has been challenged by researchers who have pointed to the limits of narrative in relation to, for example, chronic pain, dementia and traumatic experiences, which resist coherence, linearity and (happy) endings (Strawson; Garden; Woods; Belling; Wasson). Narrative, however, also enables fragmented, nonlinear stories that refuse closure and that self-reflexively point to the limits of narrative. Therefore, it seems crucial to continue to explore approaches that productively join narrative analysis with non-narrative forms of expression, such as figurative speech.

Acknowledgments

This paper was conceived as part of the research project "Body and Metaphor: Narrative-Based Metaphor Analysis in Medical Humanities" at Johannes Gutenberg University Mainz (JGU), funded by the German Research Foundation (grant no. WO 2139/2–1), and as part of the research program "The Uses of Literature" at the University of Southern Denmark (SDU), funded by the Danish National Research Foundation (grant no. DNRF127). I want to thank my colleagues at the "Uses of Literature" group and at JGU (particularly Prof. Dr. Matthias Michal as well as the students of medicine, psychotherapy and American studies) with whom I have discussed the story and this article and who have made me aware of important details. I also want to acknowledge two of my students, Alexander Popp and Jorina Charvat, who wrote inspiring term papers on Wallace's short story in the winter term 2015/2016 at JGU.

Works Cited

Belling, Catherine. "A Happy Doctor's Escape From Narrative: Reflection in *Saturday*." *Medical Humanities* 38.2 (2012): 2–6.

Biebuyck, Benjamin and Gunther Martens. "Literary Metaphor between Cognition and Narration: *The Sandmann* revisited." *Beyond Cognitive*

Metaphor Theory: Perspectives on Literary Metaphor. Ed. Monika Fludernik. London: Routledge, 2011. 58–76. Print.

Charon, Rita. "The Novelization of the Body, or, How Medicine and Stories Need One Another." *Narrative* 19.1 (2011): 33–50.

Doty, Mark. *The Art of Description: World into Word.* Minneapolis: Graywolf, 2010. Print.

Eubanks, Philip. "The Story of Conceptual Metaphor: What Motivates Metaphoric Mappings?" *Poetics Today* 20.3 (1999): 419–42.

Fitzpatrick, Kathleen. "Infinite Summer: Reading, Empathy, and the Social Network." *The Legacy of David Foster Wallace.* Eds. Samuel Cohen and Lee Konstantinou. Iowa City: U of Iowa P, 2012. 182–207. Print.

Fleischman, Suzanne. "*I am ..., I have ..., I suffer from ...*: A Linguist Reflects on the Language of Illness and Disease." *Journal of Medical Humanities* 20.1 (1999): 3–32.

Fludernik, Monika. "Second Person Fiction: Narrative *You* as Addressee And/Or Protagonist." *AAA – Arbeiten aus Anglistik und Amerikanistik* 18.2 (1993): 217–247.

——. "The Cage Metaphor: Extending Narratology into Corpus Studies and Opening it to the Analysis of Imagery." *Narratology in the Age of Cross-Disciplinary Narrative Research.* Eds. Sandra Heinen and Roy Sommer. Berlin: de Gruyter, 2009. 109–128. Print.

——. Ed. *Beyond Cognitive Metaphor Theory: Perspectives on Literary Metaphor.* New York/London: Routledge, 2011. Print.

Garber, Marjorie. *The Use and Abuse of Literature.* New York: Anchor Books, 2011. Print.

Garden, Rebecca. "Disability and Narrative: New Directions for the Medical Humanities." *Medical Humanities.* 36.2 (2010): 70–4.

Gulette, Margaret Morganroth. *Ending Ageism, or How Not to Shoot Old People.* New Brunswick: Rutgers UP, 2017. Print.

Hanne, Michael. Ed. *Binocular Vision: Narrative and Metaphor in Medicine.* Spec. issue of *Genre: Forms of Discourse and Culture* 44.3 (2011): 223–423.

Hawkins, Anne Hunsaker. *Reconstructing Illness: Studies in Pathography.* Second Edition. West Lafayette, Ind.: Purdue UP, 1999. Print.

Holmes, Martha Stoddard. "After Sontag: Reclaiming Metaphor." *Binocular Vision: Narrative and Metaphor in Medicine.* Ed. Michael Hanne. Spec. issue of *Genre* 44.3 (2011): 239–61.

Hustvedt, Siri. *The Shaking Woman: A History of My Nerves.* London: Hodder and Stoughton, 2011. Print.

Hutchings, Deanna. "Communicating with Metaphor: A Dance with Many Veils." *The American Journal of Hospice and Palliative Care* (September/October 1998): 282–4.

Kövecses, Zoltán. *Metaphor: A Practical Introduction*. Oxford: Oxford University Press, 2010. Print.

Konstantinou, Lee. "No Bull: David Foster Wallace and Postironic Belief." *The Legacy of David Foster Wallace*. Eds. Samuel Cohen and Lee Konstantinou. Iowa City: U of Iowa P, 2012. 83–112. Print.

Lakoff, George and Mark Johnson. *Metaphors We Live By*. Chicago/London: U of Chicago P, 1980. Print.

Max, D. T. "The Unfinished." *The New Yorker* 85.4 (March 9, 2009). Web. 15 January 2017. https://www.newyorker.com/magazine/2009/03/09/the-unfinished.

——. *Every Love Story is a Ghost Story: A Life Of David Foster Wallace*. New York: Penguin, 2013. Print.

Musolff, Andreas. *Political Metaphor Analysis: Discourse and Scenarios*. London: Bloomsbury, 2016. Print.

Nünning, Vera, and Ansgar Nünning. *An Introduction to the Study of English and American Literature*. Stuttgart: Klett, 2014. Print.

Outka, Elizabeth. "Dead Men, Walking: Actors, Networks, and Actualized Metaphors in *Mrs. Dalloway* and *Raymond*." *Novel: A Forum on Fiction* 46.2 (2013): 253–274.

Percy, Walker. "Metaphor as Mistake." *The Sewanee Review* 66.1 (1958): 79–99.

Reuber, Markus, Chiara Monzoni, Basil Sharrack and Leendert Plug. "Using Interactional and Linguistic Analysis to Distinguish Between Epileptic and Psychogenic Nonepileptic Seizures: A Prospective, Blinded Multirater Study." *Epilepsy and Behavior* 16 (2009): 139–144.

Richards, Ivor A. *The Philosophy of Rhetoric*. 2nd ed. London/New York: Oxford UP, 1967. Print.

Ricoeur, Paul. *The Rule of Metaphor: Multi-Disciplinary Studies of the Creation of Meaning in Language*, Trans. Robert Czerny. Toronto/Buffalo: U of Toronto P, 1977. Print.

Ricoeur, Paul. *Time and Narrative.Vol. 1*. Trans. Kathleen McLaughlin and David Pellauer. Chicago: U of Chicago P, 1984. Print.

Ritchie, L. David. *Metaphorical Stories in Discourse*. Cambridge: Cambridge UP, 2017. Print.

Schwibbe, Gudrun. *Erzählungen vom Anderssein: Linksterrorismus und Alterität*. Münster: Waxmann, 2013. Print.
Sontag, Susan. *Illness as Metaphor and AIDS and Its Metaphors*. (1978/1989). New York: Penguin, 2002. Print.
Strawson, Galen. "Against Narrativity." *Ratio* 17.4 (2004): 428–452.
Treichler, Paula (1999). *How to Have Theory in an Epidemic: Cultural Chronicles of AIDS*. Duke UP, 2006. Print.
Verghese, Abraham. "Hope and Clarity." *New York Times Magazine*. 22 Feb 2004.
Wallace, David Foster. "The Planet Trillaphon as It Stands in Relation to the Bad Thing." *The Amherst Review* 12 (1984): 26–33.
Wasson, Sara. "Before Narrative: Episodic Reading and Representations of Chronic Pain." *Medical Humanities* (January 2018): 1–7.
Weinrich, Harald. "Semantik der kühnen Metapher." *Deutsche Vierteljahrsschrift für Literaturwissenschaft und Geistesgeschichte* 37 (1963): 325–344.
Whitsitt, Samuel Porter. *Metonymy, Synecdoche, and the Discourse of Contiguity*. Padova: libreriauniversitaria, 2013. Print.
Whitehead, Anne. *Medicine and Empathy in Contemporary British Fiction: An Intervention in Medical Humanities*. Edinburgh: Edinburgh UP, 2017. Print.
Wiest-Kellner, Ursula. *Messages from the Threshold: Die You-Erzählform als Ausdruck liminaler Wesen und Welten*. Bielefeld: Aisthesis, 1999. Print.
Wohlmann, Anita. "Analyzing Metaphors." *Methods in Health Humanities*. Ed. Craig Klugman and Erin Gentry Lamb. Forthcoming.
Woods, Angela. "The Limits of Narrative: Provocations for the Medical Humanities." *Medical Humanities* 37 (2011): 73–78.
Zimmermann, Ruben. "Moralische Signifikanz durch Sprachbilder: Ein Beitrag zur 'metaphorischen Ethik' der Paulusbriefe." Ed. Ulrich Volp. *Metapher – Narratio – Mimesis – Doxologie: Begründungsformen frühchristlicher und antiker Ethik*. Tübingen: Mohr Siebeck, 2016. 9–38. Print.

Reading the Assault on the Lived Body in Hilary Mantel's *Giving up the Ghost*

Monika Class

Words need to be "ready to take their place in the world [...] to stand up and fight".[1] This is Hilary Mantel's advice for composition in *Giving up the Ghost* (2003); and her life narrative lives up to it (Smith and Watson 5–10). Her memoir tells no conventional story of literary self-affirmation and novelistic success against all odds. Rather, *Giving up the Ghost* features a battle which isn't highly regarded: the experience of chronic illness. As such the book is known as an illness memoir or autopathography (Kusek; Vickers "Illness and Femininity"; Prodromou). Culturally charged and often stigmatised (Sontag *Illness*), illness is isolating and alienating: the "condition is feared and denied by those surrounding" ill persons (Carel 48). Mantel's life narrative fights back against such ostracizing fears, developing a boldness that is far from seeking "special sympathy" (Mantel 222). On the contrary, her memoir subtly advocates the epistemic credibility of embodied states by featuring reading experiences that allow us (as readers) to imagine her corporeal identity. Taking as a starting point Mantel's distinction between "hatching" and "ready" words (70), doodling and published verbal art, this essay examines the questions of how Mantel elicits the experience of her lived body in her readers and why. Accordingly, it is divided into two parts: The first half discusses Mantel's literary acumen for conveying the experiences of her lived body to her readership and the second half contends that these experiences serve to uphold the epistemological and ethical claims of the lived body. It is in these terms that this paper will draw on the phenomenology of illness and the semiotics of reading.

---

1 | Hilary Mantel, *Giving up the Ghost* (London: Fourth Estate, 2013), 70. All further page references follow this edition.

Conceptually, the paper engages critically with, and expands, Yuri Lotman's proto-cognitive, context-sensitive reader model. Lotman proposes that reading a book like Mantel's *Giving up the Ghost* equals a back-and-forth movement along a communicative chain between the author and her readership (Lotman 69; Semenenko). That way reading entails actualisation at both ends of the communication channel, for the sender as well as the receiver, as lived experiences are being rendered and received, encoded and decoded. The experiences that are being transmitted will inevitably be altered as they move along this communicative chain (Lotman 13). Crucially, Lotman insists that encoding and decoding are never completely congruous processes and that their incongruity generates new meanings. For him, ambiguities and misunderstandings lie at the heart of communication and bring about innovation (Lotman 70). Author and readership behave as if they were partners in a dialogue, mutually activating and adjusting their bodily positions during and as a result of their encounter (Lotman 63). On the receiving end, reading automatically transforms rows of graphically expressed words into bodily and spatial imagery, as if a film were made (Lotman 70). Such readerly actualisation occurs, according to Lotman, not in a discrete entity (such as the brain in isolation) but at the boundary of collective and individual memories, and the boundary of semantic and embodied ones (Lotman 69). Thus reading is a trans-individual, context-sensitive process. Central to this model is the assumption that verbal text (here *Giving up the Ghost*) already contains an embryonic image of its ideal readership: the verbal text holds "in embryo a system of all links in the communicative chain, and just as we can derive the authorial position from it, so we can reconstruct its ideal reader" (Lotman 64). In *Giving up the Ghost*, Mantel's (extradiegetic) reflections on narration suggest that author and reader ideally bond with each other. On the one hand, her guideline for composition is to imagine intelligent readers, "at least [...] as smart as" the author (4), and on the other hand, she hopes to keep readers engaged in their conservation, "any kind readers who've stayed with you" (70). Ideally, this bond seems based on mutual respect and receptivity. This essay proposes that the image of her readership in *Giving up the Ghost* resembles the "Thou-I" encounter designed by Martin Buber within his theory of human existence in his book *I and Thou*. Irrespective of grammatical categories (first, second and third-person pronouns), the book is based on the assumption that human existence is a series of encounters. In this spirit, the "Thou-I" encounter is one in which a person enters a genuine dialogue with another, whereas the "I-It" encounter entails objectification (Carel 44). Buber notes that in the immediate, non-objectifying "Thou-I" encounter "the parallel lines of relation meet" (cited in Carel 44). The present article aims to show that Mantel's memoir contains various literary strategies to elicit such an encounter with her readership.

Part of the image of her ideal readership in *Giving up the Ghost* is Mantel's commentary on autobiography: "I used to think that autobiography was a form of weakness, and perhaps I still do" (6). Here, "weakness" indicates Mantel's scepticism towards the genre: Is it a matter of "weakness" to believe in the expression of self, the communication of lived experience? Mantel's reservations seemingly echo the tendency in structuralist and poststructuralist theory to disclose autobiography's mislead fictions of factuality, originality and immediacy (Avrahami 1). Defiantly, Mantel adds however: "But I also think that, if you're weak, it's childish to pretend to be strong" (6). This in a way sets the tone for the "Thou-I" encounter in the following illness narrative. The communication channel which Mantel establishes with her readership is less about generic (autobiographical) authority and truth claims than about throwing into relief everything that is at stake when a person suffers from a chronic condition. After all, such vital stakes expose "the crucial divide between fiction and non-fiction" (Couser 54). In this spirit, *Giving up the Ghost* does much to disarm her readership: it dismantles the normative shields Western society upholds against illness by combining her "nom de guerre [that is] persiflage" with an unsparing "trust" in the reader and, above all, a literary acumen for narrating embodied states (4). This disarming mode is central to the memoir's main purpose of "seiz[ing] the copyright in myself" (70–71) from the people—family, teachers, and medical professionals—whom she had unwittingly allowed to interpret, write and prescribe her identity. The author speculates that taking charge will exorcise her "ghosts", as she calls the recurring painful mental and physical patterns in her life. One of these ghosts is Catriona, the child she wants but can no longer have. On the last pages of her memoir, however, Mantel endorses her imaginative creatures and integrates them into the literary future she foresees for herself (251–52).

Giving up the Ghost appeals to the readers' aesthetic engagement with the text, I mean especially their immersive propensity to develop sensory imagery while reading. Mantel's approach to communicating corporeal selfhood is unflinching. She considers the unreliability of autobiographical memory, while opposing the search for "Proustian moments" emphatically: "I have an investment in accuracy" (24).[2] The source of Mantel's autobiographical confidence is the "overwhelming sensory power" of her personal memories. Mantel adds that such sensoriness makes her memories "come complete, not like groping, generalised formulations" (24). This comment tells us not only about Mantel's idea of authorship but also about her ideal readership. For her rejection of "generalised formulations" favours showing over telling, reconstructing over recording experiences. This memoir suggests, in other words, that its perusal ideally takes the form of learning to "*see* more, *hear* more, to *feel* more" (Sontag *Interpretation* 10; original emphasis). This ideal poses high demands on both partners in communication, the writer and readership, since it requires the skilful rendering of sensory experiences on the one side, and the ever attentive visualisation on the other side. Although Mantel abstains from any direct instruction of her readers, her hope seems to be that readers extend their reading experience beyond the realm of the printed page, possibly by bringing new perspectives on illness into their lives. What's more is that the author's sensory experiences make up the intriguing layering of her remembered selves which together constitute her corporeal identity in the book (as a constant process rather than a finished product). As such, reading can assume the form of an "Thou-I" encounter.

Among these versions of self, the embodiment of illness is the most challenging issue in this memoir. By "embodiment" I mean the lived body as experienced subjectively by every person. The lived body is always a subjective, personal entity. The term thus connotes embodied consciousness, which is psychological, physiological and social in kind. As such, the lived body engages and is engaged in the surrounding world. The present use of the term is derived from the French philosopher Maurice Merleau-Ponty (92–99). Trying to refute both Cartesian dualism and materialist reductionism, he posited the body and perception as the seat of subjectivity. According to Merleau-Ponty, human existence is embodied and defined by sensory experience: "To be is to have a body that constantly perceives the world through sight, touch, smell and so on" (Carel 22). Our five senses are not just a means to connect the world inside our heads with the outside.

---

2 | For Mantel, embodied memories are conscious, even if this type of memory is sometimes regarded as unconscious (Assmann 184-87).

Rather, our bodies constantly perform a double sensation acting simultaneously as perceiving subject and perceived object, seeing, touching and feeling, and being seen, touched or felt (Carel 13). Merleau-Ponty's phenomenology can give us especially nuanced accounts of what it is like to be ill. For phenomenology augments both the naturalistic vantage point that conceives of disease as a purely "biological dysfunction to be corrected by medical experts" and the purely "normativist account [that] looks to the social conception of the condition and the ways in which an illness may socially" impair or enable ill persons (Carel 12).

The phenomenology of illness distinguishes between disease and illness: Whereas disease refers to a naturalistic perspective of medical practice, illness concerns the experiential perspective and is understood as a disruption of the lived body (Toombs 203; Kleinman 5). In short, illness is what the loss of health feels like from the inside. Analogously, Havi Carel distinguishes (irrespective of narratology) between the third-person perspective of naturalistic and normativist approaches to disease and the first-person perspective on illness, that is "the perspective of the ill person herself" conceptualised by phenomenology (13). Writing on illness, Mantel describes her lived body as being under relentless attack: "Everything about me—my physiology, my psychology—feels constantly under assault" (222); "my body was staging some kind of revolt" (215). Mantel's memoir shows us how these changes to the lived body destabilise her corporeal subjectivity. Concomitantly, embodiment in this narrative is never taken for granted but under constant construction or in need of repair. Having said this, illness narrative is known to enable people to rebuild their identities by weaving their disparate cycles of hope and despair into a whole narrative fabric (Vickers "Illness Narratives" 393). Yet, the term "repair" here should not be understood as an indicator for any of the three types of illness narrative (restitution, chaos, nor quest) that Arthur W. Frank established (75–136), nor as a therapeutic means to achieve wholeness (Couser 294). Recent criticism has already covered the "textured recovery" inherent in *Giving up the Ghost*, namely to "reclaim a whole self" (Prodromou 63, 69). Mantel's memoir describes, for instance, the act of "writing oneself into being" through fragmented drafts that help to find a thread through the maze of illness.[3] However, Mantel also makes sure

---

3 | "You need to find yourself, in the maze of social expectation, the thickets of memory: just which bits of you are left intact? I have been so mauled by medical

to keep therapeutic drafts and literary outcome apart: "don't show your work before you're ready" (70). She emphasises the special challenges that life narrative entails for her as an established novelist:[4] "I seemed able to create or interpret characters in fiction, but not able to create or interpret myself" (70). Mantel's reflections on composition convey to readers her professional insights as a writer and highlight her literary sophistication and aspiration. Accordingly, my focus in the first part of this essay lies on the style in which Mantel reconstructs embodiment. The main interest lies therefore in the proto-physicality to which the memoir aspires in its conversation with its readers; I mean above all its appeal to readers to imagine her lived body as if it were a personal encounter.

Mantel's literariness is inseparable from her "investment in accuracy". Her empiricism precludes any statements about the "universalizing" implications of her illness as does, by contrast, Kathlyn Conway in *Ordinary Life* (Baena 2). Moreover, *Giving up the Ghost* defies a single classification under illness narrative. After all, the first half of the book does not even mention Mantel's disease and deals instead with her upbringing. Moreover, the memoir's resistance to closure creates inexhaustible affective and cognitive responses. Vice versa, illness narratives are highly diverse and widely resist generic classification. Illness narratives are written by patients or carers, they cover any length and manifest themselves in prose, poetry and drama; while records of illness stretch across thousands of years and across the globe (Vickers "Illness Narratives" 388). Within a context-sensitive approach, the complexity of *Giving up the Ghost* is part of a literary development in the early 2000s. According to Neil Vickers, book-length accounts of illness have arguably emerged as a distinct publishing phenomenon in the Anglo-Saxon world in the late twentieth and early twenty-first centuries ("Illness Narratives" 388–89). The post-1950s specimen were mostly self-help books intended for readers who had recently been

---

procedures, so sabotaged and made over, so thin and so fat, that sometimes I feel that each morning it is necessary to write myself into being—even if the writing is aimless doodling that no one will ever read, or the diary that no one can see till I'm dead." (222)

4 | By that time, Mantel was known as the author of *Every Day is Mother's Day* (1985), *Vacant Possession* (1986), *Eight Months on Ghazzah Street* (1988), *Fludd* (1989), *A Place of Greater Safety* (1992), *A Change of Climate* (1994), *An Experiment in Love* (1995), and *The Giant, O'Brian* (1998).

diagnosed with a similar condition. By the late 1970s, illness autobiographers like Norman Cousin in *Anatomy of an Illness* (1979) criticized the "dehumanising effects of modern healthcare" and expressed dissatisfaction with doctor-patient communication (Vickers "Illness Narratives" 388). By the early 1990s, illness gained importance in literary and philosophical memoirs, such as Philip Roth's *Patrimony: A True Story* (1991), Gillian Rose's *Love's Work* (1995), and Joan Didion's *The Year of Magical Thinking* (2005). Published in 2003, *Giving up the Ghost* contributed to this existing hybridization in highbrow autobiography.

RENDERING AND RECONSTRUCTING THE LIVED BODY AND THE EXPERIENCE OF ILLNESS

The memoir begins with Mantel's working-class upbringing in a Roman Catholic family in Hadfield, near Manchester, in the 1950s and ends with her settling down with her husband in their new home, lodged in the attic of a converted asylum in the early 2000s (241). Before school age, Hilary falls ill while on a trip to Blackpool with her parents. This is the primary instance of illness that "supplies the symbolic language for every subsequent collapse in the memoir" (Vickers "Illness and Femininity" 10). From the age of seven, young Hilary feels a constant "sick resonance within my bones and in all the cavities of my body" (Mantel 106–7). The local doctor gives her the nickname "Little Miss Neverwell" because of her frequent bouts of sickness. When she passes the eleven-plus exam, her mother, step-father and two brothers move with her to Cheshire, where Hilary attends a Catholic grammar school. Severe family tensions and financial worries (e.g. how to pay the stockings for the school uniform) outweigh all concerns for her heavy period bleeding. While in her early twenties, studying law, first at LSE London later at Sheffield University, and in a stable relationship with her future husband, the sudden attacks of shafting pain become more frequent and worsen. When she presents with excruciating pains and nausea first to a GP and then to the psychiatrist Dr G, they mistake her ambition for hysteria, medicate her first with anti-depressants and valium, and then with anti-psychotics that induce a mental disorder (akathisia), which leads to her admission into a psychiatric hospital. She takes away from this experience the resolution never to insist on a physical complaint with a physician again. Rather, young

Mantel lives with chronic pain. It is not until the final two parts of the memoir that Mantel eventually identifies her ailing as endometriosis by studying medical textbooks while living in Africa (191). Back on a visit to England in 1979, she is admitted to a London hospital with severe pains, examined and operated. After the procedure, at the age of twenty-seven, she is informed that the surgeons removed her reproductive organs. Her fertility is gone. Despite this, her endometriosis returns by 1982. Mantel has to medicate with hormones and steroids, the side-effects of which alter her lived body strangely and permanently.

It matters that the autobiographer's diagnosis occurs so late in *Giving up the Ghost*. The delay is the main cause of Mantel's medical disaster. Regarding narrative transmission, the protracted occurrence of disease sets *Giving up the Ghost* apart from other illness narratives in which the beginning of the story coalesces with the onset of disease. In breast cancer narratives, for instance, the initial discovery of a lump followed by diagnosis, surgical treatment and chemotherapy mark generic conventions of this "distinctive autobiographical subgenre" (Couser 42). However, *Giving up the Ghost* eschews the determination of a single disruptive event that would mark the onset of illness and divide the lived body in before and after. This complexity is bound up with Mantel's narrative investment in the sensory memories of her younger self. Part of the disaster of Mantel's medical history is that she felt sick before she experienced symptoms of endometriosis and long before she was diagnosed with this disease. Tellingly, her doctors' disbelief in the somatic nature of her condition was so strong that she self-diagnosed before an attentive specialist confirmed her assumption (endometriosis) in a London hospital in 1979. By that time, Mantel had sought treatment for more than seven years. Focalizing internally through the young experiencing I, the first 190 of 252 pages of Mantel's memoir feature illness without reference to the disease category endometriosis. The narrative transmission conveys to readers how Hilary's body experiences formative events as a child that take the shape of core embodied memories of being ill. These events prime her experience of suffering from endometriosis in later life (Vickers "Illness and Femininity"). Only Part Five and Six, "Show your workings" and "Afterlife", narrate the disruptions of the lived body that are distinctly connected with endometriosis. These chapters give us vivid depictions of the attacks on her lived body that Hilary experiences while seeking medical treatment in her twenties and thirties. However, the memoir initially constructs Hilary's lived body without objectifying medical terminology. The memoir reconstructs the memories of a younger self that is oblivious to pathognomonic signs. Albeit a tragic factor in Mantel's medical history, this oblivion has felicitous "side-effects" for the "Thou-I" encounter with readers. Reading *Giving up the Ghost* for the first time and learning eventually about the autobiographer's disease is one thing, and re-reading it as a case of endometriosis another. Once readers are aware of her endometriosis, re-reading the memoir seems more likely to turn symptomatic. For the diagnosis can tend to shift readerly attention away from the narrated person and selfhood towards the disease. A third-person perspective of disease might hamper the "Thou-I" relationship with readers for instance if some readers are more interested in the disease than the sufferer's personality and experience of illness. By delaying the diagnosis until late, Mantel keeps her readers' minds open to the complexity of her somatic identity irrespective of pathognomonicity. So Mantel's delay of the mention of her diagnosis is both a sign of her "investment in accuracy" and a compositional device to augment the chances for an encounter with her readership as an irreducible personality (rather than a representative of endometriosis sufferers, or a case or instantiation of the disease) (Class). And even when Mantel eventually explores and explains her disease, she asserts her lived body by deploying various immersive strategies.

Her rendering of crucial childhood memories is an important part of the "Thou-I" relation with her readers. Much of the narrative evokes her embodiment and lived body by emphasising the location of her sensory perceptions and double-sensation. This begins with Hilary's childhood. Typically, these special memories are written in interior monologue: Mantel employs the present tense to create the presence of discrete childhood experiences and focalises through the younger self, who is identified through the first-person pronoun. This "I" designates the experiencing little Hilary with very limited knowledge of health and is distinct from the narrating "I", who stands for Mantel, the expert patient and novelist, who completes her memoir in the early 2000s. Combining episodic and embodied memory, these compositional units are almost free from any extradiegetic comments and stand out like little time capsules within the chapters. As such, these memories resemble William Wordsworth's 'spots of time' in *The Prelude* (Wordsworth 1805, Book XI, ll. 258–275), but differ in theme and immediacy. Building on Vickers's article "Illness and Femininity", I will call these discrete memories "spots of bodily discomfort".

The first of these spots of bodily discomfort in the memoir consists of Hilary's consequential bout of sickness in Part Two "Now Geoffrey don't Torment Her": "The next thing is that I am in bed with a fever raging. [...] To open my eyes I have to force off my eyelids the weight of water. I am trying to die and I am trying to live. I open my eyes and see my mother looking down at me." (53) Central to the evocation of embodiment in the narrative are bodily placements and perspective-taking. The specific spatial descriptions support the deictic first person, and together these devices provide readers with a physical grid to imagine what Hilary's body feels like from the inside. The detailed depiction of the location anchors Hilary's body as the seat of subjective feelings, perceptions and sensations. In this passage, Hilary is placed in her bed, which is described as having an improvised fence "made of Mrs Scott's dining chairs" (53). Taking this travel cot as a starting point, the passage focalises consistently through little Hilary. As a direct consequence of such internalisation, it remains unclear where the said weight of water on her eyelids comes from: Is it a bodily symptom of the fever or a wet cloth placed on her forehead? Thus readers learn about Hilary's disorientation, confusion and suffering, "trying to die and [...] live" as well as about her double-sensation of looking up at her mother and being looked down upon by her. The passage suggests that all of Hilary's feelings are grounded in her body, which in turn is placed lying in this little makeshift bed.

Location and perception are also central to a previous spot of bodily discomfort. It recounts the sudden disruption of Hilary's sampling of a special sweet (depicted as wrapped in green, marzipan flavour, and branded "Weekend") when she feels as if a fly tickled inside her throat.

"I sit on the stairs, which are steep, box-like, dark. I think I am going to die. I have breathed in a house-fly, I think I have. The fly was in the room and my mouth open because I was putting into it a sweet. Then the fly was nowhere to be seen. It manifests now as a tickling and scraping on the inside of my throat, the side of my throat that's nearest to the kitchen wall." (31)

The passage starts with the place and posture that little Hilary finds herself in: sitting on the stairs. The phrase "steep, box-like, dark" associates the stairs with the candy box and her wide open mouth, intent on swallowing the big sweet. These details suggest an image of her entire body to be directed towards this sweet. Yet, this directedness is suddenly interrupted when she realises the disappearance of the house-fly that had been bothering her. A bodily discomfort located on the inside of her throat, the side "that's nearest to the kitchen", displaces this thought and induces the fear of imminent death in little Hilary: "what more sure way to die than swallow or inhale [a fly]?" (31). The passage shows sensations to lodge inside her lived body while the lived body is lodged inside the staircase of a family home. The narrated memory thus invokes the "primitive spatiality of the body beneath objective space," which is part of the primary knowledge of the body (Toombs 205).

Little Hilary's memories of sickness culminate in a spot of bodily discomfort in Part Three "Secret Garden". Hilary calls the yard of the new family home at 20 Brosscroft "the secret garden" (107). This back yard is the opposite of the place of healing and recovery in the children's book *The Secret Garden* by Frances Hodgson Burnett. Rather, Mantel prefaces the episode with her difficulties in writing about this particularly traumatic experience: "Sometimes you come to a thing you can't write" (106). What follows is a highly crafted passage, oscillating between childhood sensations and adult retrospective, describing a perception that leads to the porous boundary of the real and imaginary: "the periphery, the limit of all my senses" (106). Just like the previous spots of bodily discomfort, location and visual perception establish Hilary's bodily placement in the yard near the backdoor of the house. "I am seven and I am in the yard at Brosscroft; I am playing near the house, near the back door" (106). During this play, she is suddenly distracted by a ray of light: "Something makes me look up: some shift of the light" (106). This visual effect seems to throw her lived body off balance. As a consequence, it loses its directedness:

"There is nothing to see. There is nothing to smell. There is nothing to hear. But its motion, its insolent shift, makes my stomach heave. I can sense—at the periphery, the limit of all my senses—the dimensions of the creature. It is as high as a child of two. Its depth is a foot, fifteen inches. The air stirs around it, invisibly. I am cold, and rinsed by nausea. I cannot move. I am shaking; as if pinned to the moment, I cannot wrench my gaze away. I am looking at a space occupied by nothing." (106)

This disruptive moment brings disorientation, from which two things follow. First, Hilary believes to sense the motion of an invisible evil creature and, second, physical pain takes possession of, and installs itself in, her lived body: "Within the space of a thought, it [the creature] is inside me, and has set up a sick resonance within my bones and in all the cavities of my body" (107). In addition, Hilary's double-sensation reinforces the sense of bodily suffering: "I see myself through [my mother's] eyes: sweat running from me, my cheeks fallen in, my chest heaving" (107). Mantel communicates the lived body via location, perception and double-sensation, as well as the disruptive experience of pain. The spots of bodily discomfort render and impart unique embodied memories and thus a unique lived body. Crucially, these childhood experiences are still untouched by the third-person perspective of medical practice.

The style of Mantel's teenage and adult memories (roughly from the age of 12 onwards) is more varied than the childhood memories. In Parts Five and Six of the memoir the medical third-person perspective begins to slowly take hold over some passages of the narrative. The introduction of this medical perspective occurs usually via Mantel's retrospective (extradiegetic) comments; as such, these interjections effect a certain distance to the experience of illness and bring about some degree of objectification. However, the explicit insertion of Mantel's disease in the narrative blends the "Thou-I" encounter with the "I-It" perspective of her medical case history. In short, Mantel hybridizes the first-person perspective of illness experience with the third-person perspective of medical practice:

"The endometrium is the lining of the womb. It is made of special cells which shed each month by bleeding. In endometriosis, these cells are found in other parts of the body. (How they get there is a matter of dispute.) Typically, they are found in the pelvis, the bladder, the bowel. More rarely, they are found in the chest wall, the heart, the head. Wherever they are found, they obey their essential nature and bleed. Scar tissue is formed in the body's inner spaces and small cavities. It builds up. It presses on nerves and causes pain, sometimes at distant sites. The scar tissue forms an evil stitching which attaches one organ to another. Infertility is a distinct possibility, as the organs of the pelvis are ensnared and tugged out of shape. Endometriosis in the intestines makes you vomit and gives you pains in the gut. Pressure in the pelvis makes your back ache, your legs ache. You are too tired to move. The pain, which in the early stages invades you when you menstruate, begins to take over your whole month. Lately I had known days of my life when everything hurt, everything from my collarbone down to my knees." (190-91)

Notably, the passage integrates the second-person pronoun in the nosological characteristics of endometriosis. Here, the medical perspective detailing the (still debated) causes of the disease (the growth of the endometrium outside of the uterus, scar tissue, etc.) and symptoms (profuse bleeding, chronic pain, vomiting, fatigue, infertility) transforms via the second person into the felt experience of illness ("days of my life when everything hurt, everything from my collarbone down to my knees"). The literal use of the second-person pronoun can be said to reinforce the first-person perspective of illness if we consider our intuitive reaction to think of ourselves when addressed with "you" (Ryan 138; Macrae 65). The second-person pronoun and present tense have an immersive potential that counteracts customary resistance to illness by appealing to readers to imagine what it is like to suffer from a debilitating condition. While emphasising Mantel's lived body, this particular combination of third- and first-person perspectives creates what I will call a "first-person nosology". It helps to raise awareness for a disease that is notoriously difficult to diagnose, and sometimes still escapes detection although the condition is fairly common, affecting an estimated 10% of girls and women of reproductive age (Rogers, D'Hooghe and Fazleabas; Neudecker; Endometriosis).

Mantel deploys the same kind of first-person nosology for her rendering of akathisia, which is her designated worst experience of illness. It occurs while young Mantel is hospitalised in an asylum in the early 1970s, and the drug Fentazine induces the condition.

"And from the inside, how does it feel? Akathisia is the worst thing I have ever experienced, the worst single, defined episode of my entire life. [...] You are impelled to move, to pace in a small room. You force yourself down into a chair, only to jump out of it. You choke; pressure rises inside your skull. Your hands pull at your clothing and tear at your arms. Your breathing becomes ragged. Your voice is like a bird's cry and your hands flutter like wings. You want to hurl yourself against the windows and the walls. Every fibre of your being is possessed by panic. Every moment endures for an age and yet you are transfixed by the present moment, stabbed by it; there is no sense of time passing, therefore no prospect of deliverance. A desperate feeling of urgency—a need to act, but to do what, and how?—pulses through your whole body, like the pulses of an electric shock." (181-82)

Here, Mantel's use of the "you" and present tense gives readers not only an intuitive understanding of akathisia, but also appeals to them to enter a horrific bodily state and thus de-stigmatizes illness. Overall, Mantel's narrative does much to communicate the dissonance of the biological and lived body in nuanced ways. She introduces her disease at a crucial point in the narrative before her surgical treatment at St George's Hospital London in 1979. This treatment consists of the removal of her reproductive organs. Mantel describes the persisting feeling of loss after the surgery as follows:

"No advance in medical technology was going to produce Catriona; she was lost. But when biological destiny veers from the norm, there are parts of the psyche that take time to catch up. You understand what has happened, the medical disaster; you reason about it. But there are layers of realisation, and a feeling of loss takes time to sink through those layers. The body is not logical; it knows its own mad pathways." (230)

On the one hand, Mantel has clarity that the irreversible loss of her fertility was a consequence of the protracted diagnosis of endometriosis. On the other hand, her psyche needs time to deal with the loss. Mantel's lived body appears as a compound of bodily layers caught in the taxing process of absorbing and digesting this abstract information about her biological body. Like the spots of bodily discomfort, the passage conceives of the lived body as a cognitive agent and knower: the body "knows"; indeed, the bodily layers perform an act of knowing and understanding.[5] Mantel emphasises that somatic illness brings about the sufferers' awareness of inescapable bodily limitations or pain, even in the absence of such a diagnosis (i.e. of organic dysfunction) (Toombs 217). Before her admission into St George's Hospital, London, during Christmas week 1979, Mantel's doctors had dismissed her symptoms as a mental disorder. Mantel recounts her firm belief in the physical nature of her suffering despite the uncertainty: "I knew I was very ill, but I didn't know quite

---

5 | It is true that Mantel states that the body knows only "its own mad pathways"; yet, this phrase still connotes bodily knowledge after all, even if the attribute "mad" plays down the body's epistemic validity and thus conforms to a long tradition in Western intellectual history of derogating the body and its sensory knowledge (Smith).

how bad things might be [...] Only that it was physical; only that I had a pain and it was real" (185). She then describes how this experience of dissonance changes in the course of her official diagnosis with endometriosis and medical treatment. In doing so, Mantel's narrative consistently conveys to readers the discrepancy between the biological and lived body, giving the lived body pride of place.

Two scenes relating to Mantel's hysterectomy exemplify this. The first one recounts the communication of the outcome of her surgery in 1979:

"When I was half-awake, a day later, they came to tell me what they had done. After a general anaesthetic, you dip in and out of consciousness: sitting up and smiling, you may be the picture of alertness, but your attention has faded. They should have told me again, I think, when I was properly awake. They should have told me once or twice. They should have written me a letter, they should have written me an essay or maybe a small book." (208)

We have seen that Mantel insists on the bodily process of comprehending the sudden loss of her fertility. In addition, this passage expresses the disregard shown by her medical practitioners in the communication of this fundamental alteration of her body. The passage exposes a case of the blatant lack of empathy in the communication between doctor and patient. Initially, it voices the modest complaint that "[t]hey should have told me again, I think, when I was properly awake". Yet, Mantel amplifies her call for sensitivity towards the ill through her bitter wish list: "They should have written me a letter, [...] an essay or maybe a small book". Albeit sarcastically exaggerated, this list suggests that communications of a devastating nature like this have epic implications for the sufferer and would therefore merit a small book. The second example concerns medical objectification: "Now my body was not my own. It was a thing done to, a thing operated on. I was 27 and an old woman, all at once." (211) "Not my own" expresses the feeling of being dispossessed. The phrase "a thing done to" invokes the third-person perspective used in the medical profession, while the repetition ("thing") emphasises the alienation a person experiences when handled as a mere biological dysfunction. Furthermore, "27 and an old woman, all at once" laments the sexualizing norms that reduce femininity to functioning reproductive organs. The dissonance of lived and biological body in the memoir manifests itself in various ways. The chosen examples show that, in addition to articulating the pain and inescapable limitations in somatic illness, Mantel's memoir does much to underscore bodily intelligence and affectivity that entitle her lived body to thorough consideration, empathy and respect. Yet, Mantel's experiences of hospital show the latter to be a desideratum.

This lack, especially of empathy, in the encounter with medical professionals adds to her sufferings. One of the lessons that doctor-patient communication teaches the young Mantel is that "it was for the doctor to direct the blow, and me to absorb it" (212). Having said this, empathy isn't completely absent from any of Mantel's hospital experiences.[6] The scene with the cocoa trolley at St George's Hospital is a case in point. Freshly admitted, the medical staff takes away Mantel's painkillers, which leaves her lying in bed with her knees drawn up. It is 1979 and Mantel is in excruciating pain: "I was unable to stand up straight: some inflamed growth inside me was bending me at the waist, pulling my abdomen, knotted with pain, down towards my knees" (189). When Mantel does not respond to Panadol, "an over-the-counter remedy" (188), and laughs at the medical advice of a hot bath, the nurses offer something else as to pain relief: they let her push the cocoa trolley in the ward. In this callous scenario, it is a fellow patient, Kirsty who shouts "at the nurses. 'Look at her, look at her,' she roared. 'Give her somefin.'" (188). But Kirsty's empathic appeal is to no avail. Awash with pain, Mantel has to push the trolley anyhow. Unintentionally inconsiderate behaviour occurs when an auxiliary nurse at St George's hospital accompanies young Mantel to an ultrasonic scan. Not long before her operation the nurse tells Mantel that she has a daughter who suffered significant brain damage in a routine surgery on her hand. The nurse calls her own daughter a "vegetable" and even imitates her stammer (198–99). The nurse's behaviour adds to Mantel's distress the night before her operation. *Giving up the Ghost* contains similar encounters with medical professionals abroad. Mantel's doctor in Botswana responds to the news of the surgical removal of her ovaries in London by saying: "Oh well [...] There is one good thing, anyway. Now you won't have to worry about birth prevention" (211). Such disregard for her distress hurts young Mantel deeply.

Mantel resorts to sarcasm when memories are particularly wretched. Carel contends that the prevalent indifference, apathy, voyeurism, or

---

6 | To my best knowledge, the memoir contains three instances of attentive medical practitioners (192, 194, 218).

disgust encountered by the ill makes "learning to be rude" a necessary coping mechanism (45). Likewise, Mantel employs dark humour, calling persiflage her "nom de guerre" (4). This persiflage usually occurs when Mantel retrospectively comments on the narrated events. Such a removed level of narrative communication lends her occasional provocations more nuance than they would have if placed directly within the narrated interaction. Some of Mantel's extradiegetic comments are ironic, like that on the Botswanan doctor's insensitive remark: "—let's break open the champagne! At least I won't have to worry about birth prevention!" (212) Behind the irony lies, as Mantel admits, the thought that "sometimes one takes a little pride in endurance […] it was all that was left" (212). Other times, Mantel deploys dark humour, such as when she inserts in the narration of her operation a sarcastic allusion to the incident with the auxiliary nurse (see above): "La la la. Ma mama. December 1979: I felt the urge to leave a note by my bed: if I wake up a vegetable, put me in a stew." (208) In another instance, her nom de guerre turns into outright provocation. In the context of undergoing various hospital examinations in London, Mantel notes: "What modesty was left? I'd had more gynaecologists than I'd had lovers; alien fists in my guts" (185). This graphic statement might make her claim to delicacy seem ludicrous (189, see below). Yet this would miss a significant point. Mantel's language crosses the boundaries of politeness inasmuch as medical examinations invaded her personal boundaries. The rudeness serves thus as a rhetorical device to transfer some of the outrage that Mantel experienced onto her readers. *Giving up the Ghost* exposes how the lack of empathy impacts negatively on Mantel's lived body in its affectivity and intelligence. The rest of the present essay contends that, beyond a call for empathy, the memoir supports the view that the consideration of an ill person, both medical and non-medical consideration, should extend to her lived body.

EPISTEMIC INJUSTICE AND JUSTICE

In light of these hospital experiences it doesn't come as a surprise that anger underpins these parts of *Giving up the Ghost*. The narration of experienced injustice makes this emotion understandable for readers. By contrast, Mantel notes that at the time no one seemed to understand her situation: "I was labouring under a violent sense of injustice that may have seemed unreasonable to the people around me" (176). The narrative conveys, on the one hand, how Mantel's testimonies aren't taken seriously and, on the other hand, how difficult it is for her to testify. Central to this kind of injustice is the lack of credibility of the lived body. Miranda Fricker's notion of epistemic injustice (1) helps to analyse the medical encounters in the memoir. Fricker argues that "'there is a distinctively epistemic kind of injustice' which is a wrong done to someone in their capacity as knower" (Carel and Kidd 530–31). She distinguishes two interconnected concepts of epistemic injustice: first, testimonial injustice "occurs when prejudice causes a hearer to assign a deflated level of credibility to a speaker's testimony"; second, hermeneutical injustice happens "when a gap in collective interpretative resources puts a speaker at a disadvantage when trying to make sense of their social experiences. [In other words, hermeneutical injustice] occurs when someone's testimony is not squarely disbelieved [as is the case with testimonial injustice] but a conceptual impoverishment in a particular culture prevents that person from being able to clearly articulate their testimony" (Carel and Kidd 531, 533). Accordingly, the main difference of these two types of epistemic injustice consists in decoding and encoding. For testimonial injustice connotes a negative bias of the epistemically privileged listener (receiver) with regard to the credibility of the speaking subject (sender). Testimonial injustice is thus part of the decoding process of communication performed by expert receivers, such as health specialists, or teachers; whereas the hermeneutical injustice denotes an obstacle to the articulation of a testimony (e.g. the lack of adequate vocabulary) and thus concerns the encoding process performed by ill persons or other non-experts (sender). Carel and Ian J. Kidd argue that ill persons are especially vulnerable to epistemic injustice since they are often seen as cognitively unreliable or encounter collective obstacles to understanding and communicating their experience ("gaps in collective hermeneutical resources", 529). By contrast, epistemic justice, which incorporates both testimonial and hermeneutical justice, occurs when the interpretations of ill persons are recognised, sought out, included within epistemic consideration, judged to be relevant and articulate (where they are) and, at least in certain aspects, given some epistemic validity (Carel and Kidd 532–33). The balance in *Giving up the Ghost* tips towards epistemic injustice, while Mantel eschews any singular accusation through her rigorous self-enquiry into the social, psychological and biological causes of her "medical disaster". Yet her verdict is clear enough: "Because of the number of symptoms [endometriosis] throws up it is sometimes hard to diagnose. It is always hard to diagnose for a doctor who doesn't listen and doesn't look." (190) This marks a case of testimonial injustice.

The memoir describes how Mantel as a twenty-year old suffers repeated testimonial injustice at the hands of both her GP at the Student Health Service of Sheffield University and the local psychiatrist Dr G. This starts with her presenting to her GP with excruciating pain and nausea. When her husband asks how her appointment went, Mantel reports that her GP "'said, don't take so many aspirin. I said my legs ached and he said it was accounted for by no known disease. Except one called idiopathic some-thing-something'" (169). The GP apparently listens to Mantel's description of pain, but after ruling out pregnancy he considers her testimony about the pains in her legs epistemically inconclusive. When Mantel returns to the health services, insisting on her complaints, the GP reinforces his idiopathic assumptions. He diagnoses Mantel with depression and gives her a prescription for drugs, which have heavy side effects (169). Mantel senses that the doctor does not credit her with much cognitive credibility: "He was not on my side." (169), but she agrees to, and complies with, his epistemic authority and takes the medication: "I was depressed, so I knew it made a kind of sense" (171). Her doctor continues to disregard Mantel's pain and vomiting epistemically even though the symptoms persist. Furthermore, he unwittingly considers her gynaecological condition a psychiatric (not a somatic) illness: "No one seemed to be able to think of another disease to test me for, and if my body was not the problem it must be my mind that was acting up" (173). As such, the testimonial injustice that Mantel encounters at the hands of her Sheffield physicians is gendered. The bias against the female body is epitomised in the encounter with the psychiatrist Dr G, to whom Mantel is referred.

"Dr G, the psychiatrist, was remote and bald. He [...] soon diagnosed my problem: stress, caused by over-ambition. This was a female complaint, one which people believed in, in those years, just as the Greeks believed that women were made ill by their wombs cutting loose and wandering about their bodies." (174)

So fixated is Dr G on the misogynist codes inherent in female hysteria that he fails to consider the condition of both Mantel's lived and biological body.[7] Not only does he neither examine her thoroughly, nor listen to her carefully, he downgrades her merits as a law student to conscientiousness and calls her over-ambitious. According to Dr G, young Mantel would have been fine if she had worked as a shop assistant. The consultant denies Mantel any epistemic role in the encounters, discriminates against her as a woman and thus makes her feel "as if I had been dealt a dull blow" (176). Part of Mantel's suffering as a young woman are severe migraines. "Along with endometriosis goes, not infrequently, a hormonal disarrangement that shows itself as a severe premenstrual syndrome. In my case, it manifested in the prodromal aura of migraine headaches" (192), Mantel interjects retrospectively. When young Mantel tells Dr G about these migraine auras, which take the shape of "voices" and "morbid visions" (193), he dismisses her frightened report with the verbal ejaculation "Ah well" (193). Mantel comments that once Dr G had made his (wrong) diagnosis he stopped his epistemic consideration altogether: "At this stage, I was only a neurotic" for Dr G (193). His epistemic exclusion leads to Mantel's medication with anti-psychotics, which eventually induce young Mantel's worst experience of illness: akathisia (see above). The experience with Dr G makes young Mantel doubt that she can ever act as an epistemic agent when she uses the health services, not to mention the mental health services. The particularly strong disbelief in the somatic nature of Mantel's illness despite her testimony about bodily complaints suggests that the epistemic injustice she encountered was bound up with sexism.

Many of the consecutive medical professionals in the memoir continue to deflate the epistemic credibility of young Mantel (irrespective of gender); for instance, during Mantel's post-hysterectomy treatment with hormones and steroids: "When my next appointment with my consultant came, I said: 'I'm worried because I'm putting on weight so fast.' She shot me a spiteful glance, from amid her own jowly folds. 'Now,' she said, 'you know what it's like for the rest of us.'" (215) The physician dismisses Mantel's testimony with a remark about her own full body shape. Thus the doctor ignores Mantel's concern about her drastic weight gain that strongly affects her lived body: "It is not a matter of chest-waist-hip measurements. You get fat knees, fat feet, fat in bits of you that you never thought of." (218) It feels for Mantel as if she had to shape her bodily image from scratch

---

7 | The present article disagrees with the view that "Mantel plays with the Greek root of hysteria as ironically appropriate to her estranging illness" (Pollard 25).

every morning due to these immense physical changes: "To get out of the house for eight, I had to get up at six. I spent my scarce free time getting my hair done, lifted and teased and curled into a mane, so that I didn't look as if I had a pin-head on top of my sweetly plump shoulders." (215) In brief, the doctor belittles Mantel's disintegration of her lived body.

Another kind of epistemic injustice also occurs in Mantel's illness narrative: hermeneutical injustice. It concerns the social environment that puts a person at a disadvantage in the communication of bodily complaints with medical professionals (Carel and Kidd 533). Mantel's narrative is alert to the complex factors that together prevented her as a young woman from insisting on her symptoms with her doctors (even more than she had done): "I wonder why, despite all, I did not insist, could not insist, that doctors pay attention to me and locate my malaise. There are several possible explanations, on several levels." (226) Emphasising such intricacies, Mantel observes that "[o]ne is that, in the time and place where I grew up, expectations of health were so low, especially for women [...]. The deeper explanation is that I always felt that I deserved very little." (226) Mantel speaks of the low "expectations of health" for women and especially for herself. I shall call these expectations her "personal health horizon".

Vickers establishes a concept that suits Mantel's "expectations of health" in psychoanalytical terms; he names them "psychosomatic normality" ("Illness and Femininity" 3). The latter consists of the coping mechanisms for bodily discomforts during childhood. Mantel's psychosomatic normality seems to have put her at a disadvantage in registering and articulating her bodily complaint. The problem of her psychosomatic normality stems largely from the coalescence of Hilary's femininity and illness during childhood. She identifies with her grandfather (through a shared body schema). By contrast, Hilary's identification with her mother is fraught. Therefore it is painful for Hilary to dissociate from her shared body schema with her grandfather when her environment gradually reinforces her femininity through toys, schooling etc. (Vickers "Illness and Femininity" 12). Thus Hilary experiences femininity as an enforced bodily confinement and, concomitantly, the pressure (to assume femininity) becomes part and parcel of her frequent bouts of bodily discomfort. It seems that this broad conflation of femininity and illness hampers her ability to detect and voice the locations of her patterns of pain, nausea and migraines.

Another social component of Mantel's personal health horizon is her upbringing. By the age of seventeen, Hilary's step-father Jack and mother have established a tough regimen in the family's new home in Cheshire. According to them, being ill amounts to weakness: "It was already a weakness in my case that I was hanging about, that I was sitting down and no doubt wanting some toast; for Jack was perfect and so was his morning nausea, a spiritual quality I should emulate" (142). Mantel isn't allowed to acknowledge her bodily ailments inasmuch as Jack forces himself to ignore his "chronic colic" (142). This regimen applies to her whole family. For instance, the family cannot afford a washing machine; Hilary and her mother do the washing by hand, usually in cold water; blankets are never washed. With the benefit of hindsight, Mantel exposes her mother's lack of health awareness: "My smallest brother developed allergies, blue-faced coughs and wheezes, my mother responded by heaping more blankets on him, and placing a plug-in radiator by his bed, so the dust mites could breed better" (146). In her ignorance of health standards, her mother worsens her son's condition. Mantel's ironic use of the adjective "healthy" further underlines the unwitting disregard for health issues in her family: "I lived in the healthy cold of the box room. Once, experimentally, I set up a thermometer, bringing it down when I was twelve and still naïve, to say, look Mum, almost freezing point!" (146) These examples point to a generally impoverished concept of health in Hilary's family environment.[8]

In addition, Hilary has to make do with inadequate sanitary napkins: "Two pins were sometimes necessary to arrange my drooping sanitary arrangements" (144). The word choice "two pins" and "drooping" gives us a glimpse of her anxiety over her heavy periods and the embarrassment of spilling menstrual blood as well as her frustration and anger: "[f]or two pins, I'd land a punch" (144). Simultaneously, "two pins" indicates that Hilary had no access to the latest menstrual technology of more absorbent, thinner sanitary panties or adhesive pads.[9] Hilary's lack of access to

---

8 | Health care is "not simply a matter of medical authority and state policy, it has always been intricately intertwined with personal belief, family life and neighbourhood support systems" (Moore 969).

9 | Adhesive pads were developed in the 1960s and 70s (Stanley 215-16). Mantel describes how her mother tried to avoid any expenses for Hilary, including stockings (143).

more modern sanitary materials in 1969 suggests an impoverishment of women's health, too.

Mantel's Catholic education further increases the tendency to disregard bodily complaints. Mantel observes that Catholicism taught her to privilege life after death and disconnect from bodily reality: "[t]he whole of a Catholic life is lived in the shadow of the happy death—as if your life were to be enacted through a silvered, speckled mirror, ancient and flattering" (207–8). The damage caused by her religious upbringing seems unmistakable in her comment that "[i]n the terms of the church in which I was brought up, the body is a beast, a base, simian relative that turns up at the door of the spirit too often for comfort" (220). These depictions suggest that Hilary's conceptual disconnection from her bodily ailments was partly due to her interiorisation of family values and disciplinary power (Foucault 139). Her family environment relegates illness to weakness and bodily comfort to baseness. Such a personal health horizon appears blunt in that it fails to distinguish the experience of health from that of illness.

While at university, Hilary compares her difficulty of expressing her acute pain to "blundering through your house with the lights fused" (167). She observes that "[e]ach day I was taking, though I did not know it, a small step towards the unlit terrain of sickness, a featureless landscape of humiliation and loss" (167). The spatial imagery, "unlit terrain" and "featureless landscape", evokes a sense of dark, bodily interiority and simultaneously points, similar to the spots of bodily discomfort, to the elusive primary knowledge of her body: the humiliation and loss appear to consist in the darkness of, and the inaccessibility to, bodily knowledge. It seems that young Mantel had no concepts at hand to explain the pains to herself; nor did she recall any gynaecological nor other health codes to augment the medical relevance of her suffering in the communication with health professionals.

More than twenty years later as the author of her memoir, Mantel still finds it difficult to describe her symptoms for reasons of propriety (in the communication with her readers): "How can I write this, I wonder? I am a woman with a delicate mouth; I say nothing gross. I can write it, it seems; perhaps because I can pretend it is somebody else, bleeding on the table." (189–190) In contrast to the narrated Hilary, the narrating Mantel is an expert patient, perfectly qualified to describe her disease and thus no longer at risk of hermeneutical injustice. Nonetheless, this retrospective comment suggests, on the one hand, that she still experiences the communication of her bodily symptoms as a transgression against decorum. On the other hand, the remark relativizes the role of the lived body in this work: If Mantel deliberately dissociates from her lived body she is in the position to communicate her bleeding and other symptoms. So even if the memoir insists on the centrality of the lived body by means of focalisation through the embodied younger self, this statement indicates that the third-person perspective typically used by the medical profession is an indispensable tool for communicating illness for Mantel.

Giving up the Ghost suggests that Mantel had to become an expert patient in order to find epistemic justice. Finally, while at St George's Hospital London in 1979, her treating doctor, the professor in charge of gynaecology, recognises, seeks out and includes Mantel's testimony within his epistemic consideration (his diagnosis). He takes her self-diagnosis seriously, includes her in his consideration of pelvic inflammatory disease and cancer, and agrees with Mantel's insistence on endometriosis. During this conversation, the doctor observes that Mantel's "terminology is so precise" (190). In *Giving up the Ghost*, medical authority is shown to only share epistemic consideration on the basis of nearly equal knowledge. Indeed, epistemic justice seems only granted to the patient on the condition of her capacity to deploy the same medical codes as the doctor. Otherwise, it appears impossible to establish the epistemic relevance of her suffering. While Mantel's illness memoir draws a sense of entitlement from the epistemic satisfaction of her medically correct self-diagnosis, the overall narrative emphasises the epistemic credibility of the lived experience of illness.

Coda

Narrating for Mantel seems never only mental just as bodily discomforts are never merely somatic. Yet, she doesn't subscribe to a Romantic notion that art and literature offer recompense for physical loss along the lines of John Keats's "Ode on a Grecian Urn": "Heard melodies are sweet, but those unheard/ Are sweeter" (Keats ll. 11–12, 288). Rather, she demystifies her readers by noting: "When you stop writing you find that's all you are, a spine, a row of rattling vertebrae, dried out like an old quill pen" (223). In a review of Siri Hustvedt's *Shaking Woman or a History of my Nerves* (2010), Mantel reiterates this: Hustvedt "is not a romantic. Illness does not necessarily produce insight. Mostly it does not. It must be endured, accommodated. Our struggles towards health can accommodate what looks like disease" (Mantel "Review" n. p.). Such disenchantment underpins Mantel's "investment in accuracy". Her reception of Hustvedt's *Shaking Woman* expresses an idea that chimes with the "Thou-I" encounter that this essay has traced in *Giving up the Ghost*. As Mantel puts it: "If the shaking woman is extended a measure of tolerance, she can become a companion in endeavour" ("Review" n. p.). Likewise, *Giving up the Ghost* appeals to readers' openness, skilfully recreates the lived experience of illness and advocates its epistemic credibility. Provided that readers are sufficiently open, the reading experience of Mantel's memoir can be so embodied that reading takes the shape of prolonged multifaceted encounters and possibly even "companionship".

Acknowledgments

My thanks to Neil Vickers for the generous discussion of this topic in the Life-Writing seminar at the Department of English of University of Mainz in May 2017.

Works Cited

Assmann, Aleida. *Einführung in die Kulturwissenschaft: Grundbegriffe, Themen, Fragestellung*. Neuburg a. D.: Danuvia Druckhaus, 2011 Print.
Avrahami, Einat. *The Invading Body: Reading Illness Autobiographies*. Charlottesville: University of Virginia Press, 2007. Print.
Baena, Rosalia. "Recognition and Empathy in Illness and Disability Memoirs: Christina Middlebrook's Seeing the Crab and Harriet Mcbryde Johnson's Too Late to Die Young." *Diegesis: Interdisciplinary E-Journal for Narrative Research / Interdisziplinäres E-Journal für Erzählforschung* 6.2 (2017): 1–13.
Buber, Martin. *I and Thou*. Edinburgh: Clark, 1937. Print.
Carel, Havi. *Illness: The Art of Living*. Durham: Acumen, 2008. Print.
Carel, Havi, and Ian James Kidd. "Epistemic Injustice in Healthcare: A Philosophial Analysis." *Med Health Care and Philos* 17 (2014): 529–40.
Class, Monika. "Introduction 'Medical Case Histories as Genre: New Approaches'." *Literature and Medicine* 32.1 (2014): vii–xvi.

Couser, G. Thomas. *Recovering Bodies: Illness, Disability, and Life-Writing.* Madison: University of Wisconsin Press, 1997. Print.
Endometriosis, UK. "Understanding Endometriosis." Web. 1st January 2018.
Foucault, Michel. *History of Sexuality: The Will to Knowledge.* Trans. Hurley, Robert. Vol. 1. 3 vols. London: Penguin, 1981 [1976]. Print.
Frank, Arthur W. *The Wounded Storyteller. Body, Illness, and Ethics.* Second Edition. Chicago, London: The U of Chicago P, 2013.
Fricker, Miranda. *Epistemic Injustice. Power and the Ethics of Knowing.* Oxford: Oxford UP, 2007. Print.
Keats, John. *John Keats: The Major Works.* Ed. Cook, Elizabeth Heckendorn. Oxford: Oxford UP, 2001. Print.
Kleinman, Arthur. *The Illness Narratives: Suffering, Healing, and the Human Condition.* Basic Books, 1988. Print.
Kusek, Robert. "'To Seize the Copyright in Myself.' *Giving Up the Ghost* by Hilary Mantel as an Exercise in Autobiography." *Studia Litteraria Universitatis Iagellonicae Cracoviensis* 9 (2014): 177–190.
Lotman, Yuri M. *Universe of the Mind: A Semiotic Theory of Culture.* London: Tauris, 1990. Print.
Macrae, Andrea. "You and I, Past and Present. Cognitive Processing of Perspective." *Diegesis: Interdisciplinary E-Journal for Narrative Research / Interdisziplinäres E-Journal für Erzählforschung* 5.1 (2016): 64–80.
Mantel, Hilary. *Giving up the Ghost.* London: Fourth Estate, 2013 (2003). Print.
———. "The Shaking Woman or a History of My Nerves by Siri Hustvedt." Review. *The Guardian: The International Edition Online* (2010). Web. 30 January 2017.
Merleau-Ponty, Maurice. *Phenomenology of Perception.* Trans. Donald A. Landes. London: Routledge, 2012. Print.
Moore, Francesca. "'Go and See Nell; She'll Put You Right': The Wisewoman and Working-Class Health Care in Early Twentieth-Century Lancashire." *Social History of Medicine* 26.4 (2013): 695–714.
Neudecker, Sigrid. "'Stell dich nicht so an!' Endometriosis. Ein häufiges gynäkologisches Leiden." *Die Zeit* 5 October 2017: 39.
Pollard, Eileen J. "'But at Second Sight the Words Seemed Not So Simple' (Woolf 1929): Thickening and Rotting Hysteria in the Writing of Hilary Mantel and Virginia Woolf." *Virginia Woolf Miscellany* 80 (2011): 24–26.

Prodromou, Amy. "'That Weeping Constellation': Navigating Loss in 'Memoirs of Textured Recovery'." *Life Writing* 9.1 (2012): 57–75.

Rogers, PA, TM D'Hooghe, and A Fazleabas. "Priorities for Endometriosis Research: Recommendations from an International Consensus Workshop." *Reprod Sci* 16.4 (2009): 335–46.

Ryan, Marie-Laure. *Narrative as Virtual Reality: Immersion and Interactivity in Literature and Electronic Media*. Baltimore: Johns Hopkins UP, 2001. Print.

Semenenko, Aleksei. "Homo Polyglottus: Semiosphere as a Model of Human Cognition." *Sign Systems Studies* 44.4 (2016): 494–510.

Smith, Mark M. *Sensory History*. Oxford: Berg, 2007. Print.

Smith, Sidonie, and Julia Watson. *Reading Autobiography: A Guide for Interpreting Life Narratives*. Minneapolis, Minn.: U of Minnesota P, 2001. Print.

Sontag, Susan. *Against Interpretation and Other Essays*. New York: Farrar, Straus and Giroux, [1961] 1966. Print.

———. *Illness as Metaphor*. New York: Farrar, Straus and Giroux, 1978. Print.

Stanley, Autumn. *Mothers and Daughters of Invention: Notes for a Revised History of Technology*. Metuchen, N.J.: Scarecrow P, 1993. Print.

Toombs, S. Kay. "Illness and the Paradigm of Lived Body." *Theoretical Medicine* 9.2 (1988): 201–26.

Vickers, Neil. "Illness and Femininity in Hilary Mantel's *Giving up the Ghost* (2003)." *Textual Practice* (2017): 1–23.

———. "Illness Narratives." *A History of English Autobiography*. Ed. Symth, Adam. Cambridge: Cambridge UP, 2016. 388–402. Print.

Wordsworth, William. *The Prelude: The Four Texts (1798, 1799, 1805, 1850)*. London, New York: Penguin 1995. Print.

Contributors

Sarah J. Ablett. Studies in Philosophy, English Language and Literature, and Creative Writing at the Universities of Hamburg, Manchester, Heidelberg, and Hildesheim. Research assistant and Ph.D.-candidate working on the dramatic function of disgust and the plays of Sarah Kane at the University of Braunschweig.

Monika Class was appointed Junior Professor of English Literature and Culture at the Department of English at the Johannes Gutenberg University Mainz in 2016. Her specialisms include eighteenth and nineteenth-century studies, the theory and history of reading and the novel, and medical humanities. She earned her doctoral degree at Balliol College, University of Oxford, in 2009 for her research on the early reception of Kantian philosophy in England. After that she acted as a Marie-Curie Postdoctoral Fellow, fixed-term lecturer and co-convenor of the MSc in Medical Humanities at King's College London's English Department, before being elected as a Marie-Curie Postdoctoral Fellow at the Zukunftskolleg, University of Konstanz, in 2014. Her current second-book project is called "The Visceral Novel Reader: A Cultural History of Embodied Reading in Britain."

Dagmar Gramshammer-Hohl is Senior Lecturer in the Department of Slavic Studies at the University of Graz, Austria. She specializes in literary and cultural studies with a focus on Russian literature, gender, migration and age/aging studies. In her Ph.D. thesis (2002) she analyzed literary representations of women's aging. Her current research project focuses on narratives of homecoming in Russian and Bosnian/Croatian/Serbian literature. D. Gramshammer-Hohl was granted the Prof. Paul Petry Award in Aging Studies in 1998; she is an alumna of the Austrian Academy of Sciences and a member of the European Network in Aging Studies. Among her recent publications is the edited volume *Aging in Slavic Literatures: Essays in Literary Gerontology*, Bielefeld 2017.

Mirjam Grewe-Salfeld is a second-year doctoral student at the Department of English and American Studies at the University of Potsdam. Her research interests include (the history of) medicine, body studies and biotechnology. She finished her undergraduate degree in English Studies and History at the University of Brunswick – Institute of Technology with a thesis examining the cultural representation of Teenage Pregnancy in the U.S. and her M.A. in "Anglophone Modernities in Literature and Culture" at the University of Potsdam with a thesis on the representation of "invisible" disabilities and illnesses, such as Multiple Sclerosis, in U.S. culture. She is currently working on her Ph.D. research in which she focuses on "do-it-yourself" approaches in biotechnology and medicine, examining the cultural representation and material results of a wide range of areas from biohacking to DTC genetic testing.

Margaret Morganroth Gullette is an internationally known age critic, essayist, activist, and prize-winning writer of nonfiction. Her main work is in age studies, a field she named in 1993. Her most recent book (August 2017) is *Ending Ageism, or How Not to Shoot Old People*. *Agewise* won a 2012 Eric Hoffer Book Award and will be published in Korean. *Aged by Culture* was chosen a Notable Book of the year by the *Christian Science Monitor*. *Declining to Decline: Cultural Combat and the Politics of the Midlife* in 1998 won the Emily Toth award for the best feminist book on American popular culture. Her essays are frequently cited as notable in *Best American Essays*. She has published in *New York Times, Nation, Boston Globe, Ms, American Prospect, American Scholar, Salmagundi, Kenyon Review*, and she blogs for *Silver Century, Next Avenue, and WomensENews* A recipient of NEH, ACLS, and Bunting Fellowships, she is a Scholar at the Women's Studies Research Center, Brandeis University. Since 1997 she has found funding for adult-education programs in her Sister City, San Juan del Sur, Nicaragua and she co-founded a Free High School for Adults in 2002 which has graduated 1001 people.

Heike Hartung is an independent scholar in English Studies, associated at the University of Potsdam, Germany, and the University of Graz, Austria.

She has earned her Ph. D. in English Studies at the Freie Universität Berlin and her Ph. D. habil. in Literary and Cultural Studies at the University of Potsdam. In her publications she applies the methods of literary theory to the interdisciplinary fields of aging, disability and gender studies. Her recent publication is the monograph *Ageing, Gender and Illness in Anglophone Literature: Narrating Age in the Bildungsroman* (2016). She is a founding member of the European Network in Aging Studies (ENAS) and a co-editor of the Aging Studies publication series.

Rüdiger Kunow is Professor emeritus at the American Studies program at Potsdam University. His publications and major research interests are in transnational American Studies, theories of transnationalism as well as the cultural resonances of illness and aging. He is a founding member of ENAS, the European Network in Aging Studies. Aside from that he served as speaker of the international research project "Transnational American Studies," the European Union research and teaching project "Putting a Human Face on Diversity: The U. S. In/Of Europe" as well as the Director of a Ph. D. school on "Cultures in/of Mobility." Until 2008 he held the position of the President of the German Association for American Studies.

Ellen Matlok-Ziemann holds an MA in Sociology and a Ph. D. in American Literature and is research coordinator at the Department of Education at Uppsala University, Sweden. Her research interests include History of Science, Feminist Philosophy, Southern Literature and Aging Studies. She is working on representations of old women in American Literature.

Vira Sachenko is a researcher of forms, politics and mental life, based in Berlin. She is currently a graduate student at the University of Potsdam. Her research trajectories have been shaped by the multidisciplinary study of Values, Ethics, and Aesthetics at the European College of Liberal Arts.

Ariane Schröder is a research assistant and lecturer at the American Studies Department of the University of Potsdam. She currently writes her Ph. D. thesis on contagious disease and the fantasy of containment in American literature and culture. For her MA thesis "Write or Be Written Of(f): Reading Contemporary American Illness Autobiographies" she received the Hans-Jürgen-Bachorski-Preis of the University of Potsdam.

Her research interests include bioculture(s), body theory, Gothic literature and the history of medicine.

Anita Wohlmann is a postdoctoral researcher in American studies at Johannes Gutenberg University Mainz, Germany. As of November 2017, she will be Assistant Professor of Literature and Narrative Medicine at the University of Southern Denmark. Her research project 'Body and Metaphor: Narrative-Based Metaphor Analysis in Medical Humanities' is funded by the German Research Foundation (2017–2020). She published two monographs: *Serializing Age: Aging and Old Age in TV Series* (2016), co-edited with Maricel Oró Piqueras, and *Aged Young Adults: Age Readings of Contemporary American Novels and Films* (2014). Wohlmann has also published on the topics of age, gender, health humanities and life writing in *The Journal of Aging Studies, Age Culture Humanities, European Journal of Life Writing, Signs: Journal of Women in Culture and Society, Medical Humanities, Jahrbuch Medizin und Literatur.*

Cultural Studies

Gundolf S. Freyermuth
Games | Game Design | Game Studies
An Introduction
(With Contributions by André Czauderna,
Nathalie Pozzi and Eric Zimmerman)

2015, 296 p., pb.
19,99 € (DE), 978-3-8376-2983-5
E-Book: 17,99 € (DE), ISBN 978-3-8394-2983-9

Andréa Belliger, David J. Krieger
Network Publicy Governance
On Privacy and the Informational Self

February 2018, 170 p., pb.
29,99 € (DE), 978-3-8376-4213-1
E-Book: 26,99 € (DE), ISBN 978-3-8394-4213-5

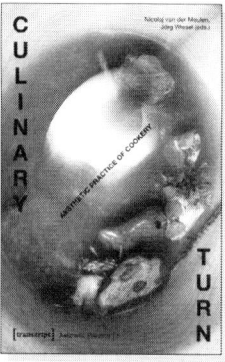

Nicolaj van der Meulen, Jörg Wiesel (eds.)
Culinary Turn
Aesthetic Practice of Cookery
(In collaboration with Anneli Käsmayr
and in editorial cooperation with Raphaela Reinmann)

2017, 328 p., pb., col. ill.
29,99 € (DE), 978-3-8376-3031-2
E-Book available as free open access publication
ISBN 978-3-8394-3031-6

**All print, e-book and open access versions of the titles in our list
are available in our online shop www.transcript-verlag.de/en!**

Cultural Studies

Martina Leeker, Imanuel Schipper, Timon Beyes (eds.)
Performing the Digital
Performativity and Performance Studies in Digital Cultures

2016, 304 p., pb.
29,99 € (DE), 978-3-8376-3355-9
E-Book available as free open access publication
ISBN 978-3-8394-3355-3

Suzi Mirgani
**Target Markets –
International Terrorism
Meets Global Capitalism in the Mall**

2016, 198 p., pb.
29,99 € (DE), 978-3-8376-3352-8
E-Book available as free open access publication
ISBN 978-3-8394-3352-2

Ramón Reichert, Annika Richterich,
Pablo Abend, Mathias Fuchs, Karin Wenz (eds.)
Digital Culture & Society (DCS)
Vol. 3, Issue 2/2017 – Mobile Digital Practices

January 2018, 272 p., pb.
29,99 € (DE), 978-3-8376-3821-9
E-Book: 29,99 € (DE), ISBN 978-3-8394-3821-3

**All print, e-book and open access versions of the titles in our list
are available in our online shop www.transcript-verlag.de/en!**